KABUL24

KABUL 24

The story of a Taliban kidnapping and
unwavering faith in the face of true terror

HENRY O. ARNOLD AND BEN PEARSON

Foreword by
MICHAEL W. SMITH

THOMAS NELSON
Since 1798

NASHVILLE   DALLAS   MEXICO CITY   RIO DE JANEIRO   BEIJING

Published in Nashville, Tennessee, by Thomas Nelson. Thomas Nelson is a trademark of Thomas Nelson, Inc.

"Ransom Song" and "In the Shelter of Your Presence" © 2001, Silke Durrkopf. Reprinted with permission.

Thomas Nelson, Inc., titles may be purchased in bulk for educational, business, fund-raising, or sales promotional use. For information, please e-mail SpecialMarkets@ThomasNelson.com.

Unless otherwise noted, Scripture quotations are taken from THE NEW KING JAMES VERSION. © 1982 by Thomas Nelson, Inc. Used by permission. All rights reserved.

Scripture quotations marked NIV are from HOLY BIBLE: NEW INTERNATIONAL VERSION®. © 1973, 1978, 1984 by International Bible Society. Used by permission of Zondervan Publishing House. All rights reserved.

Library of Congress Cataloging-in-Publication Data

Arnold, Henry O., 1966–
  Kabul 24 : the story of the Taliban's capture and imprisonment of eight western aid workers in Afghanistan six weeks before September 11, 2001 / by Henry O. Arnold and Ben Pearson ; foreword by Michael W. Smith.
      p. cm.
  Includes bibliographical references and index.
  ISBN 978-1-59555-022-4 (alk. paper)
  1. Shelter Now (Organization) 2. Taliban. 3. Humanitarian assistance—Afghanistan.
  4. Political prisoners—Afghanistan—Biography. 5. Afghanistan—History—2001–
  I. Pearson, Ben. II. Title. III. Title: Kabul twenty-four.
  HV589.A766 2009
  958.104'7—dc22   2009028898

Printed in the United States of America

09 10 11 12 13 RRD 6 5 4 3 2 1

For the Kabul twenty-four, whose faith was tested
in the extreme. They are an inspiration to us all.

CONTENTS

FOREWORD

I remember vividly hearing the news in August 2001 about some aid workers for Shelter Now International being kidnapped by the Taliban and held hostage in Kabul, Afghanistan. Word spread quickly throughout America and around the world that the plight of eight Western missionaries and their sixteen Afghan coworkers was very grave. It was a unique time in church history, when the prayers of believers all over the world were unified for one great cause. The incredible story of these hostages captured international attention and became a defining moment in the body of Christ.

This gripping story is filled with miracles and answered prayers and is beautifully told by Henry O. Arnold and Ben Pearson in this book and in the film of the same title. It is a story of a few courageous individuals who heard a particular call of God to go to a remote part of the world to serve a displaced people. It is a story of individuals going through the fire; of their faith tested in the extreme; of a dangerous journey so powerful that I believe it will capture your heart and soul in the same way it did mine.

In *KABUL24*, God's grace and provision is played out in one of the most unique settings you could ever imagine. This true story is a reminder that God hears and answers our prayers even in unusual situations that appear hopeless. It is my prayer that the story of these precious people told in this book and in the film will inspire believers around the world to listen for their own call of God . . . and respond.

—Michael W. Smith
July 2009

AUTHORS' NOTE

Our primary source material consists of raw film footage shot by Ben Pearson of interviews with the SNI hostages from 2003 through 2005. We also relied on Eberhard Muehlan's *Escape from Kabul* (Sydney: Strand Publishing, 2003), a collection of interviews with the former hostages conducted in 2002 and our source material for letters and court documents, which in some cases were translated from Pashto to German to English.

We gratefully acknowledge Georg Taubmann, for his permission to reprint his prison letters, and Silke Durrkopf, for her permission to reprint lyrics to two songs, "Ransom Song" and "In the Shelter of Your Presence."

Conditions in Afghanistan continue to be dangerous, in some areas, for Afghans who work for Western organizations. Because of this, the names of all the Afghan SNI workers mentioned in this account have been changed to protect their identities.

PROLOGUE

The thick, blue cotton fabric was little protection from the sting of the whips and the blunt strikes from the wooden rods on her body as she stumbled along the dusty streets of Kabul. Covering her from the crown of her head down to the tips of her bare toes, the *burka* was designed by law for her protection—protection from the roving, lustful eyes of other men, protection from the evil influences of the outside world. She could never enter that expansive outside world; it would always remain a mystery, although sometimes she allowed herself to imagine it. Inside the *burka*, she was anonymous to all who might care to know her; anonymous to those she might care to know too—no physical marks made visible to distinguish her beauty, no bright smile to share with others, no voice to speak to her character. She was simply a *burka*—a living, vibrant human being reduced to an animated sack, a tented Cyclops—and today nothing could protect her. No one came to her rescue. No one offered to hold her blistered, swollen hands or bathe her bloody, raw feet. Alone, contained by her *burka* and herded through the street, she did not bother to cry for mercy. She knew such cries were meaningless to hearts hardened by the strict adherence to brutal *sharia* law.

Only young girls and old women were exempt from the law of the *burka*. Women bound by the law wore the *burka* outside the home at all times to conceal identity and make recognition impossible. The nameless, faceless *burka* was never to wander the streets alone. If she were married, then the husband would accompany her; if single, a male member of her family would escort her. Her brief public forays outside the house were to the market or the home of another *burka*. The religious foibles of her husband kept the *burka* on edge. If she did anything to displease him, her position was in jeopardy. If the *burka* committed any infraction against *sharia* law and thus brought shame upon her family, she faced possible expulsion from her home. There were no educational opportunities for her, either. A Taliban *fatwa* cited the education of women as a "source of seduction and depravity." The *burka*'s place in society was that of property, totally dependent upon the interpretation of the law by the whim of the dominant male in her life. For those unmarried or widowed, the rules of the Taliban could be fatal. They had no means, no way to take care of themselves, and *sharia* law kept them in perpetual house arrest. It was no wonder that frequently a *burka* set herself on fire if she suddenly become an outcast simply because she had been unable to adhere to the burdensome demands of the law; better to burn inside a *burka* shroud than to endure a lifetime of poverty, rejection, starvation, and abuse.

But what had this particular *burka* done? What law had she broken? Whom had she displeased? There was a myriad of ways she could have broken a commandment, because there was a myriad of commandments, sixteen alone regarding dress and behavior just to leave her house. How would one keep up with them all? In the bedlam of the moment, she did not understand the accusation made against her. Whatever it was, how could it warrant such a brutal reaction?

Her vision was impaired as the crowd manhandled her down the street. The single meshed hole centered in the *burka*'s hood provided the only limited, distorted view of the chaotic world around her. She caught fleeting glimpses of her sister *burka*s watching as she moved down the street. Their fear kept them motionless and silent. What could they do? They were helpless. Calling out to their ill-treated sister or coming to her defense in any way would only bring unwanted attention upon them. The mob must take its wrath out on this victim; Allah demanded it. This religious fury momentarily deflected attention from them—but who knew who might be the next *burka* to take the journey to the stadium?

Suddenly the beatings stopped and the *burka* went airborne, her feet and legs still making frantic motions of escape. Tossed onto a ridged metal bed, she could feel the vibration and hear the rumble of the revved truck engine. The truck began to rock from side to side as the heavy weight of male bodies leapt into the bed, surrounding her and cutting off any hope she might have of getting away. Shouts and curses filled the air as the driver rapidly pumped his horn and popped the clutch on the truck, scattering the unarmed mob. The vehicle hopped down the street for several yards like a frog before smoothing out the drive. Caught up by the frenzied excitement, children trotted beside the truck, curious and fascinated by the hostility expressed toward the *burka*. Perhaps the young boys aspired to be like the men in the truck: black-turbaned, bearded, ammunition belts cross-strapped over their chests, Kalashnikov weapons jammed into the crooks of their arms, faithful followers of the Prophet Mohammed . . . *may peace and blessings of Allah be on him*, as one was required to say each time the Prophet's name was mentioned.

The drive through the streets was swift, as though a race had begun. The curves were sharp, tossing the passengers about like dolls. As the *burka* slid around the legs of the Taliban inside the truck bed, she received angry kicks from the boots insulted by the touch of the condemned. Stops were abrupt, the shouting from the armed riders intense, punctuated with occasional bursts of gunfire—a frightening advertisement of the consequences for disrespect to *sharia* law. The journey was short.

The truck sped through the tunnel leading into the soccer stadium and drove straight onto the field. The game had stopped. The teams were resting, the fans patiently waiting; but the moment the truck entered the stadium the spectators rose to their feet. Bloodlust cheers pierced the atmosphere at the unexpected halftime entertainment.

The *burka* had never been inside a soccer stadium. *Sharia* did not allow women inside, their presence somehow an affront to Allah. They yanked her from the back of the truck, and through her cloth mesh window she could see billboards with pictures of the high-ranking *mullah*s rising out of the top row of the stadium. These were her judges, the wise ones of Allah whose strict interpretation of the law had left them no choice but to bring her to this final moment of her life.

The *burka* did not resist. She relaxed her body as they dragged her to the center of the field. She could hear the amplified voice of the judge authorized to pass sentence silence the crowd with the list of her offences and Allah's justification for sending her soul to hell.

The sentence passed, the crowd of men began to roar. The *mullah* offered no chance for reprieve. The *burka* asked for none. The *mullah* offered no prayers. The *burka* asked for none. The *mullah* offered no prospect for final words from the condemned, a chance to confess. The *burka* asked for none. What had she to confess? There was no hope of pardon, and no rote prayers could change the outcome of her future. She would pray for herself, to Allah alone. She needed no *mullah* to intercede.

All was silent inside her *burka*, the raging voices in the stadium abruptly muted. For the first time in her life, she felt the *burka*'s protection—no more abuse, no more rejection, no more condemnation; she was hidden from sight and strangely comforted and warm inside it. She could take flight, and through the mesh of the hooded *burka*, her vision of the sky began to expand.

Fareed knelt on the hard ground of the playing field inside the stadium. He tried to get to his feet but could not find the strength or will to rise. He was a statue frozen in descriptive position, his right arm raised, his hand in the shape of a gun pointing to the back of his head.

"This is where it happened," he said, a hollow tenderness in his voice. "This is how they killed her." He gently tapped the back of his head with his index finger. "Before the American invasion, the Taliban bring the men here for games, they say, for the soccer . . . but no games; only death." His voice trailed off.

Fareed looked into the camera, and those around him wondered if he was finished describing what he'd witnessed and if Ben had enough footage of the scene for his documentary. Fareed had led Ben and the others through the tunnel into the stadium. A bright blue sky lay overhead. The stadium was deserted, its seats of concrete fractured and crumbling from lack of repair. The severe images of the *mullah*s on the billboards had vanished, their likenesses peeled away and deteriorated into stark white enormous postcards bleached out from the searing heat and radiant sun. The grass on the playing field was a weedy brown crust.

Fareed lowered his arm and rested his hands on his thighs. His thick curly hair waved in the hot breeze, his black moustache a bushy curtain above his white teeth.

Ben could not speak. No one could speak. He zoomed back from Fareed and began to pan over the stadium from their position in the center of the field. Flocks of morning doves circled above them or watched from their billboard perches like guardians of a sacred place.

When Ben finished his sweep of the stadium, he turned off the camera and pulled his eye away from the lens. Georg Taubmann, international director of Shelter Now International, and Udo Stolte, SNI's German director, were Ben's guides during his stay in Kabul. They had introduced Ben to several of the sixteen Afghans who had been captured that morning in August 2001 and imprisoned by the Taliban along with Georg and seven other Westerners. Fareed was one of the sixteen. He and several of his fellow Afghan SNI workers had seen too many of the executions like the one he had just recounted. Now the three of them stood in awed silence as if listening for whispered messages.

Fareed has the correct humble posture for being in this place, Ben thought as he removed the camera from his shoulder and bent over, lowering it to the ground.

When Ben rose up from carefully placing the camera on top of its case, he noticed the other three men looking at him with strange expressions. "Don't move," they said. Ben froze. There was a fluttering sound above his head. A moment later, seemingly from nowhere, a dove landed on Ben's shoulder, damp from sweat and strained from supporting the camera. The dove dug its talons into Ben's shirt, securing its position, then twisted its head back and forth, eyeing Ben with a curious scrutiny.

"From God. From God," Fareed whispered, his legs suddenly

"From God." A dove alights on Ben in the Kabul soccer stadium that was the site of Taliban executions.

filled with energy. He gradually came to his feet, not wanting to frighten the dove off Ben's shoulder.

Udo slowly raised the camera draped around his neck and took a picture of the startling moment. Everyone began to smile. How could they not smile at this gentle touch from above?

The dove cooed softly and then pushed off Ben's shoulder, taking a gyratory spin above their heads until it returned to the sky. The men watched it soar until absorbed once again into the numberless flock that circled above the stadium.

Georg came over to Ben. He was looking at Ben's shoulder as if the dove might have left a residue of something holy. He placed his hand upon the blessed spot and looked into Ben's eyes.

"God has sent you," he said. "God has sent you to us to tell our story."

CHAPTER ONE

THE ARRESTS

A guest in an Afghan home is always offered a cup of tea. It is a standard practice stipulated by the law of ancient custom. While sipping the beverage, conversation should flow as freely as the tea that flows from the spout of the exotic shaped pot—warm, stimulating, satisfying, the tea and the conversation. The Muslim concept of being a good host and offering care and protection to any and all guests that come under their roof goes back to the days of the Prophet Mohammed, who considered being a proper host a hallowed duty.

Still, Afghans are wary of outsiders, so for a foreigner to receive an invitation into an Afghan home is an honor. To receive a second invitation is possibly a greater one. It now goes beyond a cultural obligation. The foreigner has earned the trust of the host, and the host has extended that deeper level of hospitality, the Prophet's hospitality. So when that protection became betrayal—of innocent victims whose only desire was the welfare of and a friendship with their hosts—it broke a covenant held sacred for centuries.

There was nothing about the day that was unusual, blisteringly hot, the August sun baking the adobe homes in the neighborhood. A breeze blew down the dusty Kabul streets and between the houses as though originating from inside an oven. The only good effect the light wind afforded was in reducing the drying time of the fresh laundry hanging from the clotheslines.

It was not Dayna Curry and Heather Mercer's first visit to this particular Afghan family. The two young American women had worked with the children living within the home, and whenever Dayna was there, the children never failed to ask her to read from her collection of children's stories from the Bible. One of the older boys became insistent that she make a copy of the book for him, which she had finally and reluctantly agreed to do. (Because the Taliban had laws forbidding it, Dayna did not want anyone in the family to think she was trying to manipulate the young boy into converting or take advantage of his seeming enthusiasm to hear the stories.)

These two were a pair of auburn-haired Renaissance maidens, each with a cheerful shimmer in her eyes, their fresh-faced expressions in stark contrast to most of the faces weathered by dry desert air and unsympathetic sunlight. Along with other SNI coworkers, they had been regular guests in the home, and once when the matriarch of the family became ill, a SNI staff member brought her medication. The group had befriended this family and others in the neighborhood with no ulterior motive . . . yet their kindness would be betrayed by this family. On this day, the underhanded motive came from within the Afghan family.

A few weeks before, one of the uncles of the family had questioned Heather about the benefits of becoming a Christian. "What do I have to do to become a Christian?" he had asked. His interest was to the point, more in line with a fact-finding mission than anything genuine or heartfelt. "What do I get if I become a Christian? Will you pay me if I become a Christian? Will I get a visa if I become a Christian? What do I get if I convert?"

It had been a wise choice, then, to defer the conversation regarding a benefit analysis in converting to Christianity. The belligerent uncle, along with the rest of the Afghan family, would first see the "Jesus film" and then the dialogue could continue. A date and time were set when the whole family could be present for the viewing. Heather and Dayna would come that Friday, August 3, in the late afternoon.

The smell of baking bread wafted upon the stifling air as the women stepped through the gate and approached the house inside the compound. A fire was burning in the courtyard, chickens were scurrying about, mothers were washing clothes in large tubs and hanging the dripping apparel on the clotheslines, and many of the children were playing outside, waiting for the arrival of the two women.

One of the young boys raced up to Dayna. Unable to contain his enthusiasm, he bounced up and down on his legs, a human pogo stick.

"Do you have it?" he cried. "Do you have it?"

The boy's eagerness appeared exaggerated but did not alarm either of the two girls. In the Muslim culture, discussions of religious topics are the norm. Many are interested in knowing what people from other cultures believe. It is a chance to learn from others, especially when there is so little exposure to the outside world and with the illiteracy rate so high in Afghanistan. Among the Muslims, Jesus Christ is highly regarded as a prophet and teacher from God. Though Jesus does not carry the same historical or spiritual weight as Mohammed, any healthy and respectful exchange of ideas regarding Christ's teachings, in a proper theological context, would not normally be discouraged or frowned upon.

Where it could become hostile and even dangerous would be if there were overt attempts at persuading any Muslim to convert to Christianity. When Heather and Dayna came for their visit, they never intended to coerce any of the family to accept Christ, but they were certainly prepared to share the gospel story if any member of the family had expressed genuine interest. They were simply fulfilling a request that had come from within the family. Still, the whole occasion had its risks. Were any member of the family to convert to Christianity, it would be quite dangerous for them, a danger that included the possibility of a death sentence from the Taliban.

Heather and Dayna had never had so large a crowd gathered for any of their other visits. The family knew the women were coming and the word had spread. It was not just women and children but several of the adult males as well. To their surprise, the uncle who had earlier expressed so much interest in Jesus had fled the scene on a bicycle. He did not even bother to greet them when they arrived.

Heather set up her computer in the living room to play the DVD, and the family huddled around the screen with their cups of tea, watching and listening intently to the grainy film of the story of Jesus spoken in their own language. This cross-cultural home gathering—between citizens from different countries, between adherents of different faiths—to share a story of a mutually revered religious figure was no more a threat to either religion than sharing the obligatory cup of tea. There was no portentous hint of betrayal, no indication by anyone in the room that the situation might become dire.

Because of some technical difficulties with the computer and the DVD, it took longer than planned to show the film. Dayna could not stay for the entirety of the film but had to leave for an appointment in another part of the city. When the time came for her to depart, she made her exit quietly, so as not to distract the family as they watched the film.

The taxi driver who'd brought Dayna to the house had waited for her—better to have a definite fare than drive through the city in search of the rare customer—and after she got into the car, he pulled away. When they stopped at the first cross street, Heather heard a demanding voice coming from outside the car. A fearsome-looking Talib approached the passenger's side of the vehicle, flourishing his arms and insisting the driver come to a stop to let him inside the car. He grabbed the handle, his voice bellowing in the harsh, fricative Pashtun dialect, and threw open the front door.

"Drive on!" Heather screamed at her Afghan cab driver. "Don't stop. What are you doing? Go on. Get out of here!" But the cabbie ignored her insistent pleas to escape.

The Talib slid onto the front seat of the automobile and slammed the door. The driver was his first concern. The Talib's intimidating glare froze the driver's foot on the brake. He would follow whatever instructions given him to the letter. The Talib then turned his attention to Dayna, who had her feet dug into the floorboard and was pressing herself against the back of her seat.

"Who are you?" Dayna insisted. "What do you think you are doing?"

The Talib's wide, hateful eyes absorbed Dayna's shrinking frame. There appeared a glint of pleasure on his face as he observed how quickly he had cowed these two helpless people. Sweat trickled out from beneath the folds of his black turban and disappeared inside the hairy mass of his beard. When Dayna was about to give one more weak protest, he silenced her with an order to say no more. He removed a walkie-talkie from inside his vest pocket and barked an order into it. Within seconds, a carload of Taliban pulled up beside the taxi and slammed on its brakes. A Talib armed with a Kalashnikov leaped from the vehicle and forced himself into the backseat of the taxi.

The initial courage Dayna expressed dissipated in this ominous predicament. She was a woman, alone, a foreigner, one who came to this country uninvited, who barely spoke the language, who brought an infidel's culture and religion. She represented everything this Talib despised, and she knew that under these conditions asserting herself could only worsen the situation. She chose a different tactic; demands turned to pleas and expressions of frailty. Would they please take her to the organization where she worked? She was alone. She was a woman.

The Talib in the front seat ignored the visible expressions of fear on her face and in her voice. He watched as his fellow Taliban climbed out of the vehicle parked next to them in the middle of the street and surrounded the taxi. Then he stretched his arm over the back of the seat and grabbed her bag. Half the contents spilled out on the seat as he rifled through it.

"Where is it?" he shouted. "Where is the equipment? Where is the other woman?"

A kind of madness had taken hold, a madness that surrounded and engulfed the taxi, and Dayna felt as though it had infected her. Yet this seemed to calm her, even provide a spark of courage. She refused to answer his questions. She refused to give up her friend. She politely said she would not speak to him under these conditions and requested they take her to the SNI headquarters.

A final cursory inspection of Dayna's bag yielded nothing, so the Talib tossed it back to her in frustration.

"The other one must have it," he grumbled. "Go back for her."

The family was unusually quiet after the movie was over. Heather had no expectation of a response, but she thought it strange that this typically boisterous and effusive family was subdued as she packed up her computer and DVD. In the standard Afghan leave-taking, Heather kissed the women three times on the cheek and made her way out the front door of the house. In the past, the family would escort her through the courtyard and out the gate; many times the young boys would gleefully chase her taxi as it drove away. This time there was no escort. Heather walked alone through the courtyard, opened the gate, and let herself out of the compound. She could not explain this break with tradition. Perhaps the Jesus movie had offended the family. Perhaps the women were showing more than usual deference to their menfolk. Heather was puzzled but not alarmed. From the street, she looked back toward the house. Family members congregated at the doorway, but no one stepped outside, their waves of farewell restrained; then a gruff voice was heard from inside the house, and the family disappeared from sight, the front door closing with an abrupt slam. This rebuff stung more than it set off any alarm.

Her taxi driver had a male passenger sitting with him in the front seat of the vehicle. *Probably just a friend*, Heather thought, and she shrugged off her growing suspicions as she walked toward the car. The houses deflected the late afternoon sun, casting their shadows along the street lightly sprinkled with vehicular traffic and pedestrians. Heather slipped into the backseat of the taxi, apologizing to her driver for her tardiness, expecting him to laugh off the irrelevancies of time. She also expected the passenger in the front seat to get out of the car once she closed her door. Neither man met her expectations. The stranger in the front seat made no move to exit, and her cab driver was silent, offering no friendly conversation. Heather looked up and caught his terror-filled eyes in the rearview mirror. He drove for only a few feet when the door opposite Heather flew open and a man leaped inside the car. Heather immediately tried to escape, but she got no farther than opening her door and stepping out onto the street when a cadre of Taliban surrounded the vehicle. *Where did they come from?* she thought. *Why didn't I see them?* It never crossed her mind that the Afghan family hidden inside their house had betrayed her and Dayna to the feared vice and virtue police.

The passenger in the front seat ordered the cabbie to drive. The Taliban surrounding the taxi immediately jumped into the back of a truck and followed. Heather had no idea what she had done to deserve this hostile attention. She wondered if Dayna, by leaving early, had escaped this fate. She rode in silence, making no pleas for mercy, making no demands as to what might be going on. Where were they taking her? What were they going to do to her? Could death be near, around the next corner, in some back alley? Were they taking her to the desert, to violate her and leave her to die?

The journey was short. The stranger in the front seat ordered the driver to stop in a parking area between a government building and a mosque, where Dayna waited in her taxi. The stranger hauled Heather out of her car, marched her over to Dayna's vehicle, and ordered her to get into the backseat. The women were relieved to be reunited, but each regretted that the Taliban had arrested the other. Still, they took comfort in the fact that whatever their fate, they would face it together.

The stranger took Heather's bag and removed the computer, DVD, and all other suspicious objects before returning it to her. The two women began to contend with the stranger—their reunion restoring a level of courage in them both—telling him that he should call their supervisor at the SNI headquarters, giving him the address, informing him that their fellow employees were there at that moment having a meeting. The stranger disregarded their assertiveness and ordered the driver back into his vehicle. With an armed escort of at least thirty Taliban, Heather and Dayna were on their way to the women's prison of the Taliban's headquarters of the Ministry for the Promotion of Virtue and Prevention of Vice.

Georg Taubmann had an unsettled feeling in his stomach throughout the scheduled SNI meeting that Friday night. He was the director of the organization, responsible for all the SNI projects throughout the country. Eighteen years before, he and his wife, Marianne, left behind their families in Germany and lived first in Pakistan, then moved to Afghanistan to serve the victims of famine and war in this impoverished country.

Sometime before his arrest, Georg posed near a Shelter Now health clinic in Kabul. Note the suspicious Taliban with his Kalashnikov rifle on the left.

Georg was a soft-spoken, kindhearted soul, a man at peace with himself and with the God-call on his life. At average height and with a bearish physique, he was the confident yet humble leader of an international collection of people all compelled by their faith in God to be in this place, at this time, doing this work. Marianne was every bit his equal, every bit as committed to the work in Afghanistan. Her quiet voice, soft facial features, and long, flowing dark hair belied her inner strength, her ability to juggle the duties of wife, mother to their two teenage sons, and the demands of serving a beleaguered people.

Every one of the SNI staff and family members had gathered at the home of Margrit and Diana: the only ones missing were Heather and Dayna. The group ate their meal, then moved on to business, followed by a time of prayer and worship. Georg knew in his heart that something was wrong. Yes, an Afghan social gathering did not respect time. The festivity was all that mattered, and the to-and-fro of relatives plus the food preparation and consumption had its own imprecise rhythm. Yet Georg thought that being over two hours late to this scheduled meeting was beyond even the fluidity of Afghan hospitality. Someone suggested traveling over to the Afghan home just to check on the girls' whereabouts, so three SNI employees hopped into a taxi and headed to the home. They chose not to drive one of their own vehicles. It could attract unwanted attention from the Taliban.

When the trio arrived at the house, neighbors and family members commingled in the courtyard. From the vehicle, they could see there was a fair amount of bedlam and consternation, with everyone in the thick of multiple heated discussions, but until they got out of the car, it all appeared to be nothing more than a frantic, dumb show. The absence of the Taliban was a relief to the SNI workers. When they got out of the taxi, other people from the surrounding houses swarmed around them. They eventually worked their way through the crowd and spoke with the women of the family. Between the three of them, they were able to understand enough of the Dari dialect to learn what had happened. Everyone involved felt betrayed. Heather and Dayna had been arrested, and for good measure, the Taliban had taken some of the family's own men away. It appeared that the Taliban had forced the Afghan family to set this trap, and now everyone was suffering the consequences.

The three of them returned to Margrit and Diana's home and reported what had happened. Immediately the group began to pray for Heather and Dayna. They had no idea where the Taliban had taken the girls, and with only a couple of hours before the eleven o'clock curfew, Georg thought of his good friend, Haji Rashid. He was a high-level member of the Taliban, a moderate. He and Georg had developed a tight bond in the last year, and perhaps Haji could exert some influence that might help resolve this unfortunate issue. Georg took the risk of traveling the streets of Kabul, avoiding the erratic Taliban checkpoints, and imposing himself on his friend with a late night visit. Haji greeted him warmly, offering the obligatory cup of tea, and listened intently as Georg explained what had happened to the two members of his staff. In spite of Haji's concern over the girls' abduction and a genuine willingness to help in any way he could, he could do little. One phone call confirmed the girls' arrest, but any influence he might have in this situation would prove futile: Heather and Dayna had been taken into custody by the vice and virtue police. It was a special independent branch of the Taliban regime subject only to the "supreme leader of the faithful," Mullah Mohammed Omar. Feared by Taliban moderates and all Afghans, Mullah Omar based his dictatorship on an extreme interpretation of *sharia* law, and he claimed to have established in Afghanistan a pure Islamic state. It was a widely held belief that Mullah Omar had direct links to Osama bin Laden. With profuse apologies for his inability to mitigate the situation, Haji bade his friend good night, and Georg returned home in despair.

There was little sleep to be had that night for Georg. He was certain there would be repercussions. Eleven years earlier in Peshawar, Pakistan, Islamic extremists had attacked and destroyed SNI projects established for Afghan widows and orphans left homeless after ten years of fighting a war with Russia. At that time, the director of SNI, Thor Armstrong, and his young son had barely escaped an assassination attempt. Could history be repeating itself? At the very least, Georg expected a search and seizure by the Taliban of the homes of every SNI staff member.

On Saturday morning everyone shifted into crisis mode. They should destroy everything that could possibly be offensive to the Taliban, especially all things Western: magazines; religious materials, except their Bibles, CDs, DVDs; and artwork. They should clear their electronic equipment of anything Western as well. They had to destroy any item or communication of possible offense to this despotic regime. Until Mullah Omar established his autocratic rule, there had been a tolerance for most of these things, but the Mullah's strict perception of *sharia*—and his continual changes in interpretation announced regularly on Radio Sharia—made it impossible to keep up with what was accepted. What the regime might recognize one day could get you arrested the next. Better to destroy anything that could incur the Taliban's wrath.

Georg made one more attempt with Haji Rashid to see if he was able to offer any assistance, but to no avail. By making inquiries and demands on behalf of Heather and Dayna, the vice and virtue police could interpret his efforts as a display of too much sympathy given to infidels, and Haji himself could be in trouble.

The team passed the day engaged in the surreal task of destroying anything that could incriminate them. This was so unlike their countries of origin, where no such event had taken place in their lifetimes. They had read about this sort of thing in history books. Or it happened in other countries where there was no respect for personal liberties. They had to remind themselves that they were in another country with a completely different belief system from their own, one that was growing more sinister by the hour. They had known in their heart of hearts that such a thing could happen, but never thought this day would come.

The doorbell rang incessantly early on Sunday morning, waking Georg and Marianne from a night of restless sleep. Marianne rushed to the door and saw through the peephole a jeep full of Afghan men. Another stood at the gate. Georg went out alone to the gate and was immediately relieved to see familiar faces, ones who had been friendly and supported the work the SNI team had done for their people.

"They are coming, Mr. George," the man at the gate said. He and the others were very distressed, their heads twisting about like owls on the lookout for danger. "They are coming today to search your office. Be careful."

Georg barely had time for an embrace and a heartfelt thank-you for what he believed was information he could trust before the man hopped back into the jeep and sped off with the others. *Even among the Taliban there are good people*, Georg thought as he rushed back inside his house. He thanked God for this unexpected warning of danger from an unlikely source.

Australian Diana Thomas, a nine-year SNI veteran who had worked in both Pakistan and Afghanistan, welcomed the staff into her home around 8:00 a.m. that same morning. She had left her native country as a professional nurse, a sacrifice she never regretted, to work with Georg in the office, helping coordinate the many projects around the city. The choice to make such a long-term commitment was a statement of her independent streak and inner strength. Diana was worried that morning, but she knew whatever lay ahead, God would be with them all.

Diana shared her house with Margrit Stebner, a gracious, meek woman from Germany, who had spent the last year and a half in charge of the SNI correspondence. Her soft-spoken nature had a calming effect on the staff as they crammed into the living room, concerned and fearful over this sinister tide now turned against them.

"I have been told that the Taliban intends to come to our main office today to search it," Georg announced to the group. "They may decide to investigate other buildings and project sites as well. While I am not expecting the Taliban to arrest any of us, leave nothing to chance. We must be prepared to evacuate. Take care of any personal and business matters that require your attention, and we'll meet back here at two o'clock."

Everyone shifted into high gear, going their separate ways, fully intending to rendezvous back at the house at the appointed time. But when Diana and Margrit arrived by taxi at SNI's main office shortly after Georg dismissed everyone, they were stunned to see a barricade at the front gate into the building. A small group of Taliban stood nearby but did not give the impression of being ready to pounce. The blockade appeared to have been assembled in haste, thrown up overnight almost in prankish fashion, an adolescent joke played on the SNI staff. The two women got out of the taxi. Somehow, they needed to get through the barrier and past the locked gate. They had money and passports in the safe. If the need to evacuate became inevitable, they could not get out of the country without these documents and cash.

Diana and Margrit decided to downplay the situation and not act alarmed.

"We want inside our offices," Diana said stiffly, holding her agitation in check.

"Someone will get a key," the leading Talib said with a bleak little grin, so the women sent the taxi away, but not before Diana retrieved their walkie-talkie.

The Taliban group left the women alone, almost ignoring them. Even though armed to the teeth with everything from munitions belts, Kalashnikovs, knives, and whips, none of them displayed antagonistic behavior—the armaments were antagonistic enough. Once the Talib leader informed them that someone was coming with a key to unlock the barricade, there was no communication between the two parties. Religious dogma and fear made them unable to peacefully intermingle or interact at all.

After waiting an uncomfortable hour for the elusive courier to bring the elusive key to unlock the Taliban's barricade in front of the gate, Margrit and Diana decided to unobtrusively slip away, to escape before things took a turn for the worse. But as they began to walk away from the office, the Taliban group surrounded them en masse, their Kalashnikovs poised to fire, their voices growling and shouting for the women to stop.

The leader dashed in front of them, the butt of his whip firm in his grip, a menacing reminder of who had the upper hand.

"You will stay," he said, with a mad snarl on his face. "You will be interrogated."

At that moment, Margrit felt the sense of dread she had carried inside the last twenty-four hours get the best of her. All sorts of macabre scenes of underground prison cells, rank and medieval, and horrific images of abuse flashed across her mind. She imagined the worst possible outcome of this situation. How could she endure this? How could her faith stand up against such brutality? She had hoped this test would never be required of her and uttered a silent prayer for courage.

Diana had the presence of mind to turn on the two-way radio, alerting every one of the staff scattered about Kabul in a several-mile radius of this terrifying situation.

"The office has been barricaded!" she shouted into the walkie-talkie. "We are surrounded by the Taliban. They have detained us. They are threatening to take us away—"

Diana cut off her own communication; the threat to their safety was too intense. Her warning ended, she handed the radio to her captors, knowing any second it would be taken from her. Two staff members responded instantly to the disquieting announcement, but it was impossible to answer.

When those on the receiving end of the communication no longer heard Diana's voice, they knew their predicament was much worse than they'd originally thought. Continued frantic attempts to raise Diana on the walkie-talkie proved fruitless. As disheartening as these new developments were, they knew panic was out of the question. Steady heads must prevail.

The Taliban forced Diana and Margrit back toward the gate, where they crouched down on the ground. One of the younger men in the group—his scraggly bearded face burned by the sun, his black turban cocked rakishly to the side—approached the huddled, defenseless women, waving his Kalashnikov in the air like a cheer-leader's baton. Margrit knew instinctively that the young man was about to shoot at them. Whether it would prove to be a fatal shot or one only to amuse his comrades, she did not know. She gripped Diana's arm and whispered her warning. The man finished his flourishing twirl of the weapon and took aim at the women. The shot meant to entertain whizzed past them, missing their heads by inches. The Taliban laughed—they did have a sense of humor, after all—and the young marksman gloated in their approval. However, the smile soon left his face when he looked back at his intended targets. Instead of bursting into tears and cowering in fear, Diana and Margrit, stoic expressions plastered on their faces, were ignoring him. He would have little satisfaction from his attempt to frighten these captives.

Peter Bunch was one of the two staff members who'd responded to Diana's warning over the two-way radio. This mild-mannered Australian engineer, a square hulk of a man, had been working on SNI special projects in Afghanistan for the last three and a half years, and his laid-back, sanguine temperament had fit in nicely with the local culture—at least those not caught up in the extremism of the Taliban. After the staff meeting that morning, he had driven to one of the project sites. He had barely arrived when the alert came. He asked Zareef, an Afghan who was the SNI project manager, to return to the SNI office with him.

When the two of them saw Diana and Margrit waiting with their Taliban captors, they knew without question the trouble awaiting them. Zareef shouted for Peter to escape. The first instinct for most, of course, is flight, so Peter hit the accelerator on the auto-mobile. Even though the Taliban pursued them on foot, firing into the air to get them to stop, they could have escaped—but Peter's conscience got the best of him. He could not abandon the women in their plight, and so returned to the scene.

The ragged band of Taliban encircled the car the moment Peter drove up to the office. Enraged by his attempt to flee, they pointed their Kalashnikovs at Peter and Zareef from every direction. Peter had no chance to warn anyone on his walkie-talkie; the Taliban leader commandeered it the second he came to a stop. He also insisted Peter give him the keys to the vehicle, but Peter steadfastly refused. Peter even tried to negotiate with the Taliban to release the women and take him instead, but the Taliban leader was equally stubborn in his refusal. They were at an impasse—but the one with the most guns wins, so the Taliban leader forced the two women into the car, then stuffed himself and several other guards into the vehicle and ordered Peter to drive. If Peter would not give up his keys, then he could just chauffeur them all to the vice and virtue prison.

Katrin Jelinek had a wonderful energy that kept pace with all the children under her care. In the year and a half she'd spent in Kabul working with the street children's project and the orphanage, Katrin had endeared herself to scores of children who enjoyed little or no attention from a loving adult. She made each child feel as though he or she was important and valuable. She didn't want to evacuate without attempting to contact her Afghan staff and the children at the orphanage project.

Katrin and the street children with whom she worked.

Katrin knew the situation was precarious; therefore she had made her peace with it. The night before, she had placed a call to her pastor in Germany. She had originally intended to join Heather and Dayna at the home of the Afghan family to watch the Jesus film, but at the last minute another appointment prevented her from going. Now that the Taliban had arrested the two American women, Katrin felt that she, too, would be a target.

Any foreigner who came to work in Afghanistan knew there was great risk involved. With the volatile nature of the political situation—and of those in power—as well as a history of civil war, one knew going in that there was an element of danger and uncertainty. Katrin wanted to assure her pastor and herself that were anything to happen, she had prepared for the worst. She had come to this country, as had all the others, to help improve the lives of the people of Afghanistan. No one from SNI had come motivated by personal gain or glory, only for the excitement of obeying his or her personal God-call and to give back to a people in desperate need. She ticked off the list to her pastor—interrogation, deportation, imprisonment (or worse)—and in each circumstance Katrin was able to say she was mentally and emotionally equipped. This spiritual moment of taking stock was an "Ebenezer stone," a reminder of her commitment of faith.

That Sunday morning, August 5, 2001, Katrin arrived at the orphanage and children's project, a compound of two adjoining buildings with enough space to run activities and house up to two hundred boys. The vice and virtue police were waiting. The Taliban were convinced that this SNI project was nothing more than a *madrassa* (religious school) whose sole purpose was to convert the young boys to Christianity. Katrin had wanted to give a few instructions for the Afghan staff—she recently had been able to employ eight men to help in the workshops—as well as leave some money for salaries and materials in case she found herself expelled from Kabul. She had to stand by helplessly and watch the arrest of her employees and the rounding up of more than fifty young boys, before the Taliban forced her at gunpoint to return home so they could arrest her housemate too.

Silke Duerrkopf had been in bed most of that weekend, suffering from severe abdominal problems. The intensity and frequency of the meetings over the last forty-eight hours had exhausted her; therefore she was taking a few hours' rest before the next meeting that afternoon.

Silke was an artist who'd come from Germany around the same

time as Katrin to apply her artistic and teaching skills to the street children's project. Although she'd been unsure, at first, if this was what she was supposed to do with her life, on her first day working in a refugee camp, she'd met a young orphan girl who was around ten years old. The girl clung to Silke, talking incessantly, animated and vivacious, seemingly oblivious to the squalid conditions of the world she lived in, and Silke could not resist the affection she felt for this child. A necklace bearing the image of the *Mona Lisa* dangled from around the girl's neck. Excited to share with her that this was a very famous and beautiful painting and that she had seen it hanging in the Louvre in Paris, Silke inquired through the interpreter if the girl knew of the woman in the picture.

"This is my mother," the young girl had replied, her beaming face unable to conceal her pride. "She died when I was very small."

Silke's heart melted. All the things she could have said, all her wise Western words lodged in her throat. She could hear the inner voice of God challenging her: *This is not about you. Why go back to Germany? What about doing something real with your life in this place?* At that moment, Silke had felt a love for Afghanistan begin to blossom.

Now awakened from a sound sleep, Silke heard the commotion outside the house but was unsure of the source. But she knew something was wrong, so she dragged herself from her sickbed. She had no sooner gotten dressed in her *shalwar kamiz* (lounging house clothes) than her bedroom door burst open and ten armed Taliban clambered into the room. Silke was horrified and indignant. She refused to show fear and, shouting at them in three different languages, drove the intruders from her bedroom, slamming the door in their shocked faces.

Everyone who worked for SNI, especially the women, dressed

according to the norms of the Afghan/Pashtun culture, in both public and private settings. What might be acceptable attire by Western standards could be a cause for outrage to those who lived by the restrictive Pashtun code. Afghan women caught answering the door to their home inappropriately dressed could be beaten or imprisoned. For these Taliban to be so disrespectful was not only an outrage, it was an infraction of their own authoritarian law. While Silke got dressed, Katrin explained her housemate's indignation, something these men should have known without the instruction of a woman. When Silke entered the living room, dressed appropriately and wearing her *chador* (head covering), the designated Taliban leader ordered the two women to go with them to the vice and virtue police headquarters for questioning. No apologies were offered to Silke.

As she and Katrin clumped down the steps of their house under armed guard, it occurred to Silke that it might be smart to have money. It was not as if they were going out for a day of shopping, but she did not know what was ahead of them, and having a little cash might prove beneficial. Without asking for permission or trying to explain the purpose of her abrupt turn on the stairs, she pushed her way past the Taliban guards behind her and dashed back into her room. She stuffed her bag with all the cash she had. With a magician's speed, Silke was too fast for the Talib, who had followed her back into her room. He showed no interest in the bag or its contents after Silke resumed her march to the vehicles outside, waiting to carry them to prison.

It was midmorning when Georg left his house. He was unaware of the multiple arrests of his staff, which had happened just a short time before his departure. Ever the good shepherd, he took a slight detour from his route to the foreign ministry and swung his car by Silke and Katrin's house to check on them, only to find dozens of Taliban scurrying about in front of the house like skittish trolls. His heart began to sink as he drove up and stopped in front of the ominous scene. He steadied himself as he got out of the car and, with a feigned air of innocence, asked why the Taliban were there.

"Are you Mr. George?" someone from the group demanded.

"Mr. George" was the moniker used by the Afghans he knew, but Georg reacted with a gut response.

"I am Mr. Taubmann," he answered, which immediately set the Taliban off in a flurry of confusion.

Georg tried to collect his wits as the Taliban attempted to clarify who was standing before them and what they should do. Still baffled by this "Mr. Taubmann," the decision makers in the group ordered him taken into the house. Once inside, Georg realized that the Taliban had arrested Silke and Katrin and taken them away. Georg sat quietly as his captors discussed his fate. The discussion was brief. They snatched the car keys from his hands and then manhandled Georg to his car, where they tossed him into the backseat. Sitting in the backseat was a man who then opened the opposite door and put one foot out onto the ground. A small-framed man, he nodded at Georg.

"Do not worry. I'll take care of you," he said in broken English, his voice subdued, his eyes darting about, making sure no one else saw or heard him communicate with the prisoner before he stepped out of the vehicle.

The car instantly filled with Taliban. Georg was wedged between two fearsome warriors, their Kalashnikovs perched between their legs. The man who had whispered words of hope to Georg slipped into the front seat, never looking back at him. The driver gunned the engine and sped off down the road. The rest of the company piled into flatbed trucks and tore out in hot pursuit.

Left: A Shelter Now bakery in the Shalman Valley near Peshawar, Pakistan, which houses thousands of Afghan refugees.

Below: Baking naan bread at the SNI bakery.

In forty-eight hours the insanity had absorbed eight Western SNI staffers. Now the wrath of the Mullah Omar loyalists was about to be unleashed against the SNI Afghan employees and SNI projects and facilities in Kabul and other cities. The mandate was simple: destroy all things SNI.

CHAPTER TWO

IN THE BLINK OF AN EYE

W hat had taken years to build took only a matter of hours to reduce to rubble. It was not just the brick and mortar; it was equipment—from vehicles to the least expensive tool—either looted or destroyed. From Kabul to Kandahar, Herat to Khost to Helmand, the Taliban extremists unleashed their fury upon the numerous SNI projects designed solely for the betterment of the Afghan people. Factories that produced materials for refugee housing, shops to repair vehicles, projects to aid Afghan widows and orphans (including a school for girls), distribution centers for food and clothing, homes, clinics, outdoor bathroom facilities, anything with the SNI stamp on it fell to willful destruction. In Kabul, the total number of Afghan employees arrested came to sixteen adult men.

"I resisted them when they came to the office," Daoud, an

Afghan employee, said, disappointed that he could do very little to protect his friends, though he was able to hide the computers of the Kabul office before the Taliban arrived. "I tried to stop them, but they overpowered me and began to beat me."

"It was the worst day of my life," Fareed said, at a loss to explain such injustice carried out against them by their own people. "What had we done? What was our sin?"

All sixteen Afghan employees were taken to the religious police department, a division of the vice and virtue ministry, and held in a section of the prison separate from where Georg and Peter were imprisoned. When questioned by a Taliban interrogator as to why their search did not turn up any computers in the SNI offices, Georg refused to give them any information. Even though the staff had cleared all the sensitive material on the computers before the mass arrests, especially the names of any Afghan individual or family that might be compromised by association with SNI, the computers were still valuable and, given time and technological skill, some if not all of that information might be successfully retrieved. It was during this grilling that Georg learned of the plight of the sixteen employees. Now it was imperative that those computers stay out of the hands of the Taliban.

"We will beat the traitors to Islam until they confess," the interrogator said, his jaw snapping furiously. "You have turned them into infidels. We will torture the dogs, and they will confess. Then we shall hang them in the streets so everyone can see the price you pay for becoming a Christian."

In spite of the duress from the interrogator, in spite of the image of his innocent Afghan friends tortured and executed playing through his mind, in spite of any harm that might befall him for refusing to cooperate, Georg remained silent—denying the Taliban the information they demanded. Instead, he prayed. He prayed no harm would come to the Afghans. He prayed God would free the sixteen even before he and the other seven Westerners saw their release. He prayed that he could live with his own conscience if the Taliban carried out their threats against the sixteen. Even though Georg and the others had shared their beliefs about Christ with the Afghan employees, conversion was not a precondition for Afghan employment with SNI. They loved the Afghans for their own sake, and those sixteen men deeply appreciated the opportunity for work and the kindness shown them by the SNI staff without any pressure to convert. The sixteen had remained committed to their own Islamic faith, but they were loyal to Georg and the others, even when accused by the Taliban of being Christian converts.

On the Sunday after the arrests, Georg decided to go to the foreign ministry. He wanted to know why Heather and Dayna had been arrested, to see why the Taliban had taken these unusual hostile tactics against them. He left behind Marianne and their teenage sons, Daniel and Benjamin, carrying on by busying themselves with normal routines. The boys were understandably concerned for their safety and for the safety of their father driving through the inhospitable streets of Kabul. Marianne did her best to keep her anxiety from spilling over. Her voice calm and soothing, she wanted to give the encouraging impression to her boys that all would be well. Once it became clear what was going on, she was confident that their father would be able to resolve any issues of misunderstanding.

"We have many friends among the Taliban," she assured Daniel and Benjamin. "They will do all they can to help us."

The teenagers took their mother at her word. They could go on with their lives knowing their parents had everything under control, and when circumstances begin to take a turn for the worse, Marianne continued to try to shield her sons from her own awful fears. *What if the Taliban comes here to search our house?* she wondered. *What would happen if the Taliban decides to arrest our whole family? What would happen to the boys?* These thoughts only added to the level of stress she felt, and she did her best to shove them into the back of her mind.

Besides Peter, Marianne was the only other SNI staffer who had heard Diana's distress call over the two-way radio. Shocked, she immediately tried to respond to Diana, but got no answer. When Marianne gave up trying to raise Diana, she called Georg on the radio. He also did not answer. She tried again and again, but there was no response. This was unusual; Georg always had his radio with him. He never went anywhere without it. *He could not have forgotten to turn it on,* she thought. *Could there be something wrong with the radio? Is he out of range? Has he stepped inside a building that blocks the frequency? Have Taliban extremists found him? . . . Please, dear God, let him answer.*

After a few minutes she tried again, and all she heard was the sizzle of static. She couldn't believe this was happening. The panic began to rise in her stomach, and she called around to other SNI staffers. Had they seen Georg? Had he called them? Had they heard from anyone? No one had received a call from Georg. No one knew where he was. It was as if he had vanished, as if he no longer existed.

She did her best to banish these thoughts and prayed that she would know something soon.

She finally made contact with Len Stitt, an American SNI director stationed in Herat who was in charge of the SNI projects in that city. He had driven over to Kabul earlier that week with his family and the other SNI employees in Herat for meetings with all the Western staff members and Udo Stolte, the European coordinator, before Udo returned to Germany. At the time, this trip to Kabul was just part of a routine scheduled well in advance, but now it proved to be an ordained act of God.

Len and his family were staying in another house in Kabul, and Marianne stepped into the backyard to talk to Len out of earshot of Daniel and Benjamin. Len had not spoken to Georg either, nor had he heard from any of the others.

"It's very spooky, Marianne," Len said, his voice quality on the radio revealing a fragile strain. "I've tried Katrin, Silke, Diana, Peter. No one answers, not just Georg."

"What do you think is the best thing to do?" Marianne asked, fearful of his answer.

"The situation is getting hot. The Taliban know where we are staying. I don't know how much longer we can avoid . . ." He paused. He did not want to say aloud that what he feared to be Georg's fate might also be theirs. "I think we should consider leaving."

"No, I will not leave," Marianne said flatly. "I cannot think of leaving."

"Marianne, by my count, there are eight adults who have not been arrested, and eight children, including Daniel and Benjamin. Their safety is my biggest concern. The situation could get much worse for everyone. If we leave soon, we might be able to make it to Pakistan."

"No. I cannot leave the country. I cannot leave Georg. What if he gets out of prison, comes home, and we are not here?"

"Marianne, we still don't know if Georg has been arrested."

She had assumed the worst. Subconsciously, she had allowed herself to drop her guard against the worst-case scenario. Her fears had gotten the best of her.

"You're right. We don't know—so even more reason not to leave."

"I understand, Marianne, but I think we need to be prepared for anything."

Be prepared for anything. It is what one does when one leaves the safe confines of kith and kin. Be prepared for anything when venturing into a brand new culture, a foreign language, a dissimilar geography and harsh climate, when one steps into the lives of other human beings that are as strange to you as you are to them. She knew she had to be prepared for anything, but how does one prepare for this? This scenario was not in any manual she had ever read.

"All right, Len, I'll do what I need to do."

Marianne signed off the radio. What did she need to do? She stepped back inside the house and saw her boys sitting at the kitchen table with inquisitive looks on their faces, yet they were not quite sure what to ask her. She gave the boys an altered explanation of her conversation with Len; he was trying to contact their father and was expecting to hear from him, as was she, at any time.

A frantic knock on the door grabbed everyone's attention. She held out her hand to stop the boys from bolting for the front of the house. She would take care of this. The rapping on the door became a pounding, from knuckles to balled fist, an insistence that bespoke urgency. She walked briskly through the rooms, trying not to let the boys notice her apprehension. Could it be an SNI staff member with news of Georg? Could it be the Taliban? She cracked the door and saw the hard-edged face of Ahmed Habib, a dear friend who held an influential position in one of the government ministries and was a longtime supporter of the great work accomplished by SNI.

Marianne stepped outside and then closed the door behind her. Whatever the news Ahmed brought, she wanted to tell the boys herself after she had heard it first.

Ahmed performed a clumsy imitation of composure as a messenger of bad news. His eyes blinked nonstop. He wrung his gnarled hands, then pulled on his beard. He looked over his shoulder, then back at Marianne. There was no easy way to convey this information.

"Several of the Shelter Now people, men and women, have been arrested today, including many Afghan men who worked for the organization. They have even rounded up scores of boys from the children's project."

Marianne's eyes darted back and forth. Nothing distracted her from looking directly into Ahmed's stricken face. This was not culturally acceptable. Women did not look into the eyes of men. They averted their eyes until given permission. All the arrests were unacceptable, but Ahmed had not mentioned her husband. She needed news of her husband. She would not release him of her glare until he had told her of Georg.

"And Mr. George . . . ," Ahmed said, his voice a mere whisper, his own eyes averted from the intensity of her gaze. "They have taken him as well."

Marianne felt her insides disperse like vapor blasted by an unexpected wind, and she braced herself against the door. Ahmed had confirmed the nightmare. The trembling in her body would not stop. At the risk of his own position among the Taliban administration, Ahmed had come to bring her this news. It had to be the truth. It had to be the truth, or why would he risk exposure in broad daylight, coming to the home of the infidel? She had to stop trembling. She could not move forward if she continued to tremble. Marianne pushed off against the door and tried to balance her unsteady legs. She looked into Ahmed's sympathetic eyes. If she spoke, she might burst into tears.

"Mr. George is my friend," Ahmed said, his quiet tone meant to calm. "I will do all I can to help him."

"Where have they taken him?" she managed to ask without losing control.

"The prison of the Ministry of Vice and Virtue."

Marianne covered her mouth with her hand and nodded her head, registering the authenticity of Ahmed's words. She leaned back against the door. She needed to embrace someone. She needed physical support. To embrace Ahmed was impossible. When did she last embrace Georg? What were the last words they had exchanged before he left that morning? She could not remember.

"All he has with him is what he put on this morning," Marianne managed to say. She was beginning to regain a logical thought process, even if only focused on the mundane. "He needs a change of clothes. He needs personal items. He needs . . ." She stopped herself. She was treating this as if it were a business trip, as if Georg was traveling for a few days and she was helping him organize a suitcase for the journey. "He needs a bag packed with a few things."

"I will see that he gets it," Ahmed said.

He departed with the promise to return that evening.

Marianne went back inside the house. How do you tell your children that their father and their family friends and coworkers are now in the hands of the Taliban extremists and you have no idea why or what they intend to do with him or the others? How can you be strong when such inexplicable news has maimed your heart? What words do you use to explain to your sons that their dear father was now at the mercy of ruthless people? How do you explain why life has taken this sinister twist?

The boys were milling about the kitchen, preparing to make some lunch, when Marianne entered. There was no masking the agonized expression on her face, but she was not about to ask her sons to comfort her. She held out her arms like a mother hen and received her chicks under her wings. "They have arrested your father," she explained, "and many others . . . he is being held in a prison"—she would not mention the name; it could only heighten fear in her children as it did within her own heart. "We believe that it is some kind of misunderstanding and that soon everyone should be released."

She could tell by the worried looks on her boys' faces that this minimal information, even with its positive spin, was not completely satisfying, that there were more questions than answers, and that there was a time limit on their patience. She pulled them closer, said a quick prayer, then kissed their foreheads.

"I want whatever you're having for lunch," she said, a nod to normalcy deflecting the restlessness in her spirit. "Let me call Len to discuss what we need to do."

Marianne released her sons—young boys looking toward

manhood, though she was not yet keen to let them face grown-men realities. They went back to preparing lunch as Marianne stepped into the backyard and signaled Len on the radio. Once she had explained everything that Ahmed told her, it was not long before several SNI staff members converged on the house to offer her support. She still did not want to alarm her sons, so the staff distracted them while she and Len moved to a separate room to discuss their next move. Len had been in contact with the offices in Peshawar, Pakistan, keeping them informed of the latest developments. Everyone in Peshawar agreed that it would be best if the remaining staff left Kabul and tried to get out of the country. Marianne said the words—it looked like retreat was inevitable. She even agreed with her words, but her heart was not ready to accept a rational, logical decision of the mind.

Marianne spent the rest of the day destroying whatever she had in the house that she thought might offend the religious police, but some things could not be shredded or burned. These she put into a box and took outside into the backyard. She took a shovel from the garden shed and began to dig a hole in the earth. It had to be deep, deep like a burial, so scavengers would not find these treasures—items that revealed a traceable past, tangible items of past existence, such as holiday souvenirs gathered from their travels; letters from loved ones; CDs of favorite music; and photos: sons from birth to present day, parents and siblings, and of her wedding day. She gazed at a picture of her and her beloved Georg. *He had hair back then*, she mused as she rubbed her finger over the image of the two of them, tuxedoed and veiled, smiling, their hearts soaring with love. On that day, she had never imagined where their shared vows and the God-call would take them. Burying her wedding photos in the backyard in Kabul, Afghanistan, was not a specific action of the marriage vow she could have foreseen. She leaned back and looked into the sky, amazed by her marriage covenant, amazed by what it could require of a person, amazed by its power. However, God had sworn a covenant as well: a covenant to be their refuge, to be a light in darkness, to be present wherever they might be. There was no place one could go that God was not present. She sighed, confident that neither covenant could be broken, and finished wrapping her treasures in plastic before laying them in their temporary grave. She refilled the hole and tamped down the loose dirt with her foot. One day she would return to this very spot and dig up these years of memories and feel like the wealthiest person in the world.

Ahmed Habib returned later that evening. The cover of darkness was safer for all concerned. He was more agitated than he had been earlier in the day. As before, he and Marianne met at the front door of the house and spoke in hushed tones.

"You can no longer stay here," he said. "You must leave."

"But my husband. I can't . . ."

"You must understand. The order to arrest everyone involved with Shelter Now has come directly from Mullah Omar."

A pause followed, allowing the words to sink in. Even Ahmed looked bewildered by the words he had just spoken. Why would the highest-ranking member of the entire Taliban command dispense such an order? Mullah Omar led a nomadic existence throughout Afghanistan, issuing edicts and revisions of *sharia* law during his broadcasts on Sharia Radio. Few ever saw him, and hundreds of followers always protected him. Why did Mullah Omar care about these people? Why did he see them as such a threat? Yet when he gave an order, no one dared disobey.

Marianne understood. The danger had gotten much worse, something she and the others never could have anticipated. Her mind and heart converged, and she knew that escape was the only alternative.

"It is no longer safe for you to stay in this house."

"I must pack," Marianne said, her mind instantly deciding what essentials she would put into her suitcase. "I must tell my sons."

"Stay at my home tonight. Stay with my family. Let me protect you."

The offer was genuine, but she could not accept.

"You have placed yourself and your family in grave danger already, Ahmed Habib. I cannot put you at risk anymore."

"I insist. I insist. I will give you time to pack and then return."

He turned to leave without waiting for Marianne to answer. She had to raise her voice to stop him. It sounded as though she were yelling after conversing with him in whispers.

"Wait," she said, then slipped into her house. She returned holding a bag. "In case you are unable to return or if something happens to . . ." She did not want to finish that thought, so she held out the bag to Ahmed. "For Georg. He will need these things. And if you see him, tell him—say to him . . ." Ahmed waited, but she would not burden this kind man with all that she had in her heart to say to her husband. "I will see him soon, and tell him myself."

Ahmed smiled, took the bag, and slipped through the gate into the street.

It was now time to set aside the motherly instinct to shield her children from grave news. She sat her boys down and told them everything. She spared no detail of the current reality facing them. She did not, however, speculate on what might happen; she only dealt with the actuality of what had happened and what she intended for them to do right then. The situation was very serious, she told them. They could no longer stay in this house. They were going to have to leave Kabul without their father—that was the most difficult bit of news she had to break, and it nearly caused her to lose control, but she held her emotions in check. "Pack one suitcase," she continued, "one suitcase apiece, one for your schoolbooks, the other for personal things." And here she wrapped her arms around her boys. "You will leave behind things you love," she told them—dear God, must she leave behind the most important thing she had ever loved? "We are all leaving behind things we love," she continued, "and we may never see these things again"—dear God, not Georg . . . let me lose all keepsakes and treasures, but not Georg, she thought—"but we must travel light."

"Do you understand?" she said, and she looked at them knowing the clarity of her words had left no room for dissent.

The only concession she made was the family guinea pig. It would be caged and carried by one of the boys at all times.

In Marianne's heart the burden of fear had lifted. It was now a matter of keeping a cool head and being cautious and alert. The load she was unable to lift, its weight too heavy, was the thought that Georg sat in prison and she had no idea how he was doing. What were the conditions of his cell? How were they treating him? Had he eaten anything? Would she ever hear him tell her the story of his ordeal?

They waited for Ahmed an hour beyond the time she had hoped he would return for them. When Marianne felt as though it was becoming too dangerous for her to wait any longer, she told the boys to get into their car. Before locking the door, she turned on one light. She would let the outside world think life inside the Taubmann house was continuing as normal, and that when Georg did come home, there would be a light to welcome him.

It was the morning call to prayer. The familiar sound of the *muezzin* vocalist, perched in the minaret tower, calling the faithful to the mosque with his chant of praise to Allah, ushered in the early morning light. With the call to prayer came the lifting of the curfew and the removal of most checkpoints throughout the city. The remaining sixteen SNI workers and children could now attempt their escape after a sleepless night.

The most dangerous point of the journey was the beginning. The group could not leave before the authorities lifted the curfew, and that coincided with the time of day when the city would be crowded with the Taliban on their way to the neighborhood mosques. Perhaps the timing was in their favor. Perhaps the faithful would be less interested in them and more interested in keeping their religious commitment.

It was an unsettling feeling driving through the streets of Kabul in the predawn light, passing clusters of sleepy-eyed Taliban, Kalashnikovs slung over their shoulders, traversing toward the nearest mosque. It was possible at any moment for any of the Taliban to recognize the two vehicles, call out the alarm, and force the caravan to stop. Len and an Afghan driver did the driving. Everyone kept from making eye contact with anyone on the street. Quiet prayers went up from the two vans. The mosques were bustling with worshippers. The city of Kabul was alive with prayer: prayers for escape and prayers of praise, the citizenry filled with righteous expectancy.

When the two vans drove beyond the city limits without incident, there was relief and thankfulness that the immediate threat of capture was behind them. But there was no joy. How could there be rejoicing? They had left behind their compatriots, husbands and fathers, sons and daughters, brothers and sisters, Muslim and Christian, twenty-four dear friends whose families in Kabul and on three different continents would soon learn what these sixteen fugitives already knew: their loved one was a captive, held at the mercy of those not known for showing mercy. There could be no rejoicing. Their own journey was not yet over; eight hours of desert travel lay ahead, and the final impediment to freedom, crossing the border into Pakistan.

Along their journey near the Pakistani border, the company made a brief stop at a public bathroom. They had taken great precaution not to draw attention to themselves all along the way, but at this final stop before reaching the border, an Afghan friend spotted Marianne and approached them with disturbing news, bringing a moment of panic in everyone. He had just heard announced on Radio Sharia of the twenty-four SNI workers arrested by the Taliban, and he warned them to leave immediately, before someone realized who they were. Their rest stop cut short, they jumped back into the vehicles and sped for the border. There were no more stops.

They had timed their arrival at the border crossing to be in the middle of the day, when there would be the fewest number of Taliban. Most would be attending noon prayers at a local mosque, leaving a skeleton crew behind to carry out the responsibility of documenting passports. If there were to be any difficulties, it would be here. Had the local authorities alerted the border guards of a possible crossing by Western fugitives? Had they heard the news on Radio Sharia, like their friend at the rest stop?

Marianne and Len collected the sixteen passports. It was better if the whole company did not have to get out of the vehicles, especially the small children, but all the adults knew this ordeal could take a long time, something they had very little of. If they were still at the border crossing when midday prayers were over and the Taliban returned, their chance for escape became bleak.

Len entered the station carrying the sixteen passports just as the two Taliban guards were dipping their hands into their lunch bowls. When they saw Len with a stack of passports in his hands, their faces fell, disgusted at the thought of having to deal with this procedure at lunchtime. It was only the two of them, there was no one to take over, so if they were going to eat, they first had to get the job done.

The guards formed a two-man assembly line. The first would imprint the blank page with the official Afghanistan stamp, and the second would write his signature. Neither of them bothered to look at the names on the passports or asked for the passengers inside the vehicles to step into the station to confirm their identities. That would have taken too much time away from lunch. Both parties felt the sense of urgency to get through the process as fast as possible.

Within five minutes the bureaucratic routine was complete, and Len was back at the vehicles giving everyone their passports.

"They just wanted to get rid of us," Len said.

"Thank God for this miracle," Marianne said, looking at the

official stamp on her passport allowing her and the others to leave the country.

"Yes, the miracle of hunger."

They pulled away from the station, and as Len craned his neck around to see the border crossing fade into the distance, he saw in the backseat a small child asleep on his mother's shoulder, unaware of the danger he'd slept through. Len felt the weight of the world lift from his shoulders.

But for Marianne the weight became heavier. She and her boys would get safely back to Germany and remain there. The next contact she would have with her beloved husband would be to see him on the evening news in the custody of the Taliban. She was grateful for the miracle of their escape but prayed that God had more such miracles for Georg and the others.

The naked lightbulb dangled from the crumbling ceiling, its wire corroded and frayed. The diffused light from the bulb made the clammy walls, pockmarked as if someone had fired off rounds of ordinance inside the room, appear to sweat in the heat. The dirt floor of the six-by-nine cell was moist and stuck to the bottom of Georg's shoes as he paced back and forth in the cramped space. Georg could imagine all manner of vermin or snakes or scorpions slipping in through the cracks and crevices of the walls and ceiling. At any moment he expected these uninvited guests to appear. It was almost as frightening a thought as the appearance of a Taliban guard.

The room was adjacent to a kitchen where the guards prepared their food. Pungent smells that turned the stomach drifted through the connecting window. The kitchen was a source of considerable tumult during meal preparation, and the frequent appearance in the window of a scowling Taliban guard checking on the well-being of his guests was almost a comic experience, were it not for the miserable circumstances. There was no furniture in the cell, only two grimy, bedbug-ridden mattresses tossed on the soggy floor. Peter sat on his mattress in the corner, dozing, his hand occasionally giving a weary swat at the flies buzzing around him or scratching a fresh bite from a bedbug. Asleep or awake, Peter was a great comfort to Georg, a corporeal sign of God's presence when there appeared to be no other evidence. Yet as he paced alone, his thoughts took a dark and frightful turn, and his prayers were comparable to the Psalms of David:

> How long, O LORD? Will You forget me forever?
>> How long will You hide Your face from me?
> How long shall I take counsel in my soul,
>> Having sorrow in my heart daily?
>> How long will my enemy be exalted over me?
> Consider and hear me, O LORD my God;
>> Enlighten my eyes,
>> Lest I sleep the sleep of death. (13:1–3)

Georg's heart felt bludgeoned. How many others of his team had the Taliban arrested? Where were they now? And his family, where were they? Had the Taliban torn them from their home and thrown them into a cell such as this one? Were Marianne and the boys separated from one another? His thoughts and fears were excruciating.

> The pangs of death surrounded me,
>> And the floods of ungodliness made me afraid.

The sorrows of Sheol surrounded me;
    The snares of death confronted me.
In my distress I called upon the LORD,
    And cried out to my God;
    He heard my voice from His temple,
    And my cry came before Him, even to His ears. (Ps. 18:4–6)

All Georg could do was utter the words of King David. These words, written from the heart of a man who understood the meaning of fear and misery, deep crying to deep, a soul racked in agony, pleading for the smallest comfort, tumbled from Georg's lips. Would God send that small comfort? Would God provide a scrap of consolation? The noise, the smells, the insects, the confinement, and the fretfulness all contributed to an exhausting first day and night in prison for the two men.

On the morning of the second day, the door burst open and the guards flung Zareef, the SNI project manager, into the room. Georg and Peter rushed to their friend, but he winced when they touched him and drew back toward the door, clutching his chest. He refused to look at Georg and Peter, his head and shoulders bloated and tender from the torture he had endured. The exposure of a man stripped and beaten was a sickening and humiliating visual image.

There was no beneficence from the guards, no respect for Peter and Georg's appalled reaction at seeing this slender bough of a man tossed into their cell, a deformed and twisted figure. They pushed Zareef back into the room and barked an order.

"They have come for the keys to the offices," Zareef mumbled through inflated lips, his head bowed, forward and limp as though his neck were broken.

It came as a shock for Georg to realize his friend had suffered this torture to protect a set of keys. His heart ached. Then it dawned on him that it was more than the keys: Zareef had tried to protect him, the others, and the SNI property. Zareef's body was an outward manifestation of that failure, and it broke Georg's heart. It was a double humiliation.

Georg dug into his pocket and produced the keys. His natural instinct was to give them to Zareef, but the guard snatched the ring from his hand the moment they appeared. Then he grabbed Zareef by his shirt and pulled him toward the door. Zareef resisted, not because he did not wish to comply, but because of the pain that racked his body. He extended an arm to Georg, a helpless wave, a supplicant gesture as if offering to atone for his failure to withstand the beating. Georg looked into the bloodshot eyes of his friend and thanked him before the guard pulled him out the door.

Georg and Peter stood quiet and motionless in their cell, the noise of the guards shouting at Zareef to make haste becoming a slow, distant resonance. The door reopened and a different guard appeared. He looked back down the corridor before he entered, checking to be sure that no one was observing him. He lifted the back of his shirt, removed a bag, and tossed it to Georg.

"From Ahmed Habib," he said, then quickly disappeared.

The two men stood blank eyed, unsure of what they had witnessed, until Peter broke the spell by pointing to the bag in Georg's hands—the physical object left behind from the guard's appearing/disappearing act. They squatted down on a mattress, and Georg opened the bag and pulled out its contents: a change of clothes, a hand towel and washcloths for bathing, soap, and aspirin. He then upended the bag, shook it, and out fell a chocolate bar. Georg began to tremble. The thought of Marianne taking the time to pack these meager essentials for him and having them sent to him in prison was a stab of reality. Prison was a reality—his wife and sons and all the others suddenly consigned to memory, their faces and voices a jumbled, nearly incoherent force of sound and image battering his heart. Was this her last act for him before she and the boys had to . . . had to what? Go into hiding? Flee the city? Be arrested? Was yesterday's departure from his home the last sight he would have of his family? What were his last words to his sons, to his dear wife, before he dashed out of the house yesterday? Georg crumpled into a ball, and Peter wrapped his arms around his friend and held him as he expelled his grief and worry for his family.

Then it struck him, a sharp thought driving through the heartache. He looked again through the bag, pulling it inside out. He looked through the flannels of cloth used for bathing. He unfolded the hand towel. He laid out the fresh clothes and rubbed his hands over the pants and shirt, and there he felt it—in the large top pocket of the shirt. He pulled it out and then checked the window to be sure none of the guards was spying on them. His fingers trembled as he pulled back the folds of the plain white paper and saw the simple words written in haste.

Dear Georg, I am in the care of good people and we are leaving the country for Pakistan. Do not worry about us. We are safe. We are praying for you and everyone. I love you. Marianne.

Relief poured over him like a flood. His family was safe. God had heard the cry of his heart. He had pleaded for a scrap of comfort, and God had dropped this blessing into his beggar's cup. He pressed the note to his chest, rocking back and forth, his effusive gratitude tumbling out of his mouth.

"Thank you, Jesus," he gushed. "Thank you. Thank you, Jesus."

CHAPTER THREE

INTERROGATIONS

The war with Russia during the 1980s sent hundreds of thousands of Afghans fleeing into neighboring Pakistan, where they survived in refugee camps. *Madrassas* already existed in that part of the world, teaching a fundamentalist slant of the Koran. Many more schools sprang up because of the influx of refugees. Parents sent their sons to these *madrassas*, a boarding school that charged no tuition, if for no other reason than that they knew their children would be clothed and fed at no cost to them. It was a relief to anxious parents who had little or no means to provide for their male children. A young boy attending such a school was a *Talib*, which means "student." A *madrassa* not only provided religious instruction, but in some of the extreme schools, a young Talib also underwent military training as well. There was little attention paid to learning to read or write, except for the phrases and instructions found in the Koran that supported a stringent reading crucial to the religion. So most of the Taliban graduated from such a one-sided educational system illiterate in reading and writing—though clear and fanatical about good and evil. It goes without saying that a *madrassa* never accepted a girl or young woman.

In the early 1990s after the Russian military returned home with its tail between its legs, Afghanistan was free from the invaders but broken and without direction from strong, visionary leaders. No central government exercised any control. Warlords and *mujahideen* (Islamic guerrilla fighters)—who were constantly fighting among themselves in the struggle for power and geography—dominated the country. This Wild West atmosphere gave an opportunity for the strongest among them to rise to power. Such a one was Mullah Omar. He'd fought as a guerrilla with the anti-Soviet *mujahideen*. During the war with the Soviets, he was wounded four times and lost an eye. By 1996, the followers of Mullah Omar would bestow upon him the title "Commander of the Faithful." But before he was elevated to this exalted state, he and a band of twenty to thirty men—Talibs all, graduates from the extreme *madrassas*—roamed the southern part of the country. They knew the history of Afghanistan and became dismayed at the lawless, fractured state of their country since the end of the war. When some distraught parents from a local tribe came to Mullah Omar seeking justice in a family crisis, the Taliban movement was born.

A neighboring tribal chieftain had raped a couple of young girls, then proceeded to shave their heads, paint them, and display them to public humiliation. The distressed parents pleaded their case before Mullah Omar, and without hesitation, he murdered the offending commander in a public and atrocious fashion. When the commander's men witnessed such decisive and brutal action taken against their leader, they dropped their weapons and joined the Taliban. Such positive reinforcement proved to be an irresistible incentive to Mullah Omar, and he took his religious and often bloody campaign on the road. With the Koran in one hand and all manner of weapons in the other, he and his growing army success-fully dominated most of the country. He secured his power base when he gained control of the capital city of Kabul in September 1996. With the promise of a better quality of life and a lawful soci-ety, he had won majority support from the people.

But the Mullah Omar regime had a dark side. He established his rule on the strict interpretation of *sharia* law and claimed to have created the purest Islamic state since the Middle Ages. No one seemed to complain when he closed the schools (including the University of Kabul), banned all films and television, all forms of music, sports, kite flying (a traditional Afghan pastime), and all toys depicting humans or animals. That is what can happen when a dictatorship is established. And, of course, women had virtually no rights of any kind—including the right to work or be educated. They became dependent on men, and since the previous two decades of war had left Afghanistan bereft of much of the male population, most women had no husbands or male relatives to care for them. Daily life settled into a consistency of intimidation: the vice and virtue police patrolling the city streets, on the lookout for those men whose beards were not the proper length, who did not pray at the appointed times, whose attendance at the local mosque was lackadaisical; or for those women whose *burkas* were insufficient to cover their flesh. All kinds of offenses brought swift retribution, whipping being the standard punishment; for worse crimes, the Taliban held public executions—the only form of community "entertainment" besides the infrequent soccer and football games allowed in some areas. There were no protests, no "people-power" uprisings against such brutal practices of the law. Any complaints were whispered or never spoken at all.

As the Taliban began its interrogations of the SNI prisoners in Afghanistan, the Western media began interrogations of its own. Udo Stolte, the European SNI coordinator, had scheduled a 5:00 a.m. flight from Kabul for Peshawar the morning of the mass arrests. The flight was cancelled, so he hired a car to drive him to the Pakistani border. Had he not done so, he, too, would have been arrested. Udo knew Dayna and Heather were in custody but was confident the SNI team in Kabul could easily resolve the misunderstanding with the Taliban. It was not until he arrived in Peshawar, Pakistan, on Sunday evening that Udo learned of the Taliban's roundup of his fellow SNI workers. He immediately went into action setting up an emergency meeting with the SNI team in Peshawar, assigning different responsibilities to different teammates and instructing them to take necessary precautions. He also set a prayer chain to pray 24/7 for the safe release of the hostages. It was during his 3:00 a.m. prayer shift that he felt God was preparing him for what lay ahead: an onslaught of international media attention that he had no training or preparation for. Udo knew only God could give him the wisdom to deal with what lay ahead.

On Tuesday morning, Udo and his wife left Peshawar for Germany. Once back on his home turf, he was able to set up a small press conference that included two of the largest national television stations in Germany. Once these stations broadcast this interview, the floodgates were opened. Within minutes, the small Shelter Now office was overwhelmed by a relentless army of intimidating reporters from television and radio, newspaper and magazine. Udo had to field a volley of questions about the hostile takeover of SNI offices and work sites in Kabul by the Taliban and the arrests of his fellow workers.

The questions were specific: How were you able to get out, when the others did not? Have you had any contact with any of the SNI workers in Kabul? Was there any advance warning that the arrests were imminent? Will you return to Kabul? What is the motive behind the arrests? Do you expect the international community to help you? By your actions, have you not undermined international relations? Did you not know the Taliban was hostile toward your organization before now? Have you not brought this trouble on yourself? What was SNI doing in a Muslim country trying to convert people to Christianity in the first place? Were you forcing people to convert before you would offer to help them?

The validity of their faith and their motives was held in suspicion by some members of the press, but Udo never apologized for the work SNI was doing or why: "We have never forced anyone to convert. That is not our policy. We simply help people with their needs without regard to their beliefs. We do not go into the cities and hold crusades or swing our Bibles and say you must convert or you shall go to hell. We are Christians. We never deny that. We speak about our faith when asked, but only in a way that is acceptable within the culture."

The barrage of questions lobbed at him by the aggressive press was a daily education. He wanted to tell them the truth of the plight of his friends and to keep the facts straight, but at the same time not endanger the hostages in any way. It was a delicate balance of feeding the media machine and not making the situation any worse than it was already. All of this media attention did provide at least one benefit: almost overnight it established a large international prayer initiative for the safe release of everyone involved.

But the hardest task he had to perform, one he was even less suited for than facing a hostile press, was contacting the families of each person now held in captivity by the Taliban. Udo had to tell parents already frightened that their children had gone to an inhospitable country that their worst nightmare had now become a reality. It was also Udo's worst nightmare. It was the nightmare of nightmares, and though he confirmed to the distraught parents that they would take all possible measures to secure the release of their children, he could offer them scant hope of a positive outcome. While his friends struggled under the pressure of relentless interrogations by the Taliban, the press hounded Udo day and night, camping outside his home and office, attacking him with questions and accusations throughout the ordeal.

"Why are you not eating?" asked one of the guards.

"Because this place is not fit for human beings," Georg said, his patience at a breaking point. "It is a place for animals. Why are you even holding us? We have done no wrong. We have committed no crime. If you continue to hold us, then you must take us somewhere else. This place is intolerable."

After days of waiting, seeing no one but a few guards, with no information regarding their circumstances or the situation with their female associates, Georg decided to go on a hunger strike. The conditions of the cell—the heat, stench, noise, and darkness—were unraveling the nerves, and the terrible sense of isolation forced Peter and Georg to raise their complaints. The guards had made no effort to communicate to them what was happening or not happening with them, but with a refusal to eat, some headway began to be made: interrogations.

It was difficult to accept that the intense grilling by the Taliban was an improvement over their claustrophobic, rank-smelling sauna of a cell, but that became their new reality. They were transferred from the vice and virtue headquarters to a new location—first Georg, then Peter a few days later. Neither of them knew at the time that their new accommodation was the reform school prison for those requiring reeducation, and that their six female coworkers were also incarcerated there.

During his interrogation, Peter had little to offer the Taliban; he simply had not committed subversive activities against the government. He was an engineer who helped with building projects. It was a stretch for the Taliban to make any more out of it than that. After roughly five hours of trying to get him to confess to things that were not true regarding his work for SNI and his personal relationship to his female colleagues, his examiners gave up and accepted his signed general confession stating he was nothing more than a foreign employee of an organization that had fallen out of favor with the current leadership. Still, they refused to release him.

They were not so easy with Georg. They had the director in charge of the whole SNI organization—one that had been a thorn in their flesh since the despotic government had come to power, a threat to the purity of their self-imposed theocracy and the religious dictatorship of Mullah Omar. They were not about to let Georg off with an old-maid schoolteacher's scolding.

It was interrogation by committee. In the first days of the interrogations, Georg was surprised to see the mystery man who'd offered comfort to him in the car on the day of his arrest sitting on the panel, his demeanor as stern as the other panelists. It did not put him at ease. Could he trust this man to be a friend? The room was hot and cramped, bodies of several men taking up space and adding to the temperature. These men were poised to accuse and question, keeping Georg constantly on his guard. Georg learned the man was from the Ministry of Justice and chosen to be an interpreter. In spite of his dour expression, he never raised his voice, never accused, and he made a genuine effort to calm tempers when an exchange turned hostile. Georg was careful not to play off any sympathy this man might have for him; such a tactic could get them both in trouble.

Moods were constantly shifting, personalities constantly changing. A session might begin with an exchange of pleasantries with the lead interrogator, then shift without warning to vicious and false accusations. One minute a personality might exhibit interest and sympathy concerning Georg's well-being; the next minute it would frighten him with the threat of physical harm. The committee never beat Georg, but the interrogators never took the menace of it off the table. Even the mystery man did not diminish that threat.

Though Georg was proficient in Pashto, there were language barriers that complicated the procedure. Dialects and interpretations were tricky. There was a great deal of back and forth with the translator (not always the man who promised to take care of Georg) and the writing out of questions and answers. Think of a question, ask the question in Pashto, translate the question into English, write the question in Pashto, write the question in English, write the answer in English, translate the answer into Pashto . . . and so the marathon sessions went, one lasting for many hours without a break. It required incredible concentration on Georg's part. They repeated certain questions, trying to get him to confess to false charges. They repeated false charges and lies in an attempt to break him down. The exhaustion factor for Georg after each session was extreme.

Most of the members of the committee were in the room as a show of force, primarily used as a supportive cast for the more aggressive inquisitors. One interrogator stood out above the others, dubbed Long Nose by Peter and Georg for his obvious facial feature, which he used, consciously or not, to great visual effect. When the questioning turned abrasive, it was as though his pitch-black eyes were launching the query down his projectile beak as opposed to coming from his gray-bearded mouth. It was apparent that he had experience doing this type of work and took great pleasure in performing it, especially when the supporting cast nodded and mumbled their spontaneous approval.

Added to this physical distinction was the unusual fact that Long Nose was a former communist. It was out of character with the Taliban to allow someone like this into the fold, but extraordinary circumstances made for such compromises, including the presence of Muslim Arabs. Throughout the lengthy interrogation process endured by Georg and the other SNI captives, Arabs would intermittently roam in and out of the rooms during questioning. Silke later remarked that the women felt as if they were "the show of the day," Western women on display for curious Arabs who had never seen such a sight. It made them suspicious that the whole scheme to arrest them and shut down the organization was part of a much bigger plan.

"How many projects do you have?" Long Nose asked, bland as goat's milk, all the better to lull Georg into a false sense of security.

Georg answered, not quite taking the interrogator's tone as a round of friendly fact-finding, but willing to accept a momentary waiver from the intense grilling.

"How many foreign workers do you have?"

Georg answered with exact figures. He knew they had a certain number of people in custody. He knew a certain number had escaped. He did not know the exact number of either group. Therefore, he told the truth. What more damage could they do?

"How many Afghans do you employ?"

Georg answered with a rounded-off number and offered no names, though Long Nose paused as if in anticipation of a list. If they had Zareef, Georg knew they could have the others, unless some had been able to escape. He did not name names, and the demand to do so did not come as expected.

"Where do the foreign aid workers live? Where are all your houses located?"

Georg answered with neighborhoods and districts. He knew they knew the exact street address of each home, who they rent from, the neighbors on either side, and probably the names of the neighbor's pet goat.

"How far in advance have you paid your rents?

Georg answered. Rents were current; they could not accuse any SNI staff member of fiscal irresponsibility, and Long Nose could see by the response that Georg and the others were committed to their work in Kabul. They were not short-timers.

"Where are your rent contracts?"

Georg answered. Of course, after ransacking the offices and homes, they would have found all that information, and this line of questioning should be a moot point.

Georg never apologized or retracted an answer. He never became defensive. He answered each question dispassionately. To do otherwise would exhaust him more and cause him to lose focus. He could not lose focus. And just when Georg might think a line of questioning seemed headed in one direction, Long Nose would take a hard turn.

"The foreign women who work for you have confessed," he said, a swagger of triumph in his gait around the room. He gloated in his success at breaking them. The supporting cast nodded appreciation of his interrogating skills and grunted their approval in an attempt to add substance to the perception.

Yet Georg was not taken in by the ploy. He waited for the revelation. Indeed, to what had his coworkers confessed?

"Your children's projects are illegal," Long Nose said, his neutral face abruptly altered into a mask of ill-concealed fury. "The projects are illegal. They are secret *madrassas* to teach our children about Christianity. The women have confessed to teaching them. It is against the law to teach our children such things. You come to our country and break our laws and blaspheme our religion."

No new tactic here; attack, accuse, try to illicit some emotional response from the prisoner that takes advantage of fatigue and confusion so that any answer given can possibly be used against him.

"The streets of Kabul are overrun with children, between

twenty-five and thirty thousand of them . . . some dressed in rags," Georg said, careful not to appear as if he were assigning blame to the Taliban for this societal crisis. "Most of them are either orphans or fatherless. If they have fathers, many of them cannot work because war wounds have incapacitated them. The children have very little to eat at home, so when they cannot find the rare job, they beg on the streets or steal. School is not an option because the family needs what money or food they get from begging or stealing. What kind of future does this give them? If they only learn to be beggars or thieves as children, then most of them are doomed to be beggars or thieves as grown men, if they live to be grown men. We went to the government planning offices and got permission and the necessary permits to start the children's project to give opportunity for some of them to—"

"The staff of the city planning commission has no knowledge of granting permission of such a project."

"We paid for the permits," Georg replied, knowing full well how this would be twisted or denied. Still, he had to say it if for no other reason than to keep the truth straight in his own mind. "We were given permits by the planning office—"

"The planning office says they have no permits . . . that you started this illegal *madrassa* without applying and paying for the proper permits."

There was no point in calling the bluff or accusing anyone of lying. The Taliban had probably intimidated the Afghan employees on the planning commission into their current amnesia. Better to continue stating the facts, and state them honestly and calmly.

"The boys are taught skills so they can make an honest living," Georg said, a severity creeping into his tone. "They are taught how to make paper flowers and how to produce writing paper. Then they can take what they make and sell it in the marketplace. We also pay them to work an hour a day. We have at least seventy boys who are part of our program. All of them have permission from their families to work with us. Last winter we started a food and clothing distribution center in one of the buildings. We had just opened a carpentry shop that would provide work and train older boys in a useful skill. It is not a *madrassa*, and we do not force anyone to convert to our religion."

Georg had addressed his monologue to Long Nose and solely to Long Nose. He tried to detect any nuance of understanding from the power broker in the room, but Long Nose gave no indication that Georg's words might have touched a compassionate nerve, let alone a tolerant one. There was no crack in his stone-hard expression, nor did it appear to strike any chord of conscience in the members of the committee, their brows below their turbans knit grimly together.

Georg could have added a coda: *And what has your extremism taught them? What have you provided for them? What hope have you offered them? What is your plan to take thousands of children off the street and offer them opportunities to improve their miserable lives?* But wisely, he refrained.

"How many teachers do you have in your *madrassa*?" Long Nose asked, a little overzealously, perhaps to regain the upper hand by ignoring all Georg had told him.

"None."

"What are their names?"

"They have no names because they do not exist."

"Where do they live?"

In your imagination, Georg nearly blurted, but he just shrugged his shoulders and said, "There is no *madrassa* and there are no teachers."

"We know there has been Christian teaching going on. You are the director. You should know everything that is going on." Nothing Georg said could douse the eager gleam in Long Nose's eye for a confession.

"How much did you pay your Afghan employees to convert to Christianity?"

"We pay them to work. We did not ask them to convert. We did not pay them to convert. They did not convert. They are good and faithful Muslims."

"They are not Muslims. You turned them into Christians," Long Nose said with a conjuror's wave of his hands, as if to express that by some magic spell Georg had the power to make this spiritual metamorphosis come to pass. "They have confessed that you made them disavow their faith or you would not pay them."

Georg remained silent. There was no combating these lies. He knew the Afghan employees. They would not make such a confession unless the Taliban had coerced them, and after seeing the physical condition of his dear friend Zareef, Georg knew the vice and virtue police were not above torturing their victims to elicit whatever information they wanted.

"You are the director of your organization. You know everything that happens. Two of your women showed a film about Jesus, trying to convert a good Muslim family to become Christians."

"There is nothing bad about seeing this film," Georg responded. "In many Muslim countries people have seen this film. People in Pakistan have seen this film."

"It is a criminal act to show this film in our country."

"It is part of the Muslim tradition to speak of faith. It is even your belief that Jesus was a great prophet. When people ask us what we believe, we tell them that we are Christians. Why can we not talk about religion in Afghanistan?"

The tables had turned momentarily. The prisoner posed a question and the interrogator paused. It was a question of faith, if not a shared faith, and at least the question acknowledged that they were both men of faith. They were comrades in the struggle to evaluate the complexities of their faiths. Why must they do this in such a hostile manner?

"But you use your projects to turn people into Christians."

They were in parallel universes, each locked out from the other.

"This is not true," Georg blurted, the fatigue and accusations beginning to take their toll on his raw nerves. "We help anyone we can who is in need. It does not matter what religion they are. We help and we ask nothing in return."

"We have evidence," Long Nose replied, his own radar sensing that his badgering had finally gotten to his prisoner. "We have evidence of your lies. We have Bibles and Christian propaganda. We found them all in your homes."

"Produce them, here and now," Georg demanded. "Show me your evidence. And so what if we have Bibles? You have the Koran. Can we not possess the book of our faith in our own homes? Is that against the law?"

Long Nose's eyes blazed like trumpet blasts. He could claim to have succeeded in getting his prisoner to lose his temper, but it was a hollow victory, since it did not come with a confession. He looked at his audience as if they might provide inspiration for a different tactic with the prisoner, but their glum faces revealed that they were as much at a loss as he was for a new approach. No one seemed ready to relieve Long Nose, so he refocused his attention on Georg.

"You and everyone in your whole organization have come to Afghanistan to try and destroy it. You are nothing but criminals."

That was the last round in the arsenal. Long Nose fired it, the committee members gave their sycophantic harrumph, and together they waited for a response. They would be a coherent group, even if it were for incoherent reasons.

Georg was all impulse, his nerve endings throbbing from days of relentless browbeating. He would respond at this affront to everything he stood for. Accuse him of anything, but not of being a criminal. He would not allow the last two decades of his life to fall victim to such mischaracterization, even by irrational human beings. He had not sacrificed everything—put his life and the lives of others, especially his family, on the front lines—for criminal activity.

"A criminal steals from others and destroys what other people have built. A criminal kills people for personal gain or for selfish reasons," Georg said, rising out of his chair and stretching across the table, invading Long Nose's personal space. It was a powerful physical gesture made more powerful by defining the word *criminal*, and if Long Nose and the others thought Georg's definition was a blatant slap in their faces, then so be it. "It is not criminal to provide food and clothing for Afghan refugees. It is not criminal to care for widows and orphans. It is not criminal to offer hope to young boys who live in the streets. It is not criminal to build homes to live in and shops to work in for people who have neither. It is not criminal to take what is broken and try to fix it. And it is not criminal to show a film about Jesus."

Georg could have stopped there, and perhaps he should have stopped, but the compulsion to justify his whole life had not yet played itself out. He looked at his audience. They did not move. They were turbaned, bearded icebergs, frozen in the presumption of intractable beliefs.

"Go to anyone in Kabul that we have helped and ask them if we are criminals. Go to Pakistan. Go to the camps there and ask the refugees if we are criminals. Go to any city in Afghanistan where Shelter Now has an office. Go to the people who know us and have benefited from our projects in those cities. Go to them and ask them if we are criminals. If you do not intimidate them, they will tell you how much they respect us and are grateful for what we have done for them. I am not a criminal, and I resent this insult."

There was a sonorous buzz of heavy breathing in the room. The air felt thin and sour, and everyone breathed as though just finishing a strenuous physical task. Georg felt spent, but he would not sit back down in his seat. As weak as he was, he would not show any sign of frailty.

For Long Nose and the others, it was best to accept this round as a stalemate and live to interrogate another day. They would go home to their families, to well-cooked meals and comfortable beds. They could return tomorrow fresh for another round. Georg would return to his cell, his bug-ridden mattress, the stench and heat of enclosure, a meal of bread and tea and greasy soup. He would return tomorrow under another day's layer of exhaustion. Long Nose and his committee could wait. Time was on their side, and Long Nose ordered the prisoner taken away.

"You will only be here for another two or three more days. You are guests in our country," the female warden kept telling them, day after day, a mantra that became tiresome and less credible week after week.

In the early days of their incarceration, the Taliban ordered Heather and Dayna kept separate from the other SNI women. The two women received no special treatment; on the contrary, being Americans made them more vulnerable to intense scrutiny. The fact that they had been heavily involved in the children's projects and were guilty of showing the Jesus film to the Afghan family set them up for a more volatile going-over. Once the Taliban realized Heather and Dayna were of little value apart from the others, they allowed them to join their coworkers and the Afghan women held in the compound of the women's reform prison.

The warden might have referred to the SNI women as guests, but the Taliban did not support such a feature with hospitable treatment. What baffled the Taliban most—aside from their being in Afghanistan in the first place—was that all the women were single. No male was responsible for them. They did not belong to anyone like a piece of property, a durable or disposable good. This phenomenon flew in the face of the culture. Women in an Afghan world were dependent upon men. They had no distinction of their own. They had no identity other than being the wife of or the daughter of a male figure.

The interrogations of the women began in the evening and continued until late into the night. There were always six or seven men present at these group sessions, with a constant stream of Taliban flowing in and out of the room. These foreign women were the main attraction, and every male tried to sneak a peek of this unusual sight. As with Georg and Peter, the regimen of translations was the order of the day: Pashtu to English, English to Pashtu, questions, answers ... a Babel of languages and emotions that made the procedure almost humorous, were it not for the direness of the predicament. At one point, an interrogator tore up a form the women were required to fill out at each session and screamed that what they had written was all lies. The pervading confusion of multiple interrogations and language barriers could have brought this outburst of frustration on as much as anything. After days of the Taliban making very little progress in finding anything with which to charge the women, one of the interrogators asked Diana why none of them were married.

"Why do we need to be married?" she said, speaking for the group. "We have good jobs. We have cars. We have our own homes. Why do we need a husband?"

The committee of investigators sat stunned by such an assertion from a woman.

The interpreter took advantage of the silence Diana's answer created and began to talk with her about her faith.

"Why did you come to Afghanistan in the first place?" he asked.

"I believe God sent me here to work among the poor and needy," was Diana's simple response, which the interpreter seemed to understand.

"But you people believe in three gods," he said after a few seconds of contemplating Diana's answer.

"Are you a brother?" Diana asked, causing the interpreter's brow to furrow. "I mean, do you have a brother?"

The interpreter gave a cautious nod. He seemed not quite sure about the wisdom of having a theological discussion with a woman. He looked back at the interrogation panel, but they remained mute, appearing to allow him some freedom to pursue his own line of questioning, although the English words were incomprehensible gibberish to their ears.

"Then you are a brother," Diana confirmed. "Are you a husband?" Again, a guarded acknowledgment from the interpreter. "Do you have children?"

He looked at the panel once more, then back at Diana, and gave a wary nod.

"Then you are a father. You are a brother, a husband, and a father. You are the same man, but you have three different roles," Diana said. "It is simply the same with God. He is the Father, the Son, and the Holy Spirit."

Just as a flicker of understanding began to sparkle in his eyes, a couple of the panelists grew suspicious that the interpreter was not pursuing a line of questioning pertinent to the situation and demanded he stop at once. Before the others could berate the interpreter for overstepping his role, the call to prayer blared from the loudspeaker in the tower above the vice and virtue headquarters. The panel immediately rose to their feet and filed out of the room, but the interpreter lagged behind. When the room was empty he leaned closer to Diana, an aggressive move, yet nonthreatening.

"Is God real?" he whispered, his eyes vigilant for anyone who might return and catch him in this questionable discussion with the infidel. "Will he speak to me?"

Now it was Diana's time to be stunned. She might be suspicious of his motive had he asked this question in the presence of the others, but the inquiry seemed genuine.

"Yes, God is very real," Diana replied, her voice matching the soft tone of the interpreter's. "He can reveal himself to you, if you ask him."

The call to prayer continued to echo outside, and the interpreter rose up to leave. For an instant he appeared torn between religious duty and the honest inquisition into the possibility for a relationship with God. He said no more and departed. Neither Diana nor the others saw him again. A seed planted even in the unlikeliest of moments.

A startling aspect of the interrogation formula was the number of Arabs who subtly embedded themselves into the process, much like Georg and Peter's experience. They were not in any way a part of the Taliban, not being Afghan. On a few occasions their questions and assertiveness were a source of irritation to the Taliban. It appeared to be a question of who was in charge and an overstepping of territorial bounds, but the Taliban did nothing to remove them from the sessions and, indeed, always gave them deference. This aroused the curiosity of the SNI women.

Although most Americans were still a few weeks away from knowing about al-Qaeda and Osama bin Laden, these radical Muslims were not unknown to the SNI staffers. It had been common knowledge in the neighborhood that one of Osama bin Laden's wives lived just across the street from the SNI office. It would be quite easy to plant al-Qaeda spies in such a location. The uneasy but solid alliance of the Taliban and al-Qaeda made the women suspicious that the real motive behind their arrests was known only to bin Laden and his inner circle. Their interrogators, Talib and al-Qaeda alike, were probably simply carrying out orders.

After a few more sessions the women began to notice something unusual happening to them. When the questioning of one woman was complete, a kind-faced member of the interrogation team would lead her out of the room—but before he would bring in the next woman, he allowed the women a few minutes to compare their stories so each testimony would line up in nearly every detail. The women were not sure if this man was a secret ally or if this was just a natural part of the flow from one interrogation to another. It was not until much later that they found out that this man's own personal conviction did not allow him to stand by and see the prisoners mistreated. He had determined early on the grave injustices done to all the SNI employees and had spoken against this unfairness, which put him in contention with the majority of the committee and jeopardized his position as a lead investigator and translator. If he had been replaced by another—less sympathetic—translator, the SNI folks would have been quite vulnerable to the whims of their accusers. The committee criticized him for showing too much compassion toward the infidels, and it was a delicate balance to keep the delegation from turning completely against him. They told him that he should beat the prisoners during the interrogations, but he resisted and took the bold step of speaking directly to one of the Taliban ministers, arguing that they should proceed according to human rights as described by international law. It was to everyone's good fortune that the minister agreed with the translator; the threat of torture was no longer an option throughout the rest of the interrogation process. The SNI people christened him forever after their "Afghan Angel."

However, such kindnesses did not extend to the SNI Afghan employees. The Taliban beat Zareef mercilessly in the attempt to get him to confess to having been paid by SNI to convert to Christianity. After each beating, they told Hafeez that they would kill him. Each day when the guards taunted Nabi that this was to be his last day on earth, that they would hang him tomorrow, his response was always the same, "Then tomorrow I will be in paradise." And through the entire ordeal, Fareed kept praying and believing that Allah would release them.

We are clean, Fareed knew in his heart. *We have done no wrong.*

Georg and the others knew their Afghan friends would suffer terribly at the hands of the Taliban. The Westerners prayed continually for them, knowing they were in grave danger. For example, in the early days of their captivity, Georg learned from sources inside the prison that a bomb had gone off in the city, causing much damage. Unable to capture the perpetrators of the blast immediately, the Taliban had pulled five men at random from local prisons and executed them at a public hanging in the city square of Ariana Chowk. They hadn't cared about bringing the right people to justice; they just wanted the appearance of swift and decisive action. They could have easily taken any of the Afghan SNI personnel; no one would have come to their defense and no one would have known the men were innocent. It was an answer to vigilant prayers that none of those executed for the bombing were any of the SNI Afghan staff, but it was a constant strain and worry for Georg to know that these precious men he'd known for years were suffering on his account. It was an awful burden to bear.

The world had not come to an end, but its scope and size went into deep decline. Georg and Peter rarely were able to see life beyond the confines of their cell. When not being interrogated, their daily routine was simple: meals, Bible study, prayer and worship, conversations with guards and a smattering of prisoners, writing letters to family and friends that the warden ultimately destroyed after promising to deliver them, and sleep. Georg's efforts to befriend many of the guards proved beneficial. Occasionally, they would pass on tidbits of news they heard from the radio, so Georg and Peter knew that there was some diplomatic effort on their behalf. What they did not know for several weeks was that their female counterparts were in the same compound with them attached to the women's section on the opposite side. In between was a *madrassa* operated by the vice and virtue police used to reform lukewarm believers and those offenders who did not practice the law with appropriate attention to detail.

The women had restricted liberty within their high-walled compound. Along a sidewalk there were cramped rooms aligned like rooms of a roadside motel and a courtyard with a tree in one corner that provided shade against the glaring August sun. There was one public bathroom with rough-hewn stone steps leading up over an interior wall, through a tight gap that required one to bend over to successfully navigate, and then down the other side. It was easy to stumble on the steep, crumbling steps, and at night with no light in the bathroom, it was hazardous to make the journey.

As with Peter and Georg's housing, the women's cells were equally bad: cramped, dank spaces with filthy carpet, grimy mattresses, and a pungent odor curdled by the August heat and thick enough to water the eyes. They had no change of clothes with them and had to sleep for days in what they were wearing when arrested. Because of the stifling temperatures, most of the women slept outside.

The six women did not have much contact with each other. The order was to keep them separated until the interrogations were finished, so between the confinement, the sense of isolation within an abysmal environment, and the contentious interrogations, it was impossible not to feel fractured.

Late one night, once the interrogations were over, the Taliban herded the women into two vehicles packed with armed escorts, their trusty Kalashnikovs in their laps, and drove them to their homes, so they could gather some personal items. When Katrin and Silke were ushered into their home under heavy guard, they were shocked to see the aftermath of a search-and-seizure rampage. Items were strewn all over the floor, furniture had been tossed about, and most of their possessions were missing. The worst evidence of destruction was the montage of photographs Katrin had painstakingly assembled and hung on the wall. It now lay in shambles, pieces of torn photographs scattered over the floor like fallen leaves beneath a denuded tree. She bent down to collect the shredded photographic memories of her past, when a guard ordered her to stop and go pack.

"How dare you do this to me!" she screamed at the startled Talib who waved the barrel of his Kalashnikov in the direction of her bedroom, motioning for her to hurry up and get on with the business at hand. Perhaps he had been the one responsible for ripping up Katrin's photographs and viewed this picking up of scattered trash a waste of time. "How can you be so cruel, so inhumane?"

The other guards were first surprised at Katrin's reaction, but then broke into laughter at what they must have considered a childish outburst.

Katrin consoled herself with the thought that her imprisonment would only last for a few days and then she could return and try to put back together this extraordinary, archival treasure that lay in ruins at her feet.

It was difficult for Katrin and Silke to think straight with a dozen armed men standing over them, shouting for them to hurry as they threw together personal belongings they could take with them back to prison. This was not packing in haste for an unexpected pleasure cruise; they were packing for a return trip into a hellish situation. They were allowed their Bibles, card games, a few books, a couple of changes of clothes, underwear—a humiliating exposure in front of these brutish men—soaps, medicines, shampoo, the very basic necessities for surviving the squalid conditions of prison. Yet in the coming days, these mundane bits and pieces would help provide a level of normalcy to abnormal circumstances.

For the other women, it was the same experience: enter their ransacked homes (Diana and Margrit's home already inhabited by Taliban-friendly Afghans), hastily gather any personal effects that met the approval of the guards, and then pack back into the crowded vehicles for the return drive to prison. Diana was able to get a couple of extra Bibles that were smuggled into Georg and Peter's cell a few days later by the Afghan Angel. Once back at the vice and virtue prison, the women straggled through the courtyard back to their cells. The only solace they felt was in knowing that they were in this dreadful, unimaginable reality together, and somewhere, somehow, God was present, in the prison compound, in their cells, in their hearts.

"When you are constantly given false information, you have to learn to deal with it," Margrit would say later. The way the women chose to deal with it was to establish a routine.

Routine would help them stave off a temporary insanity and keep peace with each other. Heather had the greatest struggle adapting. She was the youngest of the six, and the new reality made it difficult for her to know what to do and how to interact. She lived in complete fear and felt disconnected from God and from the other women. Daily, the pressure built within her until at times she would lash out at the group and had to separate herself from the others until she regained her self-control. The faithfulness of her friends and their constant prayers for her helped in bringing peace to Heather and restoring her to a consistent and productive place in the group.

The six SNI women had to share the space in the compound with about forty Afghan women, most of them very young. The early-morning call to prayer was a natural alarm clock for the Afghan women. There was a minaret within the prison compound, so it was difficult to block out the amplified sound of the vocalist as he called the faithful to their prayers. Sweeping the courtyard was the first order of business as the Muslim women said their prayers. Invariably, it created a dust cloud inside the compound, driving the women who slept outside back into their three-by-three ovens.

Showers consisted of a can of cold water poured over the head, but in the heat it was a brief and welcomed relief. After a breakfast of *naan* bread and tea, the Afghan women had "reeducation time." They spent their morning sequestered, listening to lectures. This was, after all, a reformatory, and these women needed to receive instruction in the principals of faith, Taliban-style. It was during this time that the six Western SNI women spent their time in quiet reflection, reading from shared Bibles—the Taliban did not allow everyone to have her own personal copy—composing songs, writing, and praying. They would then come back together to converse and encourage one another, ending each time with prayer before the Afghan women returned to the courtyard.

Afternoons were too hot for much activity. Most of the women huddled in the shade and dozed. At one point, the boredom became so acute that the women staged a contest. Who would be the first to kill two hundred flies in a single day? At the end of each afternoon's competition, they would line up carcasses and count the number of kills. It was a pleasurable and utilitarian diversion. However, killing the abundant flies was not the only nasty and morbid activity. In addition, mice, scorpions, and lice seemed to overrun the place. The compound was a haven for all types of vermin, and it was a daily battle to keep them at bay.

It was hit-or-miss with the evening meal times, and by night-fall, there was little else to do but go to sleep. The only night-light in the compound was a single bulb hanging from the tree that pro-vided a pitiful illumination, certainly insufficient to radiate the path to the bathroom if one had to make that journey during the night. The next morning, the monotonous routine began again.

At first, the female overseer did not allow the six Westerners to fraternize with the other women—orders from above—but once their interrogations were completed, the overseer lifted the ban. In a short time, the SNI women were able to develop a strong bond with the Afghan women, due in part to the respect they gave them and for trying to fit into the Afghan culture by wearing the tradi-tional clothes and sharing the responsibilities of daily life in the compound. With some of the money they were able to bring with them to prison, the SNI women bought medicines for the Afghan women when they had health issues. Instead of purchasing special food outside the prison and having it brought in, they chose to eat whatever was offered to the Afghan women: *naan* bread and tea in the mornings, a couple of vegetables at midday and evening, and on occasion a soup consisting of bones and fat boiled in water. The abundance of bread helped stave off the persistent hunger pangs. The Afghan relatives of the women prisoners were supposed to provide the food for their family member, but those who did not have families or whose family was too poor to buy food often did without. The SNI women tried to share what food they had with the poorer women, but too often the overseer and guards would not allow it.

As the bond of trust began to solidify between the women, individual stories of how some of the Afghan women came to prison began to trickle out. One woman had neglected to wear her *burka* when she answered a knock on the front door of her house. An order for immediate reeducation was the pronouncement. Several women, many of them teenage girls, one only twelve, had either run away from husbands who constantly beat them or had refused to marry a Talib. Often a prospective husband demanded an exorbitant dowry, and when a family could not pay, the chosen girl ended up sent to prison. The husband of one woman disapproved of her selling handcrafted pieces of embroidery; the Taliban seized her one day, as she went from house to house selling her wares. A mother and daughter sold eggs on the street and found themselves arrested. The young daughter had two small children at home alone. She spent the first night in prison inconsolable, continually howling in agony at the thought of her terrified children locked in their house without food or water. It took a group effort of imploring and beleaguering the guards in order for them to release her long enough to go get her children and return with them to the prison. Two girls had enough gumption to dress like young boys and try to sell fruit and vegetables on the streets; the reward for their ingenuity was imprisonment in the reform school. Story after story revealed the haphazard cruelty of a justice system that showed no mercy. With no male family members willing to intercede (or unable), these women were treated no better than animals abandoned on the side of the road.

Punishment was always corporeal. The Taliban seemed to have no other modus operandi. Violence was just a part of life for many women, and there was no respite when it came to prison. The overseer always had her plastic pipe ready to end any dispute or administer discipline when she thought a prisoner required it. However, it was not always for ending disputes or religious infractions that a woman received a beating. Afghan women are by nature hospitable and generous. One day, two women were drinking tea and invited Heather to join them. Heather looked to the overseer, who said nothing; Heather took her silence as permission granted and sat down with the women. After the brief tea party, Heather got up to leave, and the overseer immediately pounced on the two women, dragging them into their cell, sealing off the door with their mattresses (to deaden the sound), and for the next half hour beat them. With each blow, Heather and the other women felt the burden of guilt: an innocent and pleasant encounter had become a cause for retribution. It was an unprovoked terrorist attack, but in microcosm. All the women outside the cell held each other as they listened to the relentless beating and the cries of pain. No one was guilty. All were innocent, but two Afghan women were paying the price for an infraction of a Taliban-style interpretation of proper

Muslim behavior—or was it just a perverse whim of the overseer, herself motivated to keep order for fear of what the Taliban might do to her and her family? A simple twist of fate and she could be on the receiving end of the plastic pipe. They SNI women wept for their sin-bearers, and prayed, attempting to mend their fractured souls.

For all the brutal mistreatment at the hands of the Taliban and, by extension, the female, pipe-wielding overseer, these Afghan women had an inner strength that could not be broken. There was an inexhaustible will to outlive the constant humiliations and unremitting hostility. It was a will not just to survive, but also to push back against the cruelty with their unique brand of resistance. When the rare opportunity came, these women would mutiny against their reality.

In one such case, the women took advantage of the overseer's absence one night after dinner and transformed the courtyard into an open-air celebration. After the sky had darkened, the women gathered beneath the tree in the corner of the courtyard, their metal and clay dinner pots and washbowls cleaned and positioned upside down on the ground or locked between their knees. Fingers and fists began a rhythmic percussive beat, each acoustic pattern crisp and decisive. One woman could not contain the creative impulse to bring laughter. She wound a piece of cloth over her head to make it appear like a turban and blackened her face with a piece of charcoal from a cooking fire to design a beard. Illuminated by the small wattage of the single lightbulb dangling from a low-hanging branch of the tree, the Talib impersonator struck her pose and began to mime forbidden activities, actions that would land one inside these walls. She fashioned an imaginary camera with her hands and arms and began to film her fellow prisoners. She whistled lascivious whistles. She acted out a pair of lovers kissing each other. Then, in conclusion, she impersonated the Taliban striking a fearsome stance against such sinful behavior. The female Talib had her audience holding their sides with laughter at her subversive antics.

The bowl drumming intensified, with fists and fingers increasing the speed of the rhythm. Inspired by the beat, women rose onto their nimble legs, unable to remain in a sitting position, and began to dance and sing, each with her own style of movement, her own vocal expression of joyfulness. Swept up in the unforgettable moment— transcending the beatings, the humiliations, the deprivations—this band of courageous sisters would not allow themselves to be broken. Their bodies might be brutalized, but their spirits refused to be crushed. From the prison courtyard into the warm night air rose the full-throated sounds of celebration, letting the heavens know that this mean and vicious place was capable of glory, that in a rare moment a light could break forth and push back the darkness.

CHAPTER FOUR

JUSTICE, TALIBAN-STYLE

H ad the world forgotten them? Did the world even know about them beyond their SNI circles and their families? The women wondered. Margrit worried about her parents. They were elderly and not in good physical condition; if they heard of her situation, it might have an adverse effect on their well-being. In a way, she hoped they were unaware, and that the Taliban would release everyone before they ever found out.

With no contact with anyone for weeks, it was impossible to know what the world knew, if anything. A simple lifestyle followed the interrogations. It was a drastic adjustment for the eight Westerners to go from the bustling activity of working on multiple SNI projects all over Kabul (and in several other cities in Afghanistan), to a routine of meals and limited interaction with fellow prisoners and guards inside a postage-stamp cell or a moderate-sized courtyard.

What could the world know? It was not complete solitary confinement, but the isolation from contact with the outside world began to take its toll on their psyches.

When they arrived at the prison, the sanitary conditions were bad enough, but with the increased number of women in the compound and a plumbing system constructed for a different century, the sanitation deteriorated to a sorry state. There was absolutely no effort made by those in charge to improve the living conditions of the prisoners on any level. It was a daily battle with vermin and parasites, one that never brought complete victory. Dayna suffered from asthma. Silke came down with bronchitis. The Afghan women had their own clinic of diseases and ailments, and the rare over-the-counter medicine that could be bought or smuggled inside did little to relieve the chronic health issues. Nearly all the women struggled with gastric problems. And with the decline of their physical health, it meant a near free fall of their mental health.

Added to the isolation and health struggles, the Taliban played a cat-and-mouse game. Their only form of communication with the prisoners was through interrogations. They accused them of illegal and criminal activities, but never charged them. They never offered to provide or allow legal counsel. The SNI workers could not receive or send out letters. The Taliban told them that they could write letters to friends and family, but they destroyed each batch once collected from the prisoners. There was no one to hold the Taliban accountable for their actions, no one to intervene. The Taliban called all the shots. They stubbornly refused to allow the Red Cross—or the diplomatic corps from several countries who had arrived shortly after the arrests—to interview their imprisoned citizens until the interrogators were satisfied they had wrung dry any useful information they could use against the prisoners.

The first indication that change was in the air was when the guards entered Georg and Peter's cell one morning and told them to get out. When they walked into the prison corridor, several of the guards were clearing debris, scrubbing down the floors, skim coating the walls with a cleaner. They replaced the mattresses in Georg and Peter's cell and cleaned the place from top to bottom. It was not because of good behavior on their part or for winning a prize for interrogations well done or out of the goodness of the warden's heart. Mullah Usaf, the director of the entire prison compound, including the *madrassa*, had a reputation for unexpected mood swings. He was never pleasant or kind-hearted. On his best days he was churlish and quiet. On his worst he could lash out for the least infraction. No, there was some ulterior motive behind this spring clean. When the order came to spruce up the facility where Georg and Peter resided, they could hardly believe it, but gladly accepted it even if they were suspicious as to the cause.

It was not twenty-four hours later that they discovered what had motivated Mullah Usaf to order the cosmetic overhaul of their cell and corridor. The guard took Peter and Georg to Mullah Usaf's office. There they came face-to-face with the six SNI women for the first time since their arrest. Georg and Peter were not sure how many women the Taliban had arrested in their sweep of the homes and offices of the SNI employees, and the surprise and joy at seeing their comrades, especially in these dreadful circumstances, reduced them all to tears.

The reunion was happy but brief, as an even greater surprise interrupted the gathering. Mullah Usaf ordered the office door opened and in walked a delegation from the Red Cross, diplomats from Pakistan, Germany, Australia, and the United States, as well as Heather's father and Dayna's mother. The Taliban Foreign Ministry could no longer deny them access to their citizens and family.

What came as the biggest surprise to the prisoners was hearing of the international coverage of their arrest and imprisonment.

"What does the press write about us in our own countries?" Silke asked in all innocence. "Do they even know about what is happening to us?"

"What do our families know? Are they aware of our situation?" Margrit asked.

It was now the diplomats' turn to be surprised: the prisoners were afraid that the world had forgotten them, and the diplomats understood the extent of their isolation from these anguished questions.

"You are headlines around the world," they told the bemused prisoners.

The news overwhelmed them. No one had forgotten them. Friends and families were not the only ones to remember them and lift them up in prayer. They were known to millions of people, and here, at that moment, this cadre of representatives of agencies and governments from around the world had stepped into their lives, if only for a moment, so they could know with assurance that the eight of them and their sixteen Afghan coworkers had not vanished from the hearts and minds of people all over the globe. On the contrary, they were constantly in their thoughts. The Christian communities from around the world were in a 24/7 vigil praying for the safety and certain release of everyone. There was unity of prayer among the Christians and a commitment on the part of the diplomats to do everything in their power to free the twenty-four prisoners. The news of the international surge, spiritual and diplomatic, mounted on their behalf raised a level of hope within them that they never dreamed would happen. And to sweeten this heartening information with even more tangible evidence, the diplomats and Red Cross representatives showered them with gifts, from cosmetics, to clothes, to candies, to medicines. It was like every gift-giving holiday rolled into one.

However, the interviews with the Red Cross and the diplomats promptly turned sour. On the orders of Mullah Usaf, the Taliban refused to leave the room during the process and did not allow the talks to take a political turn. Representatives from the Taliban Foreign Ministry listened in on every discussion, and there was nothing subtle about their eavesdropping. They constantly interrupted conversations between the individual prisoner and his or her diplomat. They ignored the Red Cross doctor's insistence that private consultations take place with the prisoners. Under international law, the Taliban should allow a doctor to examine the prisoners without interference and give them the freedom to answer direct questions as to their physical condition as well as the living conditions inside the prison. It was a tug-of-war between all the parties.

"I refuse to say anything in front of these people," Diana shouted, glaring into the eyes of a Foreign Ministry interpreter. Her outburst expressed the anger of everyone at the injustice of such treatment.

Mullah Usaf and the Taliban were quite hostile at first but finally relented. They allowed a brief physical exam by the doctors for each prisoner. During his succinct interview with the physician, Georg was able to tell about the wretched condition of the bathrooms. (When Mullah Usaf later received word of what Georg had reported, he reacted angrily and confronted Georg. He then proceeded to take it out on all the prisoners.) The diplomats and the Red Cross delegation had encouraged the eight to write letters to their families and promised they would personally deliver them once they returned to their respective countries, but the letters never made it past Mullah Usaf. He had the letters destroyed, and he did not allow the Red Cross or the diplomats to return to the prison.

One short-lived bright spot for Heather and Dayna was the opportunity to see a parent who had traveled all the way from the United States. But Mullah Usaf made the familial moments torturous. The time allowed for each visit was painfully short—just thirty minutes—and he would only allow Heather's father and Dayna's mother to see them every five days. The time in between meetings was unbearable for both women.

Such ill treatment at the hands of the Taliban could not restrain Silke's passionate temperament or her artistic skill as a painter. On the contrary, she was inspired. Angry at the way their meetings had gone with their diplomats and at how Mullah Usaf chose to torment Heather and Dayna by limiting their access to their parents, Silke decided to direct her vexation into a creative project. She took her nail file and began to carve a landscape that she intended to fill with a jungle of animals. The first to appear on the wall of her cell was a life-sized elephant. A Western viewer would naturally enjoy and appreciate such imaginative expression, but to the Taliban such images would be a transgression, and Silke knew this.

Personal conviction overrode any apprehension. She wanted to rub this offense in the faces of the Taliban. She wanted to insult and horrify them, for she was convinced in her heart it was the right thing to do. She poured out her frustration and resentment into her creation.

Once the elephant began to take shape, the other women, especially the Afghan women, quickly recovered from their shock at Silke's energetic fury expressed in this act of creation and gleefully encouraged her, throwing out suggestions of all sorts of animals to be depicted on the wall. Silke appreciated the endorsement from this one-of-a-kind sorority and stepped back to evaluate the curves and dimensions of her long-trunked, giant-eared pachyderm.

The room suddenly became smaller, dwarfed by the size of her inspiration, and she solicited the help of her sisters to clean out the cell, now turned artist's studio. It did not take long. A couple of mattresses, personal accessories, clothes, a few books, and the divided spoils showered upon them by the diplomats and Red Cross representatives were all lugged outside into the courtyard to make room for the spirited artist to carve her heated vision of revolt into the wall. Lion, rabbit, cat, dog—all appeared in their playful or majestic shapes beside the elephant. Then Silke took the only elements available to her that could create color—a chemical concoction of dirt, Vaseline, dishwashing liquid, beauty creams—and produced her palette. It was exciting and disturbing for the others to watch the artist spread the copper-colored mixture inside the carved lines of each animal. The master was at work, and the audience was in awe.

Breathless and perspiring, Silke paused to critique the work. Her manic eyes racing over the wall, she could see something was missing; an image to complete the scene had not yet appeared in her mind. The rage against the ruling powers had not yet produced a final statement in this carved and painted insurgency. She stared at the fresco and wiped the sweat from her brow. Creation was a messy work that accelerated the heart rate and opened the pores of the skin. Then it came to her.

"Pigs," she blurted, half laugh, half syllable.

Pigs. It was a stroke of genius. For each day Heather and Dayna had to wait to see their parent, a pig would appear on the mural; five days equaled five pigs. That would be the perfect sign of her disgust against the heartlessness of Mullah Usaf. It was bad enough in Islamic culture to depict an image of an animal or human in a painting or sculpture, but pigs were an anathema. Once Silke announced her intention to paint a quintet of swine, it took the multitude to bring her to her senses. Let the Taliban be offended, but not apoplectic. As bad as things were, such rebelliousness could draw a retribution none of them wanted to imagine. Silke looked at her audience, then back to the wall—a wall unfinished in her mind for the lack of the final-offense image. She let her arms drop and the palette fell to the ground. She would dissent against the system but not against her sisters. Their objections were reasonable, their solidarity a powerful force. Silke had taken the protest far enough. Clearer heads prevailed. It was not a defeat. It was a qualified triumph, and she accepted the finality.

When the female overseer made her rounds, plastic pipe in hand—there was no engraved invitation requesting her presence at the prison gallery to view the latest work of a local artist—and saw the commotion around Silke's room, she stepped inside the desecrated space. The crowd stood in fretful expectation around the door of the cell, waiting for a response as if a famous art critic had come to declare judgment on the work. Her eyes scanned the wall. She did not gasp. Her hand did not immediately go to her face to shield her eyes from the offending sight. The reaction was swift but understated.

"No one can pray in this room until the walls are repainted," she said, then turned to leave.

She did not threaten with the pipe. She did not demand to see the artist for a private consultation. Reeducation was a waste of time. She gave her pronouncement and departed. The crowd of women around the door made way for her to pass.

It was a victory without pain or bloodshed or demolition of property, a victory creating an even tighter bond for the sisterhood. There was punishment, but it was tolerable: the six SNI women were unable to share the unexpected bounty given them by the Red Cross and diplomats with their Afghan sisters. Still, they found a way around this decree by leaving small piles of treats in secret places in the courtyard or subtly dropping these prizes as they passed by a group of women. Everyone would savor and share the delight in this victory for as long as possible.

Peter and Georg sat on their mattresses, their backs leaning against the wall, their voices low, an ear cocked for the unexpected noise. Even though the Taliban were through with the interrogations, neither man could feel at ease. Their stomachs knotted each time they heard footsteps coming down the corridor, but on this particular morning the footsteps doubled, tripled, quadrupled in number, with several voices barking for the guards to open the cell of the prisoners and to step aside. Before their cell door flew open, both men knew immediately that these were ominous sounds. The regular guards never acted this aggressively around them.

The everyday guards were not always the hardcore rank-and-file Taliban. Many of them were conscripts, brought in from the country and employed in these menial capacities. Most of them received no payment for their work; their families had to help with their provisions. They were dedicated Muslims but not necessarily strict practitioners of the Mullah Omar–style of *sharia* law. Since most of them could not even read, religious instruction came from the cleric at the local mosque, and the sermons they heard on how to be a good Muslim and the inconsistencies in human behavior that they witnessed in daily life could not always be reconciled.

Georg knew the culture, and with his good command of the Pashto language, he was able to build cordial friendships with several of these young men, who knew in their hearts that something was not right in this situation. They knew of the work done by SNI. They saw how so many of their fellow Afghans had benefited from the relief programs and projects. They were getting to know the director and many of his employees, and could see the respect and love they had for them and for their culture. Out of the goodness of their hearts, several of the guards Georg and Peter befriended would secretly try to help them, even at the risk of incurring the wrath of Mullah Usaf. They would smuggle written messages and Bible verses back and forth to the women. They would bring news from the outside world that they heard on the radio. Their acts of kindness were limited but genuine.

When the door burst open, it was apparent that these new guards were on a mission.

"It is time to go," the leader shouted, waving his arms in the air like a frantic orchestra conductor. "You must go now. Time to take you away. Hurry. Hurry."

It was frightening when these guards appeared out of the blue, in a frenetic state, insisting that the prisoners must leave at once.

"Where are you taking us?" Georg asked, rising quickly off his mattress, the muscles in his legs reacting to the urgency of the guards. No one had ever answered the question before when asked, but he still asked.

"Hurry. Hurry. Time to go."

Always the same answer to the same question. There was no time to change clothes or groom themselves. They whisked the pair out the door, down the corridor, and into the brilliant sunshine. Peter and Georg stopped in front of a van with a group of Taliban scurrying between a convoy of parked vehicles. This was the farthest they had gotten since their arrest. They were outside the confines of the prison, but it did not feel much like freedom.

Moments later, the women arrived with their escort; the female overseer wore a *burka*, something she never wore while at work in the prison. The friends had not seen each other since the reunion with the Red Cross and the diplomats weeks before, but there was no time for greetings or small talk. Mullah Usaf followed the women, hopped into the lead vehicle, and ordered the convoy to follow. The eight SNI workers were crammed into a van with a Talib driver, another Talib riding shotgun, and the female overseer in the back. The van followed the pickup truck with a truck bed full of Kalashnikov-toting warriors. The passengers were pleased to have this unexpected encounter but had a mixture of feelings about what was happening. They were thrilled to finally be back into the world after more than a month of confinement, but there was still an underlying fear as to where this journey might lead.

They passed along familiar sights, even through the district where most of them lived, but they could not imagine they were being taken back home. When the lead vehicle turned onto the highway in the direction of the airport and the convoy followed, the eight dared to hope that Mullah Usaf could be taking them to an awaiting plane that would then fly them out of the country. They watched the sights go by, and when they passed the turn-off that would take them to the airport, their hearts sank. Still, it was such a relief to be together to share their anxieties, to confess their hopes and fears. Whatever might happen, it was a comfort to be in this group.

When they pulled from the main road onto a side street, they were shocked at the throng of people that jolted into action like a hive of bees the second the vehicles came into view. A sea of journalists from all over the world bustled about in front of the supreme court building. The reporters could hardly be constrained as they approached the vehicle with the prisoners. As soon as the van stopped, the Taliban guards leaped out of the truck and surrounded the vehicle, formed a phalanx around the prisoners, and marched them through the crowd. Cameras flashed and volleys of questions filled the air, as guards and captives forced their way through the horde, up the front stairs, and into the court building. The eight prisoners could not believe their eyes as they read the giant sign above the entrance: THE SUPREME COURT, with the statement written in Dari and Pashto above and below the English translation. This was the highest court in the country. This was where they tried the most important cases. This was where the judges pronounced sentence on the most heinous of crimes. There had been no mention of a trial during the interrogations. There had been a flurry of accusations, but no one had formally charged them with any crime. Why were they here? Who would decide their fate?

Row upon row of shoes lined the walls on either side of the corridor—a sign of respect for those devout Muslims who entered this venerable building. They were ushered down the hall, into an anteroom beside the court chambers, and deposited there with no Taliban chaperone except for the overseer in her *burka*. She was present to keep watch over the honor of the women, but since she spoke no English, the eight were able to converse without harassment or interruption. They were amazed that for the first time in over a month they were together as a group and in effect left alone with no supervision. They knew they had little time to waste so they instantly began to compare stories of their interrogations, bringing to light any lies the Taliban had told about their cohorts in order to extract false confessions. It did not take long for Heather and Dayna to relay the story of their experiences with the Afghan family they'd been visiting, and everyone immediately saw through the attempts by the Taliban to twist the truth about the proselytizing of the family members. This was the seminal event setting off the chain of arrests. What linked them all together was their connection to the SNI organization as employees, and being in possession of a scant amount of forbidden literature and media technology. It was all the Taliban had against them. Now they were to appear before the Supreme Court, the highest court in the land, the court that decided the most complicated judicial cases. It made no sense.

Georg began to see some kind of a pattern. Could they be players in a much bigger picture? First the arrests for innocuous crimes, followed by the interrogations that produced no confessions. Next, the Taliban denied them their confidential interviews with the Red Cross and their diplomats. They had no access to legal counsel. Something was rotten in this state of affairs, but Georg could not put his finger on it.

The door to the anteroom banged open, and Mullah Usaf's guards ordered the team to follow them into the courtroom. An army of journalists and onlookers took up most of the space in the room. The guards had to clear a path so the defendants could get to their seats at the front. The eight looked over the crowd, relieved to see the friendly, hopeful faces of their individual diplomats, as well as the parents from America. They did not feel quite so alone knowing that these dear people were present and on their side.

A large desk positioned toward the back wall dominated the room. Upon it were stacked large, thick books, weighty with centuries of Koranic wisdom and laws and interpretations of laws and wisdom collected from the *imams* and clerics over the ages. On the wall behind the desk was an expansive picture with verses of the Koran inscribed across the canvas, admonishing the faithful to revere the Prophet and be devoted to his teachings. Mounted on either side of the frame and in other places on the walls were scimitars and bladed armaments, along with an array of short-handled whips with the leather-encased steel cable flowing from its end like a spout of water spurting out of a fountain. It was the kind of whip favored by the vice and virtue police, used with little discretion when meting out punishment. This assortment of weaponry was a not-so-subtle reminder of the potential consequences to those who might stray from the path of the righteous.

Chief Justice Mullah Noor Mohammed Saqib sat behind the

desk, waiting for the eight to take their seats, his beard cascading over his folded arms, his dark eyes magnified behind his glasses, his head scrunched into his shoulders and cocked to the side as if unable to bear the weight of the enormous white turban—this high court judge's crown. To his right and left, twenty or more judges flanked Mullah Saqib, sitting cross-legged on the floor. Most of these ancient-looking, bearded wise men kept their heads bowed; the more pious mumbled prayers; many massaged their prayer beads; a few caught a late-morning nap and remained asleep throughout the whole proceeding. On the floor in front of the desk sat a row of scribes prepared to transcribe every word spoken by the participants, and to the right of the desk stood the translator, the oracle ready to enlighten the world with the translated wisdom from the chief justice. The cold, grave expression on Mullah Saqib's face never softened. This disciple of Mullah Omar was a hardliner feared throughout Afghanistan for his frequent death sentences, and due to death threats against him for his uncompromising interpretation of *sharia*, he never went anywhere without scores of bodyguards. The eight had little expectation of mercy from him.

The defendants took their seats, and Diana leaned toward Peter.

"They must have trucked these judges straight in from the farm," she whispered.

"Looks like we've got a real kangaroo court here," Peter responded. "They shook the trees and these guys fell out."

The opening speech of the chief justice was nothing more than a lengthy monologue going into raptures over the virtues of *sharia* law. His brief pauses between long-winded orations gave the translator little time to interpret the words for the courtroom; consequently, the translator mangled or dropped many phrases and sentences altogether. It was obvious that Mullah Saqib had determined the guilt level of the defendants before they had even opened their mouths when his speech shifted to a denunciation against the defendants for proselytizing and referring to Shelter Now International as a criminal organization. "They entered the homes of innocent Afghans for the purpose of converting them," he said. "The authorities collected thousands of Bibles and boxes of Christian literature as well as numerous computers, recording devices, music and movies, all of it used for the purpose of converting the faithful Muslim people into Christians." When he emphasized the possible sentences he could pass once the court determined the guilt of the eight— fines, imprisonment, deportation, even execution—it appeared that Peter's appraisal of this being a kangaroo court was not far off the mark.

At one point during the bungled translation from Pashto to English, an Afghan journalist who was sympathetic toward the SNI eight interrupted the interpreter, informing everyone in the courtroom that the words translated were incorrect, then he proceeded to give the correct translation. This intrusion into his well-crafted diatribe against the defendants infuriated the chief justice, increasing the tension in the room. It was an early sign of a loss of control that Chief Justice Saqib was quick to remedy. He scolded the journalist and threatened to have him removed unless he stopped, but the damage was done, and Chief Justice Saqib hastily concluded his speech.

"*Sharia* law is full of mercy and justice," he said. "And the defendants have the full right to defend themselves or choose a lawyer to present their case."

When Georg received permission to speak, he took full advantage of the opportunity. It was not lost on him that here was the chance to expose the fraudulent wiles of the court before the scores of international journalists in the courtroom.

"Your Excellency," Georg began in English. Georg would allow the court translator to translate his words for Mullah Saqib. He wanted the international press to know exactly what he was saying. "A month ago we were arrested in our homes and offices without any provocation. Those who arrested us entered our homes and offices without any warrants. They were physically abusive and treated us like criminals without ever stating the reason for our arrest. Then for three weeks they interrogated us, and not once did anyone say why we were in prison or what the charges against us were. You say we entered Afghan homes to convert them. Can we not enter the homes of our Afghan friends when they extend us an invitation? And where does it say in *sharia* that one cannot speak of his religion? In addition, it is no secret many Afghan and Taliban officials have the equipment to watch films and listen to music in their homes and workplaces, and yet do you bring them into court? After our interrogations, we signed no confessions of guilt to false accusations, and when we proved we had not been involved in illegal activity, they still kept us locked in our cells. Now for the first time after keeping us imprisoned for a month, we hear the crimes we have allegedly committed, and you inform us that we have the right to hire a lawyer. How could we have done that when no one told us about this court date? How could we have hired a lawyer and prepared our defense when they have denied us any access to the outside world? They have forbidden us to speak with our diplomats. They have forbidden us to speak with our families. They will not even pass on our letters to our families. They have forbidden us our rights. This is not mercy and justice described in *sharia* law."

Throughout Georg's tirade, not once did Chief Justice Saqib look at him, his whiskered face an expression of impatient disgust. But Georg knew his audience. He knew that he was not just bringing to light his ill treatment (and that of his friends) to the court, but through these journalists, to the whole world.

When Georg finished he sat down. A few of the others also presented their cases before the dispassionate chief justice but failed to move him a centimeter closer to the mercy of *sharia* law. He instructed some court bailiffs to fetch the table of evidence that incriminated the defendants. He, too, could play at this game. He could show the world what damning evidence gathered against the eight had justified their arrests and these current charges.

The collection of videotapes, CDs, DVDs, Bibles, computers, and tape and CD players brought out for the media to see barely covered the small table. Photographers focused their lenses, and video crews panned their cameras over the items on the table. The burning question that was obvious to everyone in the room . . . *Is that all there is?* Where were the thousands of Bibles? Where was the mountain of Christian literature? Where was the electronic inventory enough to stock a multimedia store? In fact, that was all of the assets, and most of the illegal booty they obtained from other foreigners, not the homes and offices of the eight SNI defendants. The majority of the confiscated items on the display table did not even belong to the defendants.

Chief Justice Saqib could barely conceal his surprise and anger when he heard that this paltry amount of evidence was all the court possessed. He had arrogantly publicized truckloads of substantive proof at the beginning of the hearing, and now he was staring at a table of materials that looked as if they were a collection of rejected items from a rummage sale. In an effort to have the last word before he adjourned the proceedings, Chief Justice Saqib announced that this investigation was ongoing, that more evidence would be produced, that once the defendants had chosen a new lawyer and the investigation was complete, a new trial date would be set. And then he dismissed the court.

In the hurly-burly of their exit from the courtroom, the eight barely had time to wave to friends and family before they were back outside the courthouse and being shepherded toward the van. More journalists awaited them outside and crowded around the vehicles like the paparazzi firing off their cameras in hopes of scoring the "money shot." And it came in an unanticipated way.

After seeing an international press gathered to document the courtroom experience, the SNI team knew for sure the world was aware of their plight. But how would the world receive it? They had no idea why their circumstance had attracted so much attention. They had little concept of what the media had said up to now or how they might report the current state of their dilemma. How would the world react to these latest events? Would this show trial work in their favor, or would the sensationalism turn off the community of nations? On the other hand, could this be a cruel manipulation on the part of the Taliban to legitimize their government in the eyes of the world and disparage the Christian faith? As they stumbled down the walk to the van, the journalists swarming around them on all sides, they did not know whether to be hopeful or to despair. They could only put their trust in God and pray for an outcry from around the world that would bring pressure to bear on the Taliban. Dare they anticipate a speedy trial, a fair judgment, and, soon, the freedom they all coveted? The control of their future was out of their hands.

Yet at that precise moment, as they were bundled into the vehicle, Georg seized an opportunity he never dreamed would be possible. It would be risky, but worth taking. There had been no direct contact with their families since the arrest, the Taliban had seen to that. But here and now in the confluence of this drama, with an international press corps focused on them, Georg would put a human face on their situation that all the showiness of the hearing had been unable to do.

Georg had a large family, with seven brothers and sisters. They always gathered as a family to celebrate birthdays. The day before their court appearance had been the birthday of Georg's father, and he knew the Taubmann clan would have gathered at his parent's home for the celebration. Given the nature of Georg's professional life, he was rarely able to attend any of these occasions, but he always made it a point to speak with his father or mother by phone on their birthdays. But under his present circumstances, he could not even send them a birthday card. He had to get a sign, communicate in some way to his father, to his mother, to Marianne and his boys, to his whole family, to all the families of the eight, that their sons and daughters were well.

The van began to pull away from the courthouse with some of the paparazzi in pursuit. Georg's stomach churned as he watched the moment slip away. He knew he would always regret it if he didn't take this chance, and he had to snatch it now. He pulled open the side window and wedged his head and the upper part of his body out the window. He would not be timid and keep his face inside the frame of the window. He would go as far as he could. He wanted to be sure that every journalist he passed would see him, so he stretched out the window as far as he could.

"Tell our parents not to worry," he cried. "Tell our families we are well."

He waved. He smiled with confidence. He had shown the world a face of optimism. By the time the Taliban driver and his sidekick realized what Georg had done, it was too late. They shouted at him to get back inside the van, close the window, and not speak to the press, but it was too late. He had spoken to the families. He had spoken to the world. The Taliban could do nothing to prevent his message from getting out. Georg sat back in his seat and closed the window. His father would know his son loved him and had given him the best birthday present he could ever have. A sigh of relief heaved from his chest. *Thank God*, he thought. Thank God, his

"Tell our families we are well." As the SNI eight are hustled out of the courthouse in early September 2001, Georg sends a message home via the international press.

father in Germany would soon see him on the television and know his son was still among the living. Georg had spoken on behalf of all the prisoners, but at that exact moment, his thoughts were only of his earthly father.

The media did its job. The world saw the grainy footage of Georg with his head and torso sticking out the window, his smiling face and waving hand, and heard his reassuring words. There it was, Georg's courageous act played over and over again on countless stations, the director of the SNI team passing before the eyes of the world as if he were royalty giving a concise blessing of hope to the masses.

Georg's instincts were good ones. In the early days of media coverage, the SNI people had been portrayed by some news organizations as crazy, Bible-waving sectarians who deserved what they got because they should have known not to proselytize in a country hostile to such things. Over time, most news organizations became more objective and sensitive about the state of affairs. However, some in the media were not always so sympathetic. The day before the hearing, a German newspaper had published a photo of Georg, Silke, Margrit, and Katrin next to a photo of three Afghan men hanging on a gallows at a public execution. Now there was a new image to replace the terrifying one. It helped equalize the insensitivity of the press. However, their ordeal was far from over. Freedom was still a distant hope. Reunion with loved ones was only a dream and an oft-spoken prayer.

CHAPTER FIVE

THE WORLD TURNED OVER

The day began as normal . . . from the minaret towers across Kabul came the morning call to prayer. In the dim light of dawn, the faithful began to stir and rise to perform their religious obligations. The tower looming above the prison compound echoed its chant, disturbing Georg and Peter's sleep. It was only a minor disturbance. They were long accustomed to this ritual and rolled over on their mattresses and went back to sleep.

Georg squinted, saw the diffuse light filtering through the window, and then returned to slumber. He did not know how long he slept before he began to hear the roar. He could not be sure of the source. He could not be sure from what direction it came. It sounded human yet otherworldly. It felt as if the roar were in surround sound, echoing in his head, yes, but also reverberating beneath his body, a jiggling sensation from head to foot. He could not be sure it was not a dream, though he could not remember a dream ever making his body quiver. Then the roar went silent. The tingling stopped. *Surely it was a dream,* he thought, then relaxed his body. However, the roaring returned, as though from a distance, a crescendo of sound played above, below, and inside his head, and then floated away. The uncanny din roused his mind. He could not go back to sleep until he discovered the source of the enigmatic noise.

Georg rolled over on his back. He wiped the grime from his eyes and looked at Peter. The sound had had no effect on him. He slept in perfect calmness. Peter did not move except for his slow, methodical breathing. *It must be a dream if Peter has not wakened,* Georg thought, and he took a deep breath and tucked an arm under his head. He tried to draw out images within the cracks and plaster flakes on the ceiling as one does when viewing the clouds in the sky, but the return of the audible commotion interrupted his playful activity. This time he knew he was not asleep. He knew this sound was not a dream. He glanced back at Peter, who remained motion-less. He did not want to awaken Peter, not yet. *Determine the source of the clamor and then rouse Peter,* he thought. He sat up and cocked his head toward the window. It returned. It intensified. It was human. *How could this hubbub not awaken Peter?* thought Georg. He got to his feet and crossed to the window. He could see nothing, but the sound now came in steady flows. Georg called to Peter, first in a forceful whisper, and when that did nothing to stir him, he barked his name.

Peter rolled over and faced Georg. He blinked his eyes in won-der—not of the clamor pouring in through the window, but as to why his friend would bother to wake him when he was in deep sleep.

"Peter, listen," Georg said and stretched his body to the window.

The sound now came in waves, and riding those waves were vocalized words and phrases. *Allah is great. Death to our enemies. The Lion of Panjshir is dead.*

"Do you hear that, Peter?" Georg asked. "It's coming from the *madrassa.*"

"What are they singing?" Peter asked.

Georg could not make out the exact declarations. He caught a word here, a phrase there. It soon became clear that the shouting was celebratory, as if they were listening to a crowd in a stadium cheering on their favorite team. The acclamations would swell and recede, surge and wane, and in the brief silence between it was as if the crowd drew a collective breath before exploding the next round from their throats.

The two men listened in awe at these sounds of triumph coming from the Taliban reform school, these voices lifted in praise to Allah for an act accredited to him.

A guard came to the door with their breakfast—a guard Georg and Peter considered a friend, and he told them that death was the cause of this celebration.

"Ahmad Shah Massoud, the Lion of Panjshir, has been assassinated by al-Qaeda," the guard said, his voice tentative, ruminating on the words as if testing the veracity of what he spoke. "The foreign minister announced the news this morning."

The Lion of Panjshir was a thorn in the side of Mullah Omar. Massoud was the last obstacle between Omar and absolute domination in Afghanistan. For years Massoud had led an Afghan resistance force against the Taliban. The Northern Alliance was a hodgepodge of non-Pashtun tribes and factions that had initially come together to form the *mujahideen* to fight against the Soviets. Once the Taliban began to control most of the country with a special vengeance toward the non-Pashtun ethnic groups, Massoud had persuaded these splinter groups to ally themselves against the Taliban. They maintained their stronghold in the northern sector of the country. Any follower of Massoud captured by the Taliban received particularly ruthless treatment.

Massoud had agreed to a television interview with an Arabic news organization shortly before his assassination. On September 9, 2001, they set up the interview site on a hill just outside the encampment. After only a few moments of answering the interviewer's questions, the camera operator detonated the explosives inside the camera, killing himself, Massoud, and a Northern Alliance official. With Massoud out of the picture, Mullah Omar could seize control of the entire country. The Taliban was now at the height of its power. For Georg and Peter, the news was like a stone in their hearts.

There was no time to lose. The eight had to get a lawyer. Since the Taliban had taken control over most of Afghanistan, Mullah Omar's sovereignty as interpreter of *sharia* law was unquestioned. *Sharia* is Arabic for *path*, and though it has its roots in the Koran, it began to take shape as a sacred addendum for legal scholars not long after the death of the Prophet Mohammed. *Sharia* grew out of the need for governments, judges, clerics, and leaders who discharged judicial responsibilities in a tribe, village, city-state, or country to have some much-needed guidance in deciding family and criminal cases and determining proper religious rituals. The intent of *sharia* was not to supplant the Koran, only to expand its spiritual and lawful discernment in relation to Allah and in deciding legal due process among Muslim communities. Over centuries, *sharia* law did not become a certified system universally understood and applied by all Muslims. Some considered *sharia* law simply a guideline to deepen one's experience and commitment to Allah. Others have embraced it as a way of governance for an entire population of an autonomous nation.

In the case of the Taliban, a fundamental extremist such as Mullah Omar came to power by the ruthlessness of the gun and remained in power by the merciless rule of his preferred interpretation of *sharia* law, with women enduring the most under such harsh rule. Without any provocation, women, foreign and Afghan, could find themselves victims of attack. Heather and Dayna had both experienced such rash and unexplainable harassment on Kabul's public streets before their arrests. It was frightening for all concerned to think that judges who interpreted *sharia* law in the cruelest of terms would now put them and their religion on trial. It felt as though they'd been thrust back in time—this could not be the twenty-first century. Now more than ever, the eight SNI workers needed someone who could not only navigate through the complexities of *sharia* but also had a knowledge and understanding of the culture.

The day after the assassination of Massoud, the diplomats from the different countries met with the eight, along with representatives from the Afghan Foreign Ministry, to discuss a choice for legal counsel. Consensus was that Atif Ali Khan, a young lawyer from Peshawar, Pakistan, might be the best selection for all parties. A conservative whose religious and legal persuasions leaned toward the Taliban, Atif had been educated in the United States, so he spoke fluent English as well as Pashtu. Moreover, he had training in *sharia* law. Enmeshed in both Western and Middle Eastern cultures, Atif had the proper comprehension of the multicultural nature of the situation, and he knew that this case would have international attention. Once contacted by the Pakistani embassy, he immediately agreed to meet with the SNI team, and a diplomat from the American embassy in Kabul arranged for him to fly to Kabul to convene with his potential clients. Even though his political sympathies might not lie with his clients from the outset, they had to put their hope in someone who would be impartial in championing their cause. However, it would be two weeks before they would be able to meet face to face.

Was it propaganda? Was it a lie? Was it sensational reporting from Arab radio and television networks? Georg and Peter could not believe what the guards told them when they burst into their prison cell: planes crashing into the World Trade Center Towers and the Pentagon, thousands dying in the destroyed buildings, chaos in America never seen before. It could not be true, yet their sources were reliable . . . sympathetic guards who listened to the radio and had kept them informed daily on what was happening in the outside world and who smuggled letters back and forth to the women across the compound. Georg was aware of an increased wariness among the more tyrannical of the Taliban in their attitudes toward the guards he had befriended. Out of the goodness of their hearts, these guards and the Afghan Angel had taken it upon themselves to look out for the well-being of the eight while at the same time trying not to raise suspicion among the hardliners, but there was a growing risk for the safety of everyone involved. So there was nothing for them to gain by telling Georg and Peter this news. In fact, it was risky: telling them this outrageous story put their lives in jeopardy. Most of their fellow guards rejoiced when they heard the reports. In their minds, America deserved this horrendous attack, and it showed how the determination of just a few people could bring this mighty giant to its knees. For these guards to show even the smallest kindness toward the prisoners by secretly giving them this information put their lives in grave danger. The news must be true.

The eight prisoners did not see the television footage of the September 11, 2001, terrorist attacks, the constant replays of the collapsing towers, the burning Pentagon, or the fiery crater in the Pennsylvania landscape where the fourth airplane had crashed. Not until much later were they able to see those horrific images. It was a grief in the collective memory of America and her allies around the world that these eight people did not share. There was this blank space in their consciousness, absent the images of the attacks. Nevertheless, once the shock of the early reports began to settle, clarity came to Georg's mind as to why he and the others might be in prison.

Georg was confident that only one man could be the mastermind behind this event: Osama bin Laden. Because of his close ties to Mullah Omar, developed when the two had fought against the Soviets, Omar had granted bin Laden safe haven in Afghanistan when he'd fled Sudan after the bombings of the American embassies in Kenya and Tanzania.

Georg began to put the pieces of the puzzle together. The first inkling that there was a concrete motivation for their capture surfaced when the Taliban and Arab interrogators began to display more interest in the whereabouts of the American employees than in any of the others. The vice and virtue police had arrested Heather and Dayna, but they knew there were more Americans who worked for the Christian nonprofit. They had consistently badgered Georg for answers, and when he refused to tell where the Americans and the others were hiding, the interrogators had been openly hostile. It became obvious to Georg that they were looking for every American they could find. It was fortunate that Len Stitt, his family, the other Americans, and Marianne and the boys had gotten out of the country when they did. Second, once the eight had been able to compare their stories at the supreme court building, it became clear that the Afghan family had betrayed Heather and Dayna. The two girls were often guests in this home, but in the visits leading up to their arrest, the Afghan women in the family had pressured Heather and Dayna to bring the Jesus film and show it to the whole family—a type of film everyone knew Mullah Omar had forbidden. It seemed odd that they would be so persistent—as was the older boy who'd harassed Dayna until she made him a copy of her children's Bible stories book—but Heather and Dayna were happy for the opportunity to show them the film. Once the two girls were arrested—right in front of the house of the Afghan family, another obvious sign of betrayal—the vice and virtue police had debriefed the family and then released them with no punishment exacted. Their quick release also pointed to the notion that the vice and virtue police had probably intimidated this family to set up Heather and Dayna. Third, within hours after their arrests, the Taliban began ransacking all the SNI offices and destroying all SNI building projects in Afghanistan. In addition, the vice and virtue police plundered the homes where the SNI folks lived. This was unlawful, since the Taliban had brought no charges against them. They ordered the confiscation and destruction of property with impunity. From the very beginning, the Taliban and al-Qaeda did not intend to permit them to go back to work, and they wanted to destroy all that SNI had accomplished over the years. Why had they not waited for the Supreme Court to pronounce its verdict before initiating this illegal action? Fourth, when the Red Cross and the foreign diplomats finally gained permission to visit the prisoners, the Taliban never gave them a moment's peace, refusing to allow them to discuss anything political or legal and constantly interrupting their attempts to discuss their physical condition. Fifth, the show trial before Chief Justice Mullah Noor Mohammed Saqib on the trumped-up charges of proselytizing Afghans was a bogus event made glaringly apparent by the ineffective court proceedings. Mullah Omar had decreed in one of his *sharia* law edicts that they would arrest anyone caught proselytizing, keep them in jail for no more than three to ten days, then deport the offending party. The eight had already been in prison for over a month for the charge of proselytizing, even though the court had produced no witnesses to back up the indictment, and the scant amount of incriminating physical evidence against them was laughable. So even by the highest authority in the land, the eight should have been released long before now and deported. Finally, when the chief justice pronounced that the court would go to trial against the defendants, it meant that the SNI folks would not see freedom anytime soon. On the contrary, the Taliban could hold them in the country indefinitely.

Repercussions for terrorist attacks were nothing new to Georg. He had firsthand experience witnessing fanatical mobs charging through the streets, destroying and looting private and public property and even murdering innocent people. These were common reactions among fundamentalists inflamed by the rhetoric of their like-minded leadership. After America struck Libya for the bombing of Pan Am Flight 103 over Lockerbie, Scotland, there were violent demonstrations in Pakistan, and the Shelter Now team had had to flee to the mountains. The response to the first Gulf War proved more harrowing. He and his team had fled Islamabad just hours before the U.S. air strikes. The war had only just begun when Islamic extremists came to Georg's house in Peshawar. After al-Qaeda bombed the embassies in Kenya and Tanzania, all the staff escaped from Peshawar and hid out with friends in Islamabad. Under the present circumstances, there was no chance of escape. Georg knew America would not negotiate with terrorists, and Mullah Omar would not extradite bin Laden to the United States. That stalemate made war inevitable, which would lead to the flight or expulsion of all foreigners in Afghanistan. The Red Cross would leave. Family members would leave. Their diplomats would leave. They would soon be the last known foreigners left in the country—and with a looming military attack from America, the eight moved from being religious prisoners who'd committed a minor crime under Islamic law to political hostages the Taliban could use as bargaining chips, or worse, human shields. It was terrifying for Georg to think that he and his seven friends were at the mercy of the Taliban and their al-Qaeda collaborators.

Over the next several days, the six women watched from the courtyard as plane after plane left Kabul. When Georg and Peter had their chance to be outside, they, too, watched as the planes carried their only advocates out of the city. The news from the guards trickled in: America was forming a global coalition against terror—the predictable first target of the coalition's wrath would be

Afghanistan, U.S. aircraft carriers were steaming toward the region; the city was feverish with activity, as anti-Western sentiment was rampant among the Taliban. From his secret allies, Georg learned that Chief Justice Mullah Noor Mohammed Saqib had led a violent, anti-American demonstration at the U.S. embassy near the supreme court building and had announced that he would seek the death penalty for the eight if the court found them guilty.

The demoralizing circumstance was no dream. Sorrow and dejection filled their hearts. It was impossible to suppress the bleak feeling of being forsaken. Could their situation be any worse? How would God help them now? Who was there to turn to now? They could look at the situation before them and believe what they felt . . . the knife stab of abandonment. On the other hand, they could choose to believe that they just might be in the center of God's will. Perhaps there was a purpose in all of this. Perhaps this was not desertion. Perhaps God had designed this exact place and time for them, that no one else could see His mystifying purpose through to the end but these eight. Being unable to depart the city meant they would be in the center of the storm and could pray for a country they loved, pray for a people they loved, pray for a work they performed that had brought so much good to so many people. No one else was better qualified to utter such passionate prayers on behalf of a nation and her people. To be present in a "fiery furnace" when there seemed to be little hope of survival might just be ground zero of God's infinite purpose for these eight people.

The first meeting with Atif Ali Khan was a surprise to the hostages. Atif was so young. In spite of his dark hair and long beard, black as

a starless night, he had the appearance and energy of a recent college graduate. A colleague who spoke Pashtu, was from the same
tribal area as the director of the prison, and had studied in the same
madrassa as the chief justice of the supreme court accompanied
Atif. This legal team raised the hopes of the hostages when there
was little hope to raise. The Taliban court officials were not pleased
with the nuisance of dealing with a defense lawyer at all, especially
one who claimed expertise in *sharia* law.

The meeting with Atif was brief. From the outset he had only
heard negative reports about the hostages, the charges against them
rankling his devout Muslim faith, and he had to set aside his judg-
mental bias. However, the more he listened to his clients' testimonies,
the more he saw the injustice of the situation. Still, he was pessimis-
tic about the outcome, and he shared his private thoughts with
Georg when they were alone.

"Since the attacks on America, the world has turned over. The
United States is sure to retaliate, and from what I know of the situation, we must be realistic," Atif said, his lawyer face on, compassion-
free and to the point. "The war will make life more complicated, but
regardless of when the war will start, they will push this to trial, and
for you, prison is likely. We may even be facing the death penalty."

Atif let the words drop with no sign of regret or sympathy for
having said them. It was the cold hard facts, and for Georg, it was a
blow to the stomach. Chief Justice Saqib's boast to pronounce the
death penalty once the court found the hostages guilty now appeared
to be realistic. Even their legal counsel appeared resigned to this
certainty. In spite of the shock to his system, Georg thought it wise
not to share this with the others, and it made a realist of him. It
became even clearer that this whole process was a sham—and that

no matter who represented them in court, the chief justice did not intend to let them go. Of course, the final authority was Mullah Omar, but the chance of his overruling Saqib's verdict was nil. *We are going deeper into the valley of the shadow of death*, Georg thought. *Dear God, be our Shepherd.*

One tangible bright spot in the whole interview was the care packages Atif brought with him from the diplomats and the SNI team in Pakistan. Before his departure, Atif presented them with packages and boxes of new clothes, underwear, socks, snacks, medicines, cosmetics, chocolates, and newspapers, but most exciting of all were the stacks of letters from family and friends.

The eight had little time to enjoy their gifts and letters. They no sooner returned to their cells before the guards rushed in and announced they were moving.

"Why must we leave?" Georg protested, knowing it was futile but not wanting to appear too willing to yield. He wanted time to enjoy the prize of letters from his boys and Marianne, and this forced move would delay the pleasure. "We don't want to leave."

"Pack all your things. The vehicle is waiting. Now move."

In typical fashion, the urgency of the guards was meant to frighten and intimidate. To create confusion and panic in the hostages was a ploy to make them move faster.

"Who gave the order to move us?" Georg replied, standing up against the bullying tactics.

"It is an order. You must leave. You can no longer stay in this place."

But Georg would not budge. It was the principal of the thing. Why did they have to treat them this way? Besides, he had his letters to read, his precious letters.

Finally, the prison warden had to come and confirm the order.

"You have no choice in this matter," the warden said. "You are to go, and we are taking you to a better place, a nicer place, a place outside the city, a more secure place."

Why a more secure place? Georg wondered.

"Are we not safe here?" he asked. "It is not a reason to move us."

"Armies are building. There will be bombing. You must be safe."

Armies and bombing. Those words were frightening to contemplate, but it solidified why the Taliban wished to move them to a more secure prison. To keep them safe, Georg realized, was to hold them out for bargaining chips for as long as possible until they had lost all value as hostages. There was no point in continuing the argument, so Georg acquiesced, and he and Peter packed their belongings to move to their safer confinement.

It was more traumatic for the women to leave behind their friends. Weeks of internment had created close bonds between the Afghans and the six SNI women. They had become family, and the dismay at this enforced removal broke their hearts. The wails of female voices filled the courtyard as the six hostages quickly packed their personal effects. They threw themselves into each other's arms, embracing for the last time, speaking words of comfort and encouragement for the last time, their display of grief compelling the female overseer to threaten them if they did not get to the waiting van immediately. There was no sweet sorrow in this parting. It was all sorrow, and the six women knew if they did not hurry and leave, it could bring the wrath of the overseer down upon the Afghan women once they'd departed. Their eyes filled with tears, the women rushed out of the courtyard, leaving behind the heartbreaking scene, the cries of the precious Afghan women echoing in their ears.

The drive to the prison was under heavy guard, with the drivers barreling through the streets as though they expected American bombs to start falling any second. The journey was short, little time for the SNI men and women to swap news and stories and share a tentative excitement that their living conditions might just improve. When they entered the district of the city where the prison was located and approached a block-long building, Georg recognized the area. The fact that the structure was located in the heart of the city and not outside the city as the warden had promised should have been the first clue that the warden had lied to them. The compound entrance always had Taliban guards milling about whenever Georg had passed by it. He never knew what the purpose was for this facility until the large, black steel gates opened for the eight hostages.

Once they drove through the archway, the eight companions twisted their necks in every direction trying to take in their new "home" as they moved through the compound. From the tops of the imposing concrete walls was another six feet of a barbed wire fence. When they entered through a second set of gates, they came to a stop in front of a small neighborhood of buildings, and the guard riding shotgun told them to get out of the van.

They stood on the outskirts of this community of buildings wondering what sort of improvement this was over their former living quarters. Steel bars in each window, cracked compound walls, clay ground packed down to a hardened surface, and everything covered with layers of dirt and discoloration. How could anyone in his right mind consider this place an improvement? They had hoped the Taliban would put them under house arrest, perhaps take them to a part of the city less hostile, but again, they had misplaced their hopes.

"This is worse than the other prison," Georg said. "You told us you were taking us to a better place."

This was the intelligence prison for the Taliban's secret service, housing political enemies considered hostile to the government and situated in the very center of Kabul, a likely target for U.S. bombers. It made sense. If the warplanes knew where the hostages were located, they would be less likely to bomb that site.

With barely enough time for a proper good-bye, their new guards separated the women and took them away, then a second set of guards hustled Georg and Peter away in the opposite direction.

The women were ushered into a small courtyard area with a building of several cramped rooms all on one floor. At the end of the building was a water pump for their drinking water, but right next to it was a wooden privy that reeked with waste. The courtyard was much smaller than the one they had been accustomed to, and it had no tree or greenery of any kind. At least they had the area all to themselves, a mixed blessing since they had grown so fond of their fellow female Afghan prisoners. Their new rooms were smaller than the ones before, the mattresses colonized by insects, and dirt and filth coated the walls and floors. Someone had even walled up the window at the back of the room. The women were in no mood to tolerate the condition of their new digs and vigorously complained. They were sure their grievances would fall on deaf ears—this had been the standard response from the overseer in their former prison—but this time prison personnel took positive action. While the women chased the shade in the courtyard, moving behind one wall after another trying to get some relief from the radiating sun, the warden was kind enough to rip out the board and plaster covering the window on the back wall and replace it with a frame and glass. They also removed the beds and brought in cleaner ones, and the guards offered them some freshly cooked vegetables. It was a pleasant surprise, and the rapid response by the warden to these simple requests lifted their spirits.

Accompanied by their armed escort, Georg and Peter tramped through another courtyard with decrepit buildings that looked as though they could not withstand the mild winds of a desert dust storm, let alone survive bombs from U.S. air strikes. Several inmates stood in the courtyard eyeing the new prisoners with trifling interest as they passed by, clutching their measly possessions to their chests like orphan children holding on to treasures. These were treasures, especially the letters. It was all they had to make them feel human.

The escort guided them through a large iron door and up some concrete steps to the first floor. The guard opened yet another iron-

L–R: Silke Durrkopf, Heather Mercer, Dayna Curry, Katrin Jelinek, Margrit Stebner, Diana Thomas [standing] taken during their 105 day captivity.

barred door and led them down yet another long corridor with cells lining either side of the hall, each one with a reinforced steel door and an eye-level peephole drilled into it. Many of these cell doors were open, and as the two men ambled down the corridor, they caught quick glimpses of the despondent residents. Were it not for the hellish conditions of the place, Georg and Peter might think a bellhop was taking them to a hotel room.

Like the compartments for the women, the cell Peter and Georg walked into had shrunk to the scale of a cubicle in comparison to their previous quarters. The trade-off was a sizable barred window that looked out over a courtyard that actually had a grassy area with some scraggly plants and flowers. There was some shelving, empty except for a thick carpet of dust. The cell walls were a crusty guest book of names and dates. There was enough space for Peter and Georg to add their signatures to the list of those unfortunate enough to have resided here in the past. A squat iron bed lay in the middle of the room, a leprous mattress of grime and holes. The two men sat on either side of the bed, shocked and dejected, unable to comprehend their new surroundings. They struggled with the feeling of humiliation that they had been so foolish as to believe the Taliban would actually take them to a better place.

Georg and Peter did not even notice when the guards departed. When they finally pulled themselves out of their stupor of disbelief, they realized they had company. A contingent of Afghan inmates stared at these foreigners in quiet amazement, respectful enough to give the new arrivals the time they needed to absorb the reality of their new world. When one in the group dared to open his mouth and ask, in Pashtu, if he could be of any assistance, he and the others were shocked to hear Georg respond in their native tongue. It was as though Georg became an instant celebrity and his fellow prisoners an eager press corps, desirous of every scrap of news from beyond the walls of their shared imprisonment.

There was much Georg could tell them: the reasons why he and the others were arrested, the terrorists attacks in America, the impending U.S. retaliation, all of it sobering information. When this impromptu news conference ended, Georg asked if they would assist them in cleaning their room and if any of them could find a second mattress. It was as if a benevolent king had made a request of his subjects. They all immediately went into action, cleaning the space as best as possible under the circumstances—it was more a matter of removing debris and skimming off the top layers of dirt. The scavenger hunt proved a success, and the inmates dragged in a second mattress like proud hunter-gatherers.

The room finished, Georg toured the corridor. The prisoners had the freedom to move about the passageway, entering each other's room like a college dormitory, but there was little else to resemble a collegiate atmosphere. At the end of the hall were the toilets, a three-hole bench boiling over with excrement. The doors had rotted and been removed, and only a threadbare curtain shielded the appalling image from view but did nothing to stop the putrid vapors from enveloping that end of the hallway. Georg quickly retreated from the horrible smell and disgusting sight and returned to his cell.

That evening, after a meal of vegetables, *naan* bread, and tea, Georg was able to read the letters from his family, the first correspondence he had received since his arrest and his family's escape to Pakistan. Just seeing the elegant handwriting of his wife brought him joy. He spent hours just looking at the words those letters

The men's atrocious toilet conditions in the intelligence prison.

formed on the front of the envelope . . . *For Georg Taubmann . . . For Papa* . . . knowing he had not been forgotten. This was all the confirmation he needed that his absence from their lives was a constant agony. There was a vacant space in each Taubmann heart that no one could fill; no replacement was possible. The vacant space would remain so until the four Taubmanns were reunited. *Dear God, let there be a reunion, and let it be soon*, he prayed.

In addition to expressions of love for their father, the boys filled their letters with descriptions of the daily agenda of life as teenagers in Germany. Georg imagined his son's mundane activities and himself in the form of a ghost, floating above them, moving through space and time as the boys went about the routine of their lives thousands of miles from his cell. How he needed them. How he needed to be there in the flesh, not as a ghost, untouchable and unseen. How he needed to be a father in their presence, and he needed his sons to affirm his fatherhood. Could God have felt this same pain when His Son was absent for a time?

From Marianne came tender words that melted his heart. The longings expressed, the secret whispers he heard in his mind's ear, intensified his isolation. Yes, she kept the message upbeat, to keep his spirits lifted, telling good news of family and how the world prayed for them at all times. But he knew his precious wife. He knew her sorrow and yearning. It was his sorrow and yearning. The two had become one, and when separated they were exiles in a shadowed world. Were it not for Peter, who embraced Georg while he wept and prayed for him, the ache in his soul would have been unbearable.

In this broken state he reached for the plump envelope Atif had brought to their first meeting, containing news clippings from around the world. It stunned him to see the international attention focused on them. In many papers they had achieved front-page status. Even the anticipated attack on Afghanistan by the United States and her allies had not pushed them to the back sections of the newspapers. Most of the reporting was factually honest, even admiring of the hostages, but a few articles rehashed the idea that the SNI staffers had been proselytizing and deserved what they'd gotten. These stories ignored Shelter Now's eighteen-year commitment to Afghanistan and Pakistan, during which SNI staff had repeatedly faced harassment and danger while they steadfastly continued to serve. The Taliban's complete disregard of human rights and zero tolerance of another's faith never crossed the minds of those who wrote these biting commentaries.

In spite of the fact that most of these articles were favorable, in his fragile emotional condition, Georg was even more dejected after he read the more hostile clippings. The slings and arrows in the Western press hurt worse than any maltreatment by the Taliban. It was hard to bear a new and unexpected element of persecution, yet it inspired a small vision of himself among the likes of the ancient prophets, the disciples, the early Christians, the apostle Paul, all of whom chose to be faithful to a God-call and suffered this type of discrimination and worse . . . esteemed company for his broken soul.

CHAPTER SIX

HAMID HOTEL

The window in their cell was a picture window compared to the small one they had had in the vice and virtue prison. That was the first improvement. Georg and Peter could look out and see sunshine, blue sky, the other barracks surrounding the courtyard. They no longer remained confined to their cell as they were in the first prison. They could move about the floor, roaming in and out of other cells and visiting other detainees. The vice and virtue warden had not allowed them to have any contact with other prisoners in the first six weeks of their incarceration, as the SNI women had enjoyed, so mingling with fellow inmates in the intelligence prison was another improvement for the two men. Even the food tasted better, with a larger variety of vegetables and scheduled servings, not erratic as in the first prison. Then a few days after their arrival, the

Georg and Peter in their tiny cell at the intelligence prison.

warden, Mullah Hamid, allowed them time in the afternoon to walk about in the courtyard.

Once when Georg was taking his afternoon stroll through the courtyard, the Afghan Angel appeared and motioned for him to approach. He could not stay but a moment, he told Georg, but he wanted to see how all of them were doing and to update them on the political and military upheavals in the city. The country was facing the prospect of war, he told them, and there had been several anti-American demonstrations in the streets, some of them led by Chief Justice Mullah Noor Mohammed Saqib, who threatened dire consequences against the Western hostages should America attack Afghanistan. Even though he was unsure of what would happen, the Afghan Angel promised to do all he could to help them. Then he gave a quick scan of the courtyard and looked around the compound for any guards before he turned his back to anyone who might be watching. Satisfied that no one was paying attention to them, he pulled opened his coat and showed Georg the GPS he had successfully smuggled into the country. He said he hoped this valuable piece of equipment would help keep the hostages safe, that he would use it to try and keep the American forces apprised of their location at all times, and then he left. It was a remarkable bit of encouragement that Georg needed. Here, a Muslim, a member of the Taliban who was supposed to be his enemy, was risking his life to help them, a wonderful reminder that God could be much more than anyone could imagine.

In spite of the fact that their cell was cramped and filthy and the bathroom vile, after being deprived of sunlight, friendly human communication, decent food, and restricted contact with the outside world for so long, these incremental improvements made everyone feel as if they had moved from the slums to a hotel. Given the amiable nature of Mullah Hamid, the SNI eight dubbed their new quarters the "Hamid Hotel."

However, not all was what it seemed. On the surface it appeared this latest location was an upgrade, but there was a dark, sinister side. Mullah Hamid was only second in command. His polar opposite was his immediate superior, Mullah Usaf, who had an impetuous temper that often led to beating prisoners for a slight infraction of the rules. And since the intelligence prison housed political prisoners accused of crimes against the Taliban government, and there were no laws against any form of torture, Mullah Usaf was free to use any means at his discretion to extricate confessions or information he deemed vital to protect the country.

It was not long before Georg heard the stories of Mullah Usaf's brutality from victims who shared their floor. He was naturally more gregarious than Peter and had the distinct advantage of speaking the language. He cultivated more friendships and, consequently, learned more about the prisoners' histories. Because of the common freedom on the floor to move about, Mullah Hamid did not mind the prisoners congregating in Georg and Peter's room. It was similar to the apostle Paul's experience when he was under house arrest in Rome. People would flow in and out of his cell . . . his prison ministry. This practice continued for a time, until Mullah Usaf heard about the gatherings and assigned some dodgy prisoners to spy on the meetings. When he received the reports of what was discussed at these gatherings, the Afghan prisoners were no longer able to have open and frequent contact with the two men. The shared disappointed grieved all but the spies, and forced Georg and Peter to be cautious with their trust.

However, before Mullah Usaf disbanded these meetings, Peter and Georg impressed the Afghans on their ward with the way they lived out their faith, and their treatment of their fellow prisoners. The two men respected the Muslim devotion to Allah and understood how this belief system meshed with Afghan culture. As the Afghans wandered in and out of their cell, they never ceased to be amazed at the amount of time the two foreigners spent reading the Bible and praying. They were not accustomed to seeing such piety from men not considered clergy. For them, religious practices were short rituals, and most of them depended on the *imam* to help them understand the sacred words of the Koran—particularly those who were unable to read. Reading sacred writings on their own or praying for a long period was not a part of their lifestyle. And when Georg chose to fast each Friday, the holy day Muslims set aside for worship, that gesture increased their respect for him.

Sometimes the Afghans would come into the cell just to look at Georg's Bible. They were familiar with sacred texts: their own Koran, the Torah, the Zabur (Psalms), and the Injil—a collection of the stories of Jesus much like the Gospels in the New Testament—but they had never seen the type of Bible Georg possessed, which contained both Old and New Testaments. Sometimes the Afghans asked if Georg would read from the New Testament, and after he did so, the men would have lengthy discussions regarding their faith. On several occasions some of the Afghans asked Georg if they could just hold his Bible, and when he offered it to them, they would rush off to wash their hands before taking it. A man might stand perfectly still, holding the Bible against his chest as if he were pressing into his heart the stories Georg had read out loud. Another might kiss it in reverence for the truths it held. It was humbling for Georg and Peter to witness the high esteem these men held for the Christian Scriptures.

Yet it was the Afghan men's wrenching stories of how they came to be in prison that pierced the hearts of Georg and Peter more than anything did. Since Georg knew the language and had been in the country for a decade and a half, he had met a great many Afghans. He had wined and dined with the wealthy, been a frequent guest of tribal leaders in villages throughout the country, and had even developed friendships among high-ranking members of the Taliban. At the same time, he was acutely aware of the daily struggles of the Afghan refugees, people forced to leave their homes due to famine and drought and war or fleeing the Taliban. Georg had exposure to the wealthy and the poor of Afghanistan, but these political prisoners were a different breed altogether. They were from a middle-class demographic that had suffered much at the hands of whatever national or local power happened to be in place at the time, dating back to the 1970s. Families like theirs—often of a minority ethnic group—had been driven from their homes, had their possessions taken from them, had been arrested, tortured, and executed simply by virtue of their differing political opinions and goals. From military coups that spawned civil war . . . to the Russian invasion and its political support of a propped-up and corrupt communist government after the army departed in defeat . . . to the tribal conflicts between the *mujahideen* . . . to the rise of the Taliban . . . this class

Georg with an Afghan prisonmate.

of Afghans had suffered for decades. These ordinary citizens endured the most under this ravaging lawlessness, with nearly every family experiencing the loss of a husband, wife, child, parent, sibling. Georg realized early on that he was building friendships with a group of men from a part of Afghan life with which he had had little contact. It only deepened his love for these people and helped him endure his own situation.

The Afghan men seemed eager to share their stories. Georg and Peter had fresh ears and caring hearts, and they listened late into the night as these men crammed into their small cell to give the details of their horrendous experiences, broken men sharing their histories in a space the size of a child's bedroom. Simple nomads who roamed the country arrested on trumped up charges for favoring the rule of a king over the Taliban, businessmen who sold items that did not meet the approval of the vice and virtue police, an engineer libeled by a neighbor and never given due process to prove his innocence. A group of elderly men, respected by their community, had taken issue with the Taliban on some negligible civil matter and now sat in Georg and Peter's cell. Young and old from all over the country—men who just happened to be part of the wrong ethnic group or had any connection (real or not) with the political opposition—wound up in the intelligence prison.

The Taliban inflicted their greatest wrath, however, upon the followers of Ahmad Shah Massoud, the Lion of Panjshir. They hunted them down and encouraged all Afghan citizens to expose anyone suspected of being a sympathizer of the Northern Alliance and its dynamic leader. The merest inference from a neighbor, a grudge from a relative, could land a man in prison without an official charge of any particular crime, and without exception, these suffered torture and beatings from Mullah Usaf's henchmen. Many of the prisoners had been through this ordeal on more than one occasion.

These tortures also were ongoing, witnessed many times by Peter and Georg, who heard the painful screams coming from the chambers on the other side of their compound, the lashing of the whips, the shouted commands to confess or the laughter and cheers from the tormentors. On one occasion Georg actually saw a man the Taliban had beaten repeatedly for several days. This man did not have the strength to make it back to his cell but instead lay on the ground in the courtyard, barely conscious and moaning in pain. His feet were swollen, face puffy and bruised, his head battered, his hands and fingers distended to twice their normal size; streaks of blood swiped across his shoulders, back, and chest. When Georg saw his wounds, he gave the man all the aspirin and medicine he had. It was all Peter and Georg could do: minister when they could, pray at all times, and try to block out the horrific sounds of torment echoing through the compound.

In a rare letter smuggled out of the prison, Georg documented this experience and others to Greg Gilmore, director of Shelter Now in Peshawar:

25 September 2001
Dear Greg,

Finally, I get the opportunity to send out some letters. One prisoner leaves tomorrow and wants to take them to Peshawar. We are not allowed to send or receive mail.

We are being held in the Intelligence Agency Prison. I'll

have a lot of horror stories to tell you once we are free. It is amazing what the women have had to endure. In the last prison, women prisoners were beaten in front of their eyes every day, and sometimes we witness terrible beatings of boys in the madrassa. It is like one huge nightmare. But please don't say anything to Marianne.

It was awful to hear about the attacks on the World Trade Center in New York and the Pentagon in Washington.

The diplomats have now gone from Afghanistan, along with all the other foreigners, and we are left with these people. We have been shifted under heavy guard to a terrible prison. Greg, if you were to see it from the outside, you'd have a shock! We were told they were bringing us to a nicer place that would be safer for us, but it is the opposite of that. When we went past the steel gates, everything was dark and as filthy as you can imagine. The atmosphere is terrible, and when Peter and I saw our cell, we were utterly speechless. It is just two meters by three meters. Three holes serve as toilets for up to fifty people; they stink and are filthy.

Then we heard the stories of the prisoners. It is very, very sad and shocking what people here have suffered . . . for nothing. It's terrible. I am afraid when I listened to their stories. Will we have to go through similar things? Who will be able to protect us then?

The prisoners are very kind to us and often try to encourage us. But, Greg, sometimes I think I can't take it anymore. Also, I think so much of Marianne, Daniel, and Benjamin. This separation is very painful for me. I have no news of them. How are they doing? How are they coping? I think of you all, the *team, the future of our projects which we built up with so much hard work. And how we are probably being kept as hostages. They don't tell us anything about what they plan to do with us.*

The situation is very tense here. The uncertainty is often unbearable. At least I'm allowed to visit the women every day. They always ask me for news of what's happening, but I can't tell them much. Greg, please tell all our friends not to stop praying for us.

There would be much more to share but that is enough for now. God has allowed us to go through this suffering, and often we've cried out to Him to make it stop . . . but things just seem to get worse. Please pray for us that we all come out unharmed.

We are in the fire and it's hot, but we cling to Him and His word and praise Him in the most trying of circumstances.

Your friend,
Georg

These tragic stories told by the prisoners were horrifying, but Peter and Georg were inspired by the depth of character of so many of their fellow inmates. Despite their own ordeals, they displayed genuine sympathy for Georg and Peter. They were helpful to them in the smallest of ways and were grateful for any kindness shown in return.

The call came early, unexpected, as usual; delivered with a sense of urgency, as usual; no mention of their destination, as usual; and included a heavily armed escort, as usual. The eight Westerners were roused out of their cells and escorted by the guards to a convoy of vehicles, engines running, awaiting them in the compound. No chance for them to clean up, no chance for them to protest, no chance for them to converse until the Taliban crammed all eight of them inside the vehicle. The sentries opened the gate and the caravan burst onto the street, raising a dust cloud that floated over the roofs of the expansive prison development.

The difference in this departure was that the guards had not ordered them to collect their possessions as they scurried out of their cells. A good sign? A bad sign? It was difficult to tell. All chattered excitedly as they were chauffeured through the streets.

Georg kept his own counsel, looking out the window, observing the districts and neighborhoods they sped through, keen to pick up any signs of a potential destination. Wherever it was they were headed, this heavily armed fleet drew a great deal of attention zipping through the streets. As they passed pedestrians, heads bowed quickly, the subservient gesture of deference to the glaring eyes of the Taliban. Georg first assumed they were being taken back to the supreme court building. It had been several weeks since their first hearing, and Atif Ali Khan, their lawyer, had informed them that they should hear a formal declaration of the specific charges against them at their next court appearance. Atif could only guess when that exact date might take place. Times, dates, summons, rulings . . . all were at the whim of the chief justice. It was a test of everyone's patience.

When the lead vehicle took an unexpected turn, Georg quickly abandoned his hope that they might be going to court to hear the charges against them. On this new route, neither the Supreme Court nor—hope of hopes—the airport was in front of them.

Georg looked at the profiles of the driver and his partner in the front of the van. They gave no visual sign that they even knew where they were going. He leaned forward and strained an ear to see if he could pick up any tidbit of information as they spoke, but the communication between them was minimal and centered on the landmarks they passed.

Then Georg's spirits sank. He realized they were heading in the direction of Ariana Chowk, a public square in the heart of Kabul. This public square did not have eye-catching statues, ornate fountains, or manicured landscapes that drew crowds. No, since the Taliban had come into power, Ariana Chowk was famous for one thing—public executions—and the crowds that did gather on this bloody plot of earth did not come of their own free will. Once the Taliban had captured the city of Kabul in 1996, the first act performed by the new leadership had been to hang President Najibulah, his brother, and an aide in Ariana Chowk.

There were always the morbid curiosity seekers who would be present at any public execution, but to ensure a capacity crowd with rivers of people flowing in from every point of the compass, jostling for the best line of sight, screaming anti-Western slogans, and burning flags of hated countries—always dramatic images for the worldwide media—the Taliban demanded that all government employees attend these events. Fervent nationalism played its part to whip up the frenzy, but primarily these staged events were an instructive reminder to the Afghanis that their own mortality was always at risk by those who controlled their lives. So Georg knew that if the vehicles were to slow down as they approached the square, it would be because of the teeming foot traffic pouring into the square for a public hanging. Theirs.

Georg glanced about at his fellow travelers. They did not appear anxious, nor did they even seem aware of the direction the convoy was heading. They continued to focus only on their current circumstances—why they had not heard from Atif in several days, who was sick, who had recovered, when the Americans might start bombing . . . would someone try to rescue them, could they be going to court, were they still front-page news around the world . . . and, *Georg, why are you not paying attention?* Georg faked his interest in the conversation, keeping his eyes peeled for the crowds. He could not express his fears. He could not confess to his friends the cause for the rising pain in his chest. *They could not actually be taking us to Ariana Chowk to hang us,* he thought. *They cannot be finished with us and ready to execute us for their international propaganda.*

Georg placed his hand upon his chest as they approached Ariana Chowk. He pressed against his breastbone in anticipation of a stout heart palpitation. He strained his neck from side to side, looking for grim-faced crowds walking in one direction, streaming toward the execution site. Georg felt that he and the others were characters caught in a bad novel, and now he was about to know whether or not this would be their final scene.

When the square came into sight, it was virtually empty—who in their right mind would want to gather in this square? Who would bring family and friends to this square for pleasure? *Empty. Thank God,* Georg thought. *Thank God. Thank God, no one is here, no one has come. Empty. Thank God. We are safe a little while longer.* The relief came in heavy sighs, almost laughter. After this, he could face anything.

The rest of the company took in the view. All chatter stopped. They, too, had finally seen the gravity of their situation as they approached the square. It was a powerful landmark and could have been the last place they would see on this earth.

The walkie-talkie squawked and Georg looked at the Taliban riding shotgun in the front of the van. He acknowledged the order to take the next turn off the square, and the driver obeyed. Then driver and shotgun exchanged glances, and Georg thought he saw sadistic grins slicing through the middle of salt-and-pepper beards—an acknowledgment of this cruel enjoyment at the expense of their passengers. Georg felt the Taliban had planned this detour just to raise their stress level and create undue panic among the SNI hostages. Could they complain? To whom? Who would listen? Could

In 2003, Ben filming Georg (in center of doorway) leaving the site where the trial of the SNI eight was held.

they even prove what had happened—and who would care? It was a joke played upon them for the amusement of others. How does one prove harassment when it is only a joke—regardless of the level of cruelty? The sense of their powerlessness was an unpleasant reminder that once again, they were characters written into a drama in which they had no voice.

Atif Ali Khan stood outside the supreme court building when his clients pulled up. This time the front of the building was not jammed with journalists. One lone reporter from the Al Jazeera network stood in front of the building, his microphone in his hand, his camera crew milling about, waiting for something to shoot. They went into action the moment the convoy stopped in front of the building. The reporter began to speak, and the camera operator filmed the hostages climbing out of the vehicle and entering the building. That was all there was to the performance. It was comic in comparison to the last time the SNI eight had arrived at the supreme court building: hundreds of reporters from all over the world tussling for the best angles and bombarding them with questions, as if the SNI eight were royalty instead of hostages. The Al Jazeera reporter asked them no questions, and the only footage shot was of a human procession from vehicle to entrance, hardly exciting television.

Inside the courtroom the comedy continued, though due to the imminent threat of allied bombing, Chief Justice Mullah Noor Mohammed Saqib and the rest of the court played the grumpy foils opposite the main characters. Since Atif had not appeared in the court until now, the SNI eight had to formally declare him as their attorney and have the chief justice and the other judges approve of him. Interestingly, many of the judges who had been little more than decorative plants in the first hearing had fled the city in the expectation that bombs would be falling from the sky any day now; those who were in the room appeared to have no understanding of what was going on. They sat cross-legged in their judge's chairs, worried their prayer beads, and tried not to draw attention to themselves.

Once Atif received approval from the chief justice as an acceptable defender for his clients, the court had the SNI eight fingerprinted and the mark of their thumbprints stamped next to their photos, as if this routine were somehow relevant to a case the prosecution intended to build. They had not stolen anything. Were Taliban detectives going to dust for fingerprints at the SNI offices and building sites? If it was just for the sake of positive identity, why had they not done this before now and not two months into the process? Moreover, how was this to clarify whom they charged with what crime? It soon would become apparent that over half the SNI team had committed no crime but were guilty simply by association with Shelter Now International.

To add to the circus atmosphere, the court had written the charges in the Dari dialect and proceeded to read the charges in Dari. Atif only spoke Pashto and English. All but Georg spoke some words or phrases in the Dari dialect (he spoke Pashto), but none of them spoke it fluently, and certainly not proficiently enough to be able to help Atif argue their case in this type of hostile atmosphere. What had happened to Pashto, the language used at the first hearing—when the whole world had been present to see the great show of Taliban judicial sovereignty? Georg suspected it was a tactical change due to the translation fiasco in their last court appearance, when a perceptive journalist had exposed the court's clumsy handling of the first hearing. So be it. But why had the court not communicated with the hostages and their lawyer that it intended to write and read the indictment in Dari? Would the court write and speak Dari in all further proceedings? The chief justice rattled off the charges with his growling voice, not giving the plaintiffs the courtesy of a glance, while the judges who flanked him listened passively. But Georg had had enough.

"This is outrageous!" he blurted, interrupting the formal reading of the charges. "We need a translator. We cannot understand what the charges are against us."

"We need an English translation of the document," Atif added.

"How can we respond if we don't understand what you are saying?" Georg said.

But their protests fell on deaf ears. The court just continued to read the charges as if Atif and the others were yapping children trying to disrupt adult conversation. The chief justice closed the hearing by stating through his translator that Atif had fifteen days to prepare his defense and then departed the courtroom, leaving the SNI team and their lawyer frustrated and bewildered at what had just taken place.

The guards hustled the hostages out of the courtroom and into the waiting convoy. The single Al Jazeera reporter, microphone in hand, spoke into the camera as they boarded their van. He continued to talk into the camera as they sped away. For all they knew, he could have been describing the weather in Kabul.

To everyone's surprise, four days later Atif received an English translation of the court documents spelling out the charges. But the translation was so atrocious, it was like trying to crack a highly classified, complex code in order to make sense of whom the court was charging with what crime; to add insult to injury, the court had mismatched the defendants' names in the attempt to connect them with the crimes that they had supposedly committed.

When Atif arrived at the intelligence prison with the documents in hand, Mullah Hamid had Peter and Georg brought from their cell over to the women's barracks. They met in the room where the women stayed, and Atif went over the charges point by point, giving the prisoners the opportunity to clarify their positions.

Excerpt from the Indictment of
Afghanistan's Supreme Court:
4 October 2001

FACTS

That Heather Mercer and Dayna Curry were arrested outside the home of [family X], *located in Shairpoor* [Kabul], *where they had shown a CD on the life of Jesus Christ (may peace and blessings of Allah be on him*) and gifted copies of a children's book containing the stories of Jesus Christ (may peace and blessings of Allah be on him) as stated in the Bible. The said copies were in the languages of Persian and English.*

That this incident led to the closure of SNI and the arrest of the six additional foreign workers and sixteen local workers on the charge of proselytizing.

INDIVIDUAL CHARGES

Georg Taubmann:

1. *That it was his responsibility to prevent his staff from illegal activities;*
2. *That it is clear from the things belonging to* [a former

Shelter Now employee] *found in the house of Georg Taubmann that he was involved in proselytizing; and*

3. *That no formal permission was granted for the Children Project hence it is clear that the aim from the said project was to proselytize among the children.*

Heather Mercer:
1. *That she visited* [family X];
2. *That she showed them a CD in which Jesus Christ (may peace and blessings of Allah be on him) is depicted as the son of God;*
3. *That she gave them a Christian children's book.*

Dayna Curry:
1. *That she gifted a radio to* [family X];
2. *That she gave a radio card to* [family X];
3. *That she gave copies of a children's book on the life of Jesus Christ (may peace and blessings of Allah be on him); and*
4. *That she had shown a CD on the life of Jesus Christ (may peace and blessings of Allah be on him).*

Katrin Jelinek:
1. *That she visited two houses in the Shairpoor area and showed CD;*
2. *That she left a Dari Bible in the Afghan house.*

Diana Thomas:
1. *That a radio card was found in her personal office; hence it is clear she was proselytizing.* [A radio card was nothing

more than a piece of notepaper with the frequencies of
forbidden radio stations written on them.]

Silke Duerrkopf
1. *That she visited Afghan houses and that she is an official
of SNI.*

Peter Bunch and Margrit Stebner:
1. *That they are Shelter Now employees and on the ground
they were involved with the Children's Project.*

* A Muslim always adds the blessing of Allah when mentioning a prophet's name.

Atif listened as the hostages refuted the misconstrued charges.
The court could not accuse Georg of proselytizing simply because
another SNI employee had left behind some personal articles with
an Afghan family. The illegality of the children's project was absurd;
Georg had argued vociferously with his interrogators when faulted
for opening the SNI children's project illegally. He had been careful
to comply with all the requirements before opening the project and
had gone the extra mile by securing written permission from the
parents whose children participated in the program. Of course,
Georg was confident the Taliban had destroyed or confiscated all
these records when they had ransacked SNI offices, and that those
moderate Taliban who had prepared and signed the appropriate
documents for the opening of the children's project had been
intimidated to ensure they remained silent.

The list of inaccuracies went on and on. Diana never possessed a radio card or gave one to any Afghan. She had stated this fact to her interrogators and had written that specific point several times into her numerous signed confessions. Peter and Margrit had nothing to do with the children's project. Silke never went to the Afghan house in question. Katrin had visited the house but was not present at the showing of the Jesus film and had not given any member of the family a Dari translation of the Bible.

The list of charges against Heather and Dayna were only partially correct. They both had visited the Afghan family in question. Against her better judgment, Dayna had given a copy of her children's Bible stories book to the young boy after he had worn her down by his unrelenting determination to have it. Both Dayna and Heather were responsible for showing the Jesus film at the home of the Afghan family [Family X], but they assumed the family was genuinely interested in understanding the girls' faith. It was an innocent desire to fulfill the persistent requests from the adult members of the Afghan family, both male and female.

This incoherent list of charges was nothing more than an attempt to appear legitimate in the eyes of the world, although some would argue that the Taliban could not have cared less about justifying their actions to anyone or to any country. After all, just a few months earlier they'd proudly destroyed the centuries-old Buddhist statues carved into a mountainside in the Bamyan Valley, totally disregarding any cultural and historical significance the statues bore—an act that shocked and dismayed the world. So why might this situation be any different? Perhaps, on the brink of invasion from several Western countries, they hoped to gain a modicum of sympathy from other Muslim states, states that might even come to their aid. Whatever the Taliban's reasoning, it was an ill-conceived and risky strategy.

So the SNI hostages found themselves caught up in this out-landish circumstance not of their own making, with no control and no leverage with the opposition. Even if all the charges were legitimate, and every one of them had confessed guilt, in the past, none of these charges would have carried a sentence any harsher than minimal jail time, a small fine, and expulsion. The German embassy in Islamabad had sent Atif a copy of Mullah Omar's signed decree stating that very thing.

Excerpts from official English translation of Mullah Omar's decree:

All foreigners in the Islamic Emirate of Afghanistan should take note of the following points:
1. *They should not smuggle drugs.*
2. *They should not meet with or interview Afghan women . . .*
7. *They should not copy or distribute magazines, books, newspapers or cassettes that are against the policies of the IEA.*
8. *They should not invite Afghans to other religions . . .*
11. *They must respect the religion, faith and culture of the Afghans and should not work against the IEA.*

In case of contravention of the articles 7, 8, and 11, the foreigner may be subject to 3–10 days in prison and then thrown out of the country within 48 hours.

Signed by Servant of Islam
Mohammed Omar

[The original decree was undated, but its official receipt in Kabul was June 30, 2001.]

However, the SNI eight had been drawn into a surreal concoction of twisted politics, military schemes, judicial contradictions, and the religious notions of a theocratic despot. There seemed little reason for hope.

Atif wrote his defense immediately following his meeting with the hostages. After revising a final draft with input from the SNI team, Atif presented the case—the hostages were not present at this hearing—which included a copy of Mullah Omar's decree written in Dari and Pashtu. But the chief justice and his court appeared indifferent. Then Mullah Usaf, the top warden at the intelligence prison, not only matched the indifference of the court, but raised it to the level of hostility. Without warning or offering a logical reason for his decision, he abruptly denied Atif access to his clients after a brief and final meeting. When he returned to the court to file a complaint, Atif found the indifference had turned into an unexplainable lack of clout to alter the situation. *The court cannot undermine the authority of those in charge*, they told Atif. In addition, the court clerks suddenly came down with an ailment of complete incompetence when it came to processing the documents and briefs Atif had filed on behalf of his clients. It was one obstacle after another, so Atif decided to return to Peshawar. He sent word that he would continue to work on the case there and would return soon. When the hostages received the message that Atif had left for Pakistan, the feeling of abandonment was transparently painful. Georg had been able to write a letter to Udo Stolte, the director of

Shelter Now in Germany, and get it to Atif in their last meeting before he departed for Pakistan.

Kabul, 3 October 2001
Dear Udo,

Greetings from Kabul. Tomorrow somebody is leaving the prison and has agreed to take this letter. I felt it was a good opportunity to update you on our situation. The few times we were allowed to write officially sanctioned letters, we could only write how well we are, that everything is okay, etc. I once complained about the state of the toilets here, and the next day the boss came by and was very cross with me. He is incredibly brutal and in charge of all the interrogations here.

All the prisoners are beaten with steel cables and others undergo torture. About two hours ago four inmates walked past us in the corridor in a terrible state: their hands and feet were all swollen and they could hardly walk. It looked awful. That is our current environment—horror is ever-present. Little wonder that I can hardly sleep at night.

The situation in Kabul has deteriorated. There have been a number of anti-American demonstrations. We could hear the people shouting on the streets from our prison. The demonstrators then burned down part of the American embassy. One of the high-level officials from our prison was among the crowd.

We were extremely afraid during the demonstration and prayed a lot. Our guards would certainly have made no attempt to protect us had the mob decided to storm our prison.

Thankfully, we have not yet been in any life-threatening situations. If the United States were to launch a full-scale attack, all hell would break loose here. We're praying with everything we've got that we'll be free before things really get going here. Some of the team is already close to the breaking point. We really need a miracle . . .

We have often felt we were at the end of ourselves, unable to hold out another day. But God has continually given us new strength to carry on . . . We have a strong suspicion that most people have no idea of what we are going through. We often only pass on the more positive things so that our relatives won't worry about us even more.

Your close friend,
Georg

Georg did not want to appear unusually anxious to get outside for the prisoners' daily walk in the courtyard. He did not want to give any indication to the guards that something might be different on this particular occasion. It should be like any afternoon, so Georg took his place in line when the guard at the end of the corridor opened the barred door and announced it was time for their afternoon strolls.

The prisoners wandered through the door and stumbled down the stairs, their stiff bones and aching muscles awakening to the freedom of movement. His friendly manner ever in place, Georg spoke to his fellow prisoners, helped anyone hobbled by age or torture down the stairs, and nodded to the guards, but once inside the courtyard he could hardly contain himself. Word had come. He had to verify the message delivered from a prisoner in a hushed voice in a secret corner on the second floor corridor, the same information given him days before by other prisoners equally cunning in their delivery. He had to know the truth, yet he was afraid of what that truth might reveal.

Outside he forced his legs to meander along the pathway around the rectangular garden in the center of their set of buildings, but at each window in the other barracks opposite his, he would pause. With a casual air, he checked to see where the guards were located and if any were paying undue attention to him. He did not want anyone to notice him. He did not want the guards to wonder what he might be doing or question any action that could be out of the ordinary.

Each window had heavy bars across it, preventing a clear view inside. Added to the steel fortification, the glass itself was opaque with age and caked dust. With no light coming from within any of the cells, it was almost impossible to see who might be inside, unless one got close, unless one could step off the path and onto the forbidden no-man's-land between the path and the barrack. It was so close, only a few yards from the path to the first-floor windows, but Georg could not risk it. He could not step off the path and move closer to the windows. It was too dangerous, and he felt he could not linger. Day after day he strolled around the courtyard, peering into the windows, eyes narrowed, looking for movement of any kind, any sign of human life. It was no longer just an outing, a chance to stretch his legs. For Georg, it was a quest, a mission.

One day in early October, the clouds had diminished the glare of the sun, thus reducing the reflection off the glass. When Georg paused along the path, he glanced at the center first floor window of the barrack and thought he saw the wave of a hand. He looked around, checking to see if the guards had observed him. He spoke to a trio of prisoners as they passed by him on the path, and then he turned back to the window. He saw a second wave, and then a face appeared in the glass. Georg checked again to see if it was safe to risk closer inspection. The guards seemed preoccupied with conversation, so he stepped off the path a few feet and looked into the window. The eyes brightened on the face behind the glass, a smile appeared, the lips moved, and Georg could feel his chest tighten. He looked away from the window, vigilant in his caution, and saw that the guards were disinterested in any activity in the courtyard. He would have called to Peter, but it could have roused the guards from their banter.

Georg moved one step closer to the window. The single face had tripled in number. Three faces appeared in the window, all smiling. Zareef stood in the center. Hafeez's face floated on one side and Nabi on the other. The reports were true. His Afghan employees were alive—at least three of them.

The guards signaled that the break was over; it was time to return to their cells. Georg stepped onto the path as if the force of this sighting had pushed him backward. He marked a spot in the dirt with his shoe and looked about him one last time. The prisoners were leaving the courtyard and entering the barracks. He had to acknowledge that he had seen them. He could not return to his cell and leave them wondering if he had recognized them. Georg looked back at his dear employees. He smiled. He nodded. He raised his hand, only waist-high, and waved. It was enough. The three faces smiled and waved in response, then disappeared.

Each day that followed, Georg and Peter paused in their walk at the same spot in front of the window. One would watch for the guards while the other waved, nodded, and smiled at the Afghan staff when they appeared at the window. Attempts to clean the inside of the glass for better visibility provided little improvement, since a skim of dust always covered the exterior side of the window. A smile, a nod, and a wave, this discreet form of physical communication between the men, carried the weight of heartbreak and anticipation. When both Peter and Georg finished the brief exchange with their friends, they would move on down the path—no reason to make the guards suspicious; no reason to bring any more harm upon their friends—and pray. They would pray with all their souls for the peace and healing of their Afghan friends, for their safety against the threat of more torture, for their quick release, and for the protection of their families.

"I've counted eight," Georg whispered to Peter before climbing the stairs to their floor. "I think there are only eight in that cell."

Indeed, there were eight in the cell, and it was only by good fortune that they discovered where the other eight were located. One warm evening as the day's intense heat evaporated, Georg stood by the opened window, trying to inhale some fresher twilight air, when he thought he heard familiar voices coming from the annex just above and to the left of his barracks. He scanned the top floor and thought he recognized another of the Afghan SNI employees standing in a window. Georg had to resist the impulse to shout out the man's name; instead, he called to Peter.

"Peter, get out of bed . . . come," Georg whispered, the sense of urgency in his voice impossible to ignore. "I think it's Fareed in the window, second floor."

Peter scrambled out of bed and rushed over beside Georg. Georg pointed to the lit window where Fareed stood.

"Make sure no guards can see us," Georg said, and after a quick search of the courtyard to see if any guards were milling about, both men began trying to make their friend aware of them, waving like survivors desperately hoping to draw the attention of circling rescue planes. After several moments of frenetic beckoning, they finally got his attention, and Georg and Peter could see Fareed signaling for his cellmates to join him. When seven men appeared with him at the window, it was all Peter and Georg could do to keep from weeping at this wonderful sight. They now could account for all of them. All were alive. God had spared them, and to a man, they seemed genuinely happy to see Georg and Peter. From then on, the custom was established. Each afternoon Georg and Peter would take their loop around the courtyard, pausing to wave to Zareef and the seven with him. In the evening just at dusk, they would wave to Fareed and his company. These daily silent signals, packed with meaning far beyond the simple wave of a hand, were a spark of human communication that defied all confidence in verbal expression. The ritual took on spiritual weight.

When Georg first discovered the locations of the Afghan employees, he attempted to speak up on their behalf the next time he encountered Mullah Usaf, but the prison director had no sympathy. He accused the Afghans of being criminals and traitors to Islam and to the country. It devastated Georg when Mullah Usaf informed him that since their arrest, the sixteen Afghanis had been locked up the entire time, not allowed to go outside except when they were hauled over to the interrogation ward to be tortured. Two groups of eight men squeezed into a single cell—the same size cell Peter and Georg shared—day and night, no chance to step into the daylight except for their individual torture sessions, for over two months. It was inhuman treatment beyond human belief.

A guard confirmed Georg's worst fears when he informed him that the sixteen had endured beatings with sticks and cable whips by their captors and that they would be hanged for their crimes. The mental torture was worse than the physical. The Taliban hoped to extract false confessions from the Afghan employees—that the men would state that Shelter Now had coerced them into converting to Christianity or had bribed them in some other way. Yet to a man, they never betrayed Shelter Now. If they had, Georg and the rest might themselves have been tortured, or worse. These innocent, faithful Muslim employees stood in the gap for their Christian friends; they endured the torture that might have fallen to the Westerners. It was a sacrifice Georg and Peter could not comprehend, and it was difficult for both of them to be kind to those guards they suspected were responsible for hurting their Afghan friends, or the prisoners sharing their corridor. They were helpless to do anything more than pray; others suffering on their behalf was a test of faith they'd never expected to bear. However, Georg did express his frustration and anger in a note to Udo Stolte regarding the sixteen: *They're being treated like saboteurs, mass murderers, and hardened criminals. It's absolutely crazy and totally unjust! When I tried to speak on their behalf, I was pushed aside with a brusque: "They're bad criminals."*

Georg did not want to pressure the prison warden for any kind of leniency. He knew this would only make matters worse for the sixteen and could prove, in the eyes of their captors, that what they accused them of was true. So he wisely chose a different approach and began to seek ways to make direct contact with the Afghan employees.

It was a standard practice for the Taliban guards to assign prisoners the task of standing watch at night in each corridor and wing of the barracks. Georg began building relationships with these prisoners, in hopes that at some point he would be able to communicate with the sixteen. In a short time a guard agreed to smuggle a note from Georg to the Afghan staff: *I am so sorry that you have to suffer because of us*, he wrote. *Please don't worry about your families. Our staff at the Peshawar office are providing for them.* (Before the Taliban had transferred the hostages to the intelligence prison, word got back to Georg that most of the relatives of the sixteen employees had escaped to Pakistan and that the SNI staff in Peshawar was providing accommodation for all of them, as well as paying the salary of each employee to his respective family. It was a small level of consolation for them all.)

Early one morning Peter and Georg stood at their cell window and saw a prison bus pull into the compound. They first suspected it might be for them; they wondered if Atif had returned and if they would be going back to the court building. Then they noticed the sixteen SNI employees filing out of their barracks and stumbling down the pathway toward the bus, the effects of interminable confinement and brutal torture marking the faces and bodies. The men shielded their eyes from the sunlight long denied them. Most could walk under their own power. A few needed assistance, an arm slung over a shoulder or a joined-at-the-hip walk when damage done to a leg or abdomen from excessive torture made it impossible to maneuver on their own. Georg and Peter had to stifle the urge to wave or cry out. The fear of reprisals for any contact with them was too great.

A guard entered their cell with a message.

"They go to Pul-e-Charkhi," he said and then slipped out.

Entrance to Pul-e-Charkhi prison, where the sixteen Afghan
SNI employees were held (photo taken 2003).

It felt as though Peter and George were watching a death march. Pul-e-Charkhi housed six thousand inmates and was located several miles outside the city of Kabul; it was the largest prison in the country and a likely target for reprisal attacks from advancing Northern Alliance forces or allied bombing whenever it might begin. It was a miracle that their friends had lived through the last two and a half months, but their chances for surviving beyond this point had dropped significantly. Did God still have a miracle for their friends? Did God still have a miracle for any of them?

They watched as the sixteen climbed onto the bus and were driven out of the compound. Would they ever see their friends alive again?

"Dear God," Georg whispered. "Have mercy on them. Have mercy on us all."

CHAPTER SEVEN

UNUSUAL PRISONMATES

The Taliban was not inclined to show respect and consideration to Afghan prisoners—at least not until the arrival of Mohammed Sharif. At first, the Taliban thought they had rounded up a prize catch: several students suspected to be sympathizers of Ahmad Shah Massoud. They thought these students were spies for the Northern Alliance, and would have treated them as such, until Mullah Hamid and his superiors learned that Sharif was the son of a prominent tribal leader in the region. This tribe was well-known and well respected, and after discovering that this dashing young man with his outgoing and winning personality was an important member of this tribe, Sharif had carte blanche inside the prison. Treating Sharif like a common prisoner or making the mistake of torturing him as a spy could have come back to haunt the Taliban, so until the people that worked for the Ministry of Justice could straighten out the problem with Sharif and his fellow students, his stay in prison would be made as comfortable as possible.

The old adage "It's who you know" certainly proved to true for Georg and Peter. It happened that Shelter Now had been quite active in the region of the country where Sharif was from. In Sharif's hometown, Shelter Now had set up a factory that manufactured prefabricated concrete sections for building houses. This business benefited many people in the surrounding area, and because Georg had visited the factory on several occasions, he had developed strong personal relationships with many of the members of Sharif's tribe. The local population was very grateful for what SNI had done for them.

Before his arrest, Sharif had heard on Radio Sharia that the Taliban had arrested some foreign aid workers and charged them with forcing their Christian faith onto Afghan Muslims. He wondered if they could be the ones who had helped the people of his tribe. After Sharif arrived at the intelligence prison and once he found out that Georg and the others were within the compound, he requested to meet the man who had done so much to deserve the praise and respect of his tribe.

Imagine Georg's surprise when Sharif introduced himself, speaking near perfect English, mentioning the mutual connections they shared. It was an instant bond. And since Sharif could speak English so well, Peter was able to be a part of the daily and lengthy conversations. Sharif had his own surprise when Georg astounded him with an astute understanding of the history of his country and its unique social order, and he was intrigued to know more about Shelter Now and why Georg, Peter, and the others had chosen to come to Afghanistan to help her people. It was a wonderful way to occupy the time and build a lasting relationship that could prove useful in the future.

Afghanis do not forget a kindness and will do all they can to repay it, and Sharif was no exception to those cultural mores. Because of his minor celebrity status, Sharif was able to move freely about the prison—including frequent visits to the prison offices, where he was able to keep up with the news on the radio and listen to the talk among the Taliban. He could tell the anxiety levels were rising among the ranking officials, especially among the guards, who were concerned about their immediate future once an invasion began; the Taliban authorities seemed to care little about their rank-and-file soldiers. Sharif shared all the information he heard on the radio or overheard among the Taliban with Georg and Peter.

Sharif also wasted no time petitioning Mullah Hamid on behalf of the hostages. Since Mullah Hamid was already well disposed toward the hostages, he agreed to requests for Georg and Peter to have more freedom within their barracks and compound, to share their meals with Sharif—the quality of the food now much improved—and to have regular visits with their female counterparts in the women's compound, not just when Atif, their lawyer, was in town and needed to meet with them to discuss their case. Since there were no women but the female foreigners housed in that barrack, it was easy to make the accommodation; however, Hamid did expect the utmost discretion on the part of everyone. He did not want to risk Mullah Usaf finding out about the clandestine meetings with the six SNI women. Fortunately, Mullah Usaf spent much of his time at Riasat 3, the high-security division of the intelligence prison, so he was absent for long periods. All parties agreed to keep the secret.

The women themselves had requested numerous times for the prison warden to grant permission for Georg and Peter to visit them, and at last the meetings began to happen. In the late afternoons, the Taliban guards would escort Georg and Peter to the women's compound and allow them to stay for about thirty minutes per visit. These brief meetings improved everyone's spirits. It was something to look forward to, and the women did their best to play the perfect hosts. It was their "tea time": they brewed tea and coffee, and shared a plate of biscuits if they were lucky enough to procure them. Not only was it an opportunity for these friends to be reunited, but it gave the women the chance to hear the personal stories relayed to Georg and Peter from the prisoners in their ward, as well as hear of the political events happening around the world.

Day 105: the day before their escape
L–R: Georg, Peter, Silke, Margrit, Dayna, Diana, Heather, Katrin.

Their seclusion was total, so what news Georg and Peter could gather from Sharif and the Taliban guards, they passed on to the women. For them, it was like having their evening news delivered in person.

For the six SNI women, the intelligence prison was a mixed blessing. When they'd first arrived, there were only a couple of Afghan women, one with two children. Within a few of days, the Afghanis had been removed, and the SNI women had the run of the modest-sized barracks and courtyard, though they were all required to sleep in one room.

The improved conditions included an improved menu, compliments of Mullah Hamid's personal chef. Another amenity was a hot plate to cook small portions of food, brew tea, and heat water pumped from the outdoor spigot for bathing. But the major difference was that they did not have to share their confines with forty or more Afghan women. Silence and a less hectic environment came with the isolation, but in some ways they missed interacting with and ministering to the Afghan women they had come to love in that first month and a half of their imprisonment. They appreciated having their privacy, but it also created a new dynamic: there was no escaping each other. The internment required of them a new kind of patience and discipline. They still had to deal with the strain of captivity, their lack of freedom, and the underlying fear of never getting out of Afghanistan alive to see their families again. That fact alone was enough to break one's spirit. Tempers would flare from time to time. It was impossible to avoid personal conflicts when six distinct personalities with a widespread age range found themselves crammed into one diminutive space for such a long period. It was easy to become frustrated and bitter with one's cellmates when the strain of confinement took its emotional toll, and frequently one or another in the group had to experience a self-imposed time-out just to calm down.

To help with this, Diana became the de facto leader. She was the oldest of the group and had been working for Shelter Now in Afghanistan and Pakistan for the last nine years. Her seniority and leadership skills made her a natural. Under her guidance they drew up a duty roster designating individual chores. Then, to help provide a structure to their day, they instigated two scheduled meetings, one in the morning and one in the afternoon. The small assembly devoted their time to prayer, singing hymns, studying the Bible, and sharing personal anecdotes.

These sessions also gave them the option to live out the godly mandate of asking forgiveness of each other when anyone felt slighted by another. Equally difficult was the requirement to forgive when one cellmate asked pardon of another. The extreme and appalling conditions of living in this imposed communal lifestyle gave them all the frequent opportunity to put the teachings of Christ into practice—particularly the virtue of forgiveness. Ironically, they found that by extending forgiveness to one another, it began to open up their hearts not only to consider forgiving their captors but broadening it to include the Taliban regime. It was a true test of their faith, and they realized that in the harshness of their current reality, only God could have conditioned their hearts to accept the possibility of forgiving their enemies.

One thing they all agreed upon was having a clean toilet. There was no forgiveness extended toward filth. After the initial arrests, the Taliban had allowed the women to return to their homes to collect some personal items. A few of them were able to grab some cash and bring it with them, which proved helpful throughout their ordeal with the purchase of medicines and food, but at this juncture, they unanimously decided they would spend some of the money on bottles of bleach. The daily scoured privy was a point of pride, and they could boast of having the "cleanest bathroom in Afghanistan."

Their situation was serious, could even be characterized as dire, and they all took it seriously, but they committed themselves to making the best of a bad situation. In the "Hamid Hotel," the Taliban allowed the women to have the books sent them by Heather's and Dayna's parents, as well as their respective diplomats, and there was ample time to read. They were able to write letters, although very few of them ever made it to their destination and they received very few from their families. They composed songs: worship songs and songs of prison life. They joked that once they were free they could start a band and name it the Kabul Six.

It was important for them to laugh and play games. Card games, charades, games of their own invention, all of this provided necessary diversion. They celebrated birthdays as well. Dayna, Peter, and Diana all had birthdays during their captivity. They even threw a party for Georg on Marianne's birthday, and though he appreciated the gesture, it grieved him because it intensified his longing for his wife and children. For these events, they ordered cakes and had them delivered to the prisons. The hostages always shared their cake with their fellow prisoners and the guards, which only gained them more respect among the prisoners and those guards who were not quite such hardliners within their government. All of this activity was therapeutic to their souls. And on the subject of therapy, Dayna once shared a letter from her mother who said that they would undoubtedly need some form of counseling when all this was over—and that world-class psychiatrists would line up to offer their services. However, Diana quipped, "I don't need a psychiatrist. I need a hairdresser!"

From then on, the joke was that each woman would be willing to see a psychiatrist as long as he could coif her hair as well.

Mullah Hamid had such a favorable impression of the six SNI women that he told Georg he considered them his sisters. This was high praise, and his esteem placed them in a more secure position against those who hated the Westerners. These women won Mullah Hamid's admiration because of their total regard for the culture and their adherence to the basic principals of respectful behavior, something Afghan men prize. The women were always polite to the guards, speaking to them in their native Pashtu. They never went out into the courtyard without wearing a head scarf. When they gathered for their group worship time, Mullah Hamid could hear them singing from his office window. Their religious devotion to God and kind treatment of others had a profound impact on him.

Then one day a bombshell dropped into this peaceful existence, the very day they received the official English translation of the charges the government had against them.

They heard the human shouting, the hustle and bustle of a crowd stampeding along their barracks and down the corridor, angry, threatening voices, male and female, and then the profanity, in English, no less . . . perfect English. The six women had no idea of the cause of this commotion and were hesitant to burst out of the room to investigate. But when they heard the cell door next to theirs thrust open and a second round of screaming and cursing ensued, it was impossible to ignore. They quickly put on their head scarves and rushed out of the room and saw several guards, Mullah Hamid, and a handful of representatives from the foreign ministry cowering before an aggressive, angry woman dressed in a wardrobe of Western and Afghan mishmash, yelling at them for lying to her about putting her on a plane for Pakistan, decrying their broken promise of housing her in a nice hotel, accusing them of breaking a host of international laws, and demanding her immediate release. It was quite a performance, all punctuated with a barrage of profanity. When the woman refused to enter her cell, the Taliban looked at her like little boys who happened upon the old hag living in a ramshackle house in the forest. In a final dramatic touch, the woman spat at the feet of the men, and they all jumped back in horror. The gesture was viler than any profane language she had used to curse them, since cursing the Taliban in English was like cursing the deaf. The spittle from this woman drove the men from the scene and they stumbled away cautiously, as though backing away from one possessed.

Left alone, the women stared at one another, unsure of who should speak first.

"Are you from the Red Cross?" Heather asked hesitantly.

"What person do you know from the Red Cross that uses language like that?"

The woman's rhetorical answer and her behavior with the Taliban erased any hope that she might actually be there to assist them.

"They lied to me. They said they were taking me to a nice hotel. Instead they bring me to this dreadful, third-world prison and stick me in a cell not fit for an animal."

No. It was clear. She had no idea who her audience was. Her only concern was herself, but in spite of her theatrical entrance, salty language, and self-absorption, it was wonderful to hear someone from the outside world who spoke a language they all understood. Nevertheless, why on earth was she here? How did she come to this place? As far as the six women knew, they were the last Western women in Afghanistan—yet here this very Western woman showed up on their doorstep all in a rage, emasculating her captors with her profane insults. And what news of the outside could she tell them?

"Do all of you speak English?" the woman asked the group, and when the six replied in the affirmative, she was stunned. "Are you the Christians the Taliban arrested and threw into prison?"

For six pairs of ears, it was a thrilling question. Abandoned, yes, held in the thoughts and prayers of relatives, friends, and colleagues, yes, but this strange woman's question seemed to imply the world at large had not forgotten them.

"I am Yvonne Ridley from London. I am a reporter for the *Sunday Express.*

Weary of listening to politicians and diplomats giving the same vague news briefings in Islamabad, Yvonne had stolen into the country in search of a story. She quickly realized fate had dropped her into the middle of the mother of all stories. Still, she did not appreciate her current circumstances, regardless of how fate had brought her to this point. She refused to accept the cell offered by her captors, and when the six invited Yvonne into their cell, she took one look at the revolting living conditions and threw up her hands in disgust.

"I don't do squalor," she announced, though there was a crack in her bluster.

The two sides were nearing an impasse. There was not much more the six women could offer Yvonne except tea. They were all equals in this situation, and there was no possibility of an upgrade in the accommodations. Not "doing squalor" was not an option. She could accept the cell the Taliban offered or sleep in the open. When this reality hit home, it broke her; Yvonne burst into tears and collapsed in the middle of the floor.

"They said a nice hotel, with computers and videos," she sobbed. "They said they were taking me to the hotel where they were holding the eight Western hostages."

The eight Western hostages were still waiting to see that nice hotel themselves. But they knew that it goes against the grain of the Afghan culture to be the bearer of bad news. Afghanis say one thing and reality proves the opposite. The SNI women could empathize with Yvonne.

"First they say they are going to send me home, but they bring me to Kabul instead. Then it's to a nice hotel, and now this."

Yvonne waved a limp arm about the room, her eyes blurry with tears. For the moment, the moisture prevented her from seeing the construction flaws in her new digs or the compassion on the faces of the six women surrounding her. She had put up a defiant front and it was all for naught. The Taliban had broken her spirit.

Yvonne's story was simple. Shortly after 9/11, the *Sunday Express* had sent her to Islamabad. It was a foregone conclusion America and her allies would retaliate for the terrorist attacks, and the paper wanted her to cover the lead-up to the invasion. She sat around in Islamabad for two weeks, listening to the same political double-speak, filing the same stories, and getting frustrated with the inertia. She made three attempts to get a travel visa from the Taliban embassy in Islamabad, and each time they denied her request. Not lacking for ingenuity, Yvonne took matters into her own hands. If she could not get into Afghanistan legally, then she would slip through under the radar. There was only one way to accomplish that: wear a *burka*.

To become invisible in Afghanistan, one need only to put on the *burka*. Yvonne bought herself a standard issue and attached herself to a wedding party at a border crossing. At each checkpoint, she passed under the noses of the Taliban without the guards giving her a second glance. After a brief time in Jalalabad interviewing the locals, she felt she was pressing her luck and thought she should return to Pakistan, but she was not as fortunate getting out as she had been coming in. An observant guard stopped her at the border and had her arrested. For six days the Taliban held her in prison, interrogating her. When Mullah Omar heard that the British reporter they were holding in this all-male prison was, in fact, a female, he was horrified at such a breach in *sharia* law and ordered her taken immediately to Kabul, where she could be interned with the other Western hostages. Yvonne had tried to play the system, and the system did not appreciate the attempt—and that was the simple and uncomplicated way she learned how the Taliban treated foreign captives: with lies, male dominance, and a not-so-subtle exploitation of religious law.

Telling her story did not relieve her angst, so she pulled a cigarette out of her bag, but before she could light up, the other women informed her that she was in a nonsmoking cell.

"What kind of Christians are you?" she said. "You won't let me smoke when I'm really, really distressed." In all of Asia, Yvonne had landed in the one cell where the inmates did not allow smoking. There was always some trade-off to getting a great story.

"You may smoke in the courtyard," Diana offered politely. "But we are about to have our meeting. We meet twice a day, and you are welcome to join us."

She could not resist the invitation to a meeting. Her journalistic instincts to gather the juicy details in this international scoop kicked in, so the calming effects of the nicotine fix would have to wait. They met twice a day. Surely it was to discuss an escape plan; how much farther did they have to dig the tunnel before they were outside the walls? And since Yvonne had spent the last six days absent any female companionship, it was a wonderful relief to be with six women who understood her background, who were delighted to have her as a guest, and who spoke her language. They could discuss the most trivial of subjects and she would welcome the conversation.

However, if it was the details of an intricate escape plan Yvonne

The six SNI women thought they might find an opportunity to escape, and kept these burkas at the ready, just in case.

hoped to learn and later report on for her paper, she was sorely disappointed. The six sat in a circle and pulled out their Bibles, and instead of discussing the progress of a plan to rival *The Great Escape*, each woman read the latest passages from Scripture that had pertinent meaning to her. Yvonne kept watching the door, thinking that any minute now the Taliban would burst in, confiscate their Bibles, and punish them for their sedition. They were in enough trouble as it was, and if caught openly reading their Bibles, it could only make their situation worse, she reasoned.

There seemed to be little regard for Yvonne as she sat in the corner listening to the six women read from their Bibles and share their thoughts. She was a welcomed observer who did not inhibit this vital spiritual moment. After about twenty minutes, the women pulled out their handwritten song sheets, with the original songs they had composed during their incarceration, and began to sing in a loud, robust manner. The women were not singing sweet Bible nursery songs. This was heartfelt adulation sung in full voice with enthusiastic hand clapping.

> Lord, you've assigned me my portion and cup,
> You've made my lot secure.
> The boundary lines have fallen for me
> In pleasant places, oh yes.
> Surely I have a delightful inheritance
> You've shown me the path of life.
> You fill me with joy in Your presence . . .
> Surely you ransom me. Surely you ransom me.
> Surely you ransom me. Surely you ransom me.
> Surely you ransom me . . . unharmed.

If reading the Bible was not risky enough, Yvonne thought for sure this spirited worship would raise the Taliban. Fear of worsening her situation with her captors, coupled with a growing nicotine craving, caused her to excuse herself. She went into the courtyard to smoke.

Yvonne lit up one of her last cigarettes outside in the courtyard and filled her lungs with smoke. Her immediate concern was her low supply of cigarettes, as she counted the remaining number in her pack. This was not a time for her to quit, but she did not expect there to be an easy tobacco source, nor could she expect the Taliban to offer her any, given her recent behavior. As she pondered her quandary, the singing coming from the cell in the background, the call to prayer came over the loudspeaker from a nearby mosque. She heard melodic singing floating out the windows from inside the prison and the singular chanting from the minaret reverberating from outside the prison walls. Yvonne marveled at her unique place in the middle of this sanctified, parallel universe: religious fanatics on one side; religious fanatics on the other. She had been raised a Christian— the quiet type, hymns sung softly, prayers whispered on one's knees at the altar rail—but this dual worship was loud, filling the airwaves. When the six women began to pray, it got even louder, almost as if competing for God's attention. One of the six shouted, "Lord, show us the way out of here," and Yvonne felt the impulse to shout back, "It's straight down the corridor, but there is a bloody big Taliban at the door." Yvonne was in the middle ring of a spiritual circus. The bewildering moment was worthy of another cigarette, and she lit her second one off the butt of the first.

That night in their cell the SNI women listened to an exceptional storyteller tell them the tragic events of 9/11. These women had no television images in their heads. They had to imagine the smoking, crumbling Twin Towers . . . the scorched hole in the side of the Pentagon . . . a wide burnt out crater in a barren Pennsylvania field . . . as Yvonne described the whole story of the terrorist attacks. They knew it had taken place. Georg had gotten the news from the prison guards, but it was scant on details; friends and family had informed them in the few letters they received, but it had been impossible to comprehend the scope of the tragedy. Now, as though she were reporting for her paper, Yvonne described in vivid narrative and without bias all that had happened that day, and how the world had reacted. The response from the six women was somber and emotional, especially for Heather and Dayna, and in some small way, all of them listening to this tale in the dark of that isolated cell thousands of miles from Ground Zero felt an inextricable link with that horrific event. It broke their hearts.

Yvonne thought that perhaps the situation was not so primitive after all when Katrin asked her if she would like to take a hot shower. Yes, it was not the Hilton, but the place at least had a shower.

The next day Katrin put on her head scarf and led Yvonne outside into the morning light, but the "shower" Katrin pointed to was not what Yvonne had in mind: it was a water pump and a bucket. Katrin demonstrated how to use the crank handle, and after several vigorous pumps water gushed out of the spigot into the bucket. Katrin then showed her how to use the hot plate to heat up the water and offered her some soap and bathing cloths. The process to get a hot shower was a rude awakening, but to Yvonne's complete surprise, the bathroom was the cleanest she had ever seen. She was quite impressed with the SNI women's commitment to improve their circumstances any way possible. It helped diminish the disappointment of not having a real shower. It also helped Yvonne's disposition when Diana offered to help her purchase cigarettes through their connections with the guards. However, the women still prohibited her from smoking in the cell. A clean bathroom and a tobacco connection—a cold shower and no smoking in the room. Life was full of compromises, and Yvonne could learn to adapt.

Yvonne decided that it was a good time to do some washing as well. Six days in a Jalalabad all-male prison had not given her an opportunity for washing herself or her few clothes. The only clean change of clothes she had was a wedding dress, not something originally packed for her trip; while in Jalalabad, her interrogators had presented her with a copy of the Koran, a wedding dress, and an offer of a husband. The irony was unmistakably obvious: here Yvonne shared a prison cell with six women accused of attempting to convert Muslims to Christianity, yet she had not been in Afghanistan for six days when the Taliban authorities offered her a new religion, a new dress, and a new husband. She'd accepted the Koran with a promise to read it, the dress because it was a unique gift and—who knew—it might come in handy. But she declined the offer of the husband. And it seemed highly unlikely that many suitors would line up anyway.

Since they were in the female compound of the prison, Yvonne did not think twice of hanging her undergarments on a line to dry in the warm sunshine after she had finished washing them in the bucket. She did not realize the inappropriateness of this domestic task—and it did not take long to get a reaction from the authorities. Mullah Hamid knew that his "sisters" would never do anything so offensive, and given the new arrival's quarrelsome nature, he was not inclined to attempt to resolve this issue on his own.

Representatives from the foreign ministry arrived to deal with the problem, led by a man named Mr. Afghani, whom Yvonne referred to as the "smiling assassin." She did not trust the permanent grin striking a crease through his beard; he was an all-in-one good cop/bad cop. Mr. Afghani had been directly responsible for Yvonne once she arrived in Kabul. He had accompanied her to the intelligence prison and probably hoped he had seen the last of her when she'd spit at his feet the day before.

Mr. Afghani ordered the SNI women to tell Yvonne to take her undergarments off the line and get them out of sight. The Taliban guards and officers could see them flapping in the breeze from their second-story barrack windows. When Yvonne heard the interpretation, she found it amusing at first, but anger trumped her initial response. But Yvonne had made up her mind to transform herself into the "hag from hell." She chose to adopt a very aggressive style in dealing with the Taliban in general and Mr. Afghani in particular. It was a calculated tactic on her part not to be cooperative. She hoped to wear down the Taliban so they would be glad to see the back of her once they had had enough of her tirades. The SNI women took just the opposite position in dealing with their captors. Diana made the decision to resist Yvonne's bellicose approach. After translating the order to remove her undergarments, Diana stated flatly that she did not want to be included as a player on the side of Yvonne's argument. She would translate, but she would distance herself from Yvonne's antagonistic manner. She would have to fight this battle alone.

"It's just a black bra and black underwear," Yvonne said, puffing herself up with deep breaths. "It's not lacy or sexy. What is their problem?"

Diana tried to explain the delicate nature of the situation, but Yvonne ignored her.

"You've never done washing in your life," Yvonne said, turning to the smiling assassin, his smile hardening into a more sinister contour. "I feel sorry for your soldiers. Tell them to stop looking out their windows and to get a life."

Yvonne had been here for only a couple of days. The six women were into their third month of captivity. It was a fight Diana did not want to take on, and she explained to Yvonne that she was not going to translate everything she said.

"Tell him if he wants them down he can take them down himself," Yvonne cried, her ramrod posture not about to show compliance.

Diana reduced Yvonne's communication down to its basic information, leaving out the profanity and all risqué innuendos regarding the soldiers and their looking at the undergarments. However, she could not cover for or clean up Yvonne's spitting at Mr. Afghani's feet again. That gesture required no translation, and for once, the smile disappeared from the smiling assassin's face. He turned and left.

"You know, instead of bombing Afghanistan, the Americans could just bring in women to wave their knickers in the air and the Taliban would run away," Yvonne shouted. Diana stood silent beside Yvonne. The smiling assassin had had enough. Diana knew not to add any more fuel to that fire.

Yvonne refused to accept her position as a prisoner, so she had to remain consistent by refusing to cooperate with the Taliban. When Georg and Peter joined the women later that day, Georg advised her to calm down and be more respectful, but she declined to back down. She had established her modus operandi, and there was no way she would change now.

Because of her refusal to behave any differently with the Taliban, Yvonne was isolated, on her own. There was sure to be some form of punishment. The SNI women were polite but distant with Yvonne. Peter and Georg did not warm up to her or try to be of any help. Still, when a female representative of the Taliban came to the women's compound and announced that Yvonne could not treat someone in high authority with such disrespect, and that they would flog her for such behavior, Yvonne was truly frightened. She began to tremble, a symptom of panic no amount of nicotine could calm, and three of the SNI women fell at Yvonne's feet and began to pray for her.

The flogging might have been a scare tactic; two could play at this game of showing toughness. It might have been a ploy to make Yvonne squirm in a stew of her own making for a while. The real punishment Yvonne received was a lot less severe. Mr. Afghani returned to the women's compound later with a satellite phone in his hand and the smile back on his face. He would get the last word.

"Everyone can phone home to her family except the English woman," Mr. Afghani said, the smile curling into contempt as he looked at Yvonne.

Katrin came to Yvonne's defense, begging mercy for Yvonne to use the phone.

"No," Mr. Afghani said bluntly. "She is a very bad woman. She spat at me and she has to be punished."

Spared the physical punishment, Yvonne could endure the disappointment of denied phone privileges. Her relief actually allowed her to enjoy the happy atmosphere that filled the cell as each woman had the opportunity to speak with her family on the satellite phone. It was a small sacrifice in comparison.

The experience, however, did not cause her to soften her method with the Taliban. When Mullah Usaf came to the compound the next day and asked for her name, she refused to give it. Usaf then told Diana to tell Yvonne he only wanted her name so he could allocate food for her, but if she was going to persist with her obstinate manner, then she could just starve. Diana was reluctant to translate the *mullah*'s edict, but Yvonne insisted Diana tell her, boasting that she was tough and could take the news. When Yvonne heard the translation it sobered her, but she refused to back down. Any sign of weakness now would mean the Taliban had won, and Yvonne could not live with that.

On Sunday afternoon, October 7, Yvonne, smoking a cigarette, took a stroll through the courtyard. The other women were also outside, going about their own business of reading alone, performing domestic chores, or just visiting with one another. Yvonne could hear the hum of an engine. She knew it was not coming from inside the prison; it was too far away for that. It was like the buzz of an insect hovering close to the ear. Suddenly the buzzing sound was replaced by a loud explosion, then followed by an eruption of heavy artillery fire. Yvonne shielded her eyes from the sunlight, scanned the sky, and spotted the American drone high above the city. It had fired a missile at a target deemed important by Allied forces, and it sounded like everyone in Kabul who had a weapon was firing back at it. The strain had been mounting for weeks. Everyone knew an invasion was imminent, although Heather kept holding out hope for a rescue before that happened. Troops were amassing on border states, aircraft carriers cruised the Indian Ocean, and the Taliban took the opportunity to release some tension.

It did nothing but that—and the enemy drone flew off unharmed.

Yvonne drew her attention back to the courtyard as the gunfire in the city kept following the departing plane. The women (with the exception of Heather) gave little reaction to this cacophony; they remained unruffled, looking up into the sky. It was as if they all had a tranquil resolution to the inevitable. But Heather was distraught and highly emotional. The others tried to reassure her, but it was problematic. She kept screaming for the guards to put them inside a bunker—which was unlikely to happen, and not what the others wanted anyway. Heather's hopes for rescue or release before the invasion had been dashed, so the current reality was difficult for her to accept. When Georg and Peter came to the women's cell later that day to discuss the English translation of the court transcripts, they also tried to calm Heather down, but their efforts had little effect. While the group went over the transcript, Heather remained hidden under the bed.

That night, before the women settled in, the guards barged into the room and ordered Yvonne to collect her things. In typical Taliban fashion, the guards acted as though it was a life or death situation, shouting at her to hurry. They had prepared a cell for her on the second floor of a neighboring barrack and hastily escorted her up the stairs and into this new cubicle. It was actually an improvement over where she had spent the last three days: there was a chair, a small table and lamp, and a rickety bed. Still, it was a far cry from a nice hotel.

There was not a great deal of effort made to settle in. She arranged her belongings on the chair and floor and lay down to read a Ken Follett novel given her by her former cellmates. Yvonne was not long into the book before the bombing began in earnest. Cruise missiles began to roar overhead, and once more Kabul erupted in response. What she could see of the sky and the city was ablaze with antiaircraft fire and the fiery tails of cruise missiles streaking through the night above the tops of the buildings speeding toward their programmed targets. She thought briefly of Heather hiding under her bed, of the other women and their resolute, inner strength. With those women surrounding Heather, Yvonne felt confident the group would survive even the worst of what lay ahead.

Her thoughts then turned toward the people of Kabul, innocent people with no ties or loyalty to the Taliban, huddled together, taking shelter from million-dollar missiles and the fallout from antiaircraft rounds. It seemed futile and unnecessary, certainly overkill; bombs—no matter how "smart"—could still strike indiscriminately. It was terrifying to sit at the window, watching and listening to the destruction.

At some point during the bombing, guards burst into her room. They always burst in, never knocked; she wondered if they even knew how to knock. They ordered her off the bed, and Yvonne assumed she would be moving yet again and began to pack. Instead they flipped the bed into a corner, lifted up a trap door, and began hauling out caches of weapons and rocket-propelled grenades. When they had emptied the storage place, they left. Other than the initial order for her to get off the bed, the Taliban were oblivious of Yvonne's presence. They departed without further communication.

Yvonne collapsed onto the chair, staring at the empty hole in her floor, her overturned bed a casualty of the raid. Unaware of what lay beneath her, she realized that with one careless flick of her cigarette, she could have started the war single-handedly.

Early the next morning the guards whisked Yvonne out of her

room—barely given enough time to pack—out of the women's compound, and into a waiting vehicle. She did not see her six SNI companions and was not able to bid them farewell. The drivers received their instructions, which Yvonne could not understand, and then drove out of the compound as if a race had begun. At least the bombing had stopped. Yvonne was grateful they did not have to dodge explosions as they sped through the streets, though it was unsettling not to know where they were taking her. Before long it became clear that the driver was making a dash for Jalalabad and the border. When they arrived at the border crossing, the driver ordered her out of the vehicle and then sped away.

When the Taliban foreign ministers gave a press conference the next day in Peshawar, Pakistan, a reporter happened to ask about the fate of Yvonne Ridley. The Taliban representative responded, "We are releasing the English woman. She is a very bad woman with a very bad mouth."

Mullah Hamid gave Georg and Peter permission to meet with the SNI women before the bombing began in earnest. The spy drone was merely the prologue, and Georg sensed the bombing was only hours away. They gathered in prayer, imploring God to protect them. They hoped and prayed that by some chance the American forces knew their location and would try to avoid targeting the intelligence prison. This thought provided some level of comfort as the eight huddled in prayer, before the guards hustled Georg and Peter back to their barracks.

On the first night of the bombing, they crammed all the men in Georg and Peter's barracks on the first floor and locked the doors.

Had any of the bombs made a direct hit on their barrack, no one would have survived. Each day the bombing intensified. Each day the war progressed, the more dangerous it became for the hostages. When the warplanes passed overhead, the guards would point their Kalashnikovs in the sky and then at Georg and say, "Here are your friends coming again." Yet most of their fellow prisoners had a different attitude. Instead of being agitated or frightened by the bombing, these Afghanis shared a sense of excitement. With the war, their chances for freedom increased. Many of the Afghan inmates told Georg, "We pray to Allah five times a day that this regime will be toppled."

Night after night, the percussive shock waves of exploding bombs throughout the city shook the prison barracks. Georg, Peter, and the other prisoners would dash from window to window on the first floor to watch the fireworks display. There were so many explosions and flashes of light it was as though night and day had reversed.

One night was exceptionally bad. The targets chosen for that particular night were much closer to the prison than before. The noise and shock waves were so intense, so repetitive, Georg felt as though any second a stray bomb could fall on them. He looked at the barricaded steel doors at the end of the corridor. There was no way of escape. Trapped inside a cage, he knew that one misguided missile could finish them all. The next day they learned that the bombs had hit the Sharia Radio tower next to the prison.

On another raid, the fighter planes destroyed the television and radar towers located on a mountain above the city. When Georg and Peter returned to their cell the following morning, they could see the smoldering ruins of the tower and station scattered over the top of the mountain. The Taliban were particularly shamed when they heard through the news service of a foreign radio station that an American female pilot had fired the rockets destroying the radar and television. Women in Kabul could not drive cars—yet a woman had flown a fighter jet over the city and bombed a high-value target.

The nights of bombing were also a nerve-wracking experience for the SNI women. The first few nights, they moved out of the room and into the corridor of the barracks. The walls in their cell had floor-to-ceiling cracks so wide that the constant shock waves alone would be enough to bring the ceiling down upon their heads. A whistling sound preceded each explosion, followed by a deafening reverberation and the ground shaking beneath them. A lifetime was reduced to mere seconds: jets flying overhead, the high-pitched shrill of guided bombs before impact, the flash of light, the ear-splitting explosion, and finally, the earthquake vibration racing up the spine into the skull. The terrible uncertainty of it all kept the women in a constant mode of prayer. When one of them would lose control, seized with panic, the others would gather round her to comfort and console. There was no running away; no other shelter to hide in except the tinderbox they inhabited. It was either face one's mortality, trust God, or go mad.

At the end of the first week of bombing in mid-October, Atif returned to Kabul, met with his clients, and went over all the final changes that were necessary in his written defense. When he presented this defense to the court, Chief Justice Mullah Noor Mohammed Saqib, the disdain and indifference on his face painfully apparent, told Atif he required time to review the case. Atif returned to Pakistan to await the opinion of the court. When he came back a week later, he arrived with a Pakistani diplomatic contingent of a half dozen delegates. He hoped the increased number of his party might add some extra pressure on the chief justice to conclude a quick and favorable outcome for his clients. But when Atif and his delegation arrived at the supreme court building, the court bailiffs would not even admit them into the courtroom. The chief justice also refused to see him, sending word that "the court has more important cases to consider." Atif returned to the intelligence prison to convey the disappointing news to the hostages.

"This is not about having a fair trial," Georg told Atif when they all met together. "The judges will do as they please, no matter what you submit. It is futile to wait for proper court proceedings. We are hostages. We need to think of something else."

"We have reached a dead end," Atif replied, hating to state the obvious. "The court has no interest in justice. The only hope you have now is that your Western governments will apply extreme diplomatic pressure."

There had been some diplomatic overtures on the part of the Taliban to begin negotiations on behalf of the SNI employees. The Afghan foreign minister, Wakil Ahmed Muttawakil, first offered a prisoner exchange—the SNI eight for Sheikh Omar Abdel-Rahman, serving a life sentence in the United States for planning several terrorist attacks (including the first attack on the World Trade Center in 1995). Muttawakil's second offer came the day before the bombings: do not attack Afghanistan in exchange for the SNI eight. If anyone had any doubts that the SNI eight were anything other than hostages, these two offers were proof positive.

The only thing Atif could do for his clients before his final departure was take letters from the hostages back to Pakistan and see that the Shelter Now offices in Peshawar received them. However, it proved to be a daunting task to get the letters past Mullah Usaf. If the daily bombing raised the anxiety level among the Taliban, it also raised the level of security around the hostages. The hostages had written letters before, had them scrutinized, censored, and often destroyed; offhand comments had come back to haunt them, so they were careful with what they wrote. But this time Georg decided to throw caution to the wind. What did he have to lose? He would write whatever he wanted and hope that Atif could smuggle the letters out of the prison with no one knowing.

Mohammed Sharif, who had been so helpful to Georg and the others, would soon prove to be a godsend in this case. He and his fellow students had received their release papers shortly after the bombing began. Sharif could have left, but instead went straight to Georg and said he would stay with him until Georg and the others were free. His father and grandfather both agreed with Sharif's decision. This demonstration of sacrifice stunned Georg and the SNI hostages. Such a risky decision could prove to be fatal, but Sharif was determined.

"Thank you, my friend," Georg said, moved with emotion. "I know there are more Afghans who love us than those who want to harm us."

It was in this context that the hostages composed their final letters to family and friends. Georg unleashed a torrent of complaints against Mullah Usaf. Others wrote of similar grievances, in much softer language, but Georg pulled no punches regarding Mullah Usaf's cruel treatment of his fellow prisoners—especially the sixteen Afghan SNI employees. Complaints about the unsanitary conditions of the toilets paled in comparison. But Georg did not stop there. He took it upon himself to describe in detail where in Kabul they were located, and included a crude drawing of the prison with surrounding landmarks. When Atif prepared to leave the prison, Mullah Usaf had the guards search his briefcase. When they discovered Atif was smuggling letters, and even a second drawing of the prison (much to Georg's surprise), the prison warden rounded up the hostages and brought them to his offices. Mullah Usaf was unpredictable, with a vicious temper; if he were to ascertain the true contents of Georg's letter, the exact purpose of the drawing, or learn of any negative thoughts expressed in the other's letters, the situation could turn quite ugly.

Enter Mohammed Sharif, the only person present who could translate the letters into Pashtu. Georg wondered about the hand of God: if Sharif had chosen to leave when his release papers had come through, if he had not been arrested in the first place, if Shelter Now had not gone to his region and served the people of his tribe years before, if Georg had not gone out of his way to establish relationships with the leaders of Sharif's tribe . . . so many factors came together in this moment.

Mullah Usaf summoned Sharif to the offices. The first order of business was to determine the artist of the drawing and its purpose. Mullah Usaf was furious, his inflamed eyes scrutinizing each hostage as he waved the artwork in the air, accusing them all of being spies and demanding to know who was responsible. Everyone was quiet for a few seconds, allowing the echoes of Usaf's ranting to diminish. Then Heather stepped forward and confessed to the drawing. The shock in the room had a tangible thickness; no one was able to move. Even Mullah Usaf did not react immediately, as if he required a moment to weigh a number of heinous options in response to this espionage.

Georg broke the silence, knowing a quick and plausible answer might dispel the awe and bewilderment at Heather's brave confession. "It was drawn so the Americans would know where we are," Georg said. "That's true, but we wanted them to know exactly where we are so they would not bomb the prison. It would keep us all safe."

Mullah Usaf looked at Heather. She said nothing, keeping her eyes cast on the floor, the deferential appearance of respect coupled with terror burning through her heart. He looked at the drawing, turning it in his hand, studying the outline and seeming to grade it for inaccuracies. If this answer were true, his prison could be the safest place in Kabul. He placed the drawing on the table beside the letters and nodded his head; he seemed satisfied with Georg's clarification. Everyone breathed a sigh of relief.

Now Sharif was directed to read each letter—and it was his time to shine. Beginning with Heather's letter and the rest that followed, he performed an extraordinary feat of extemporized translation. In each letter—with each written articulation of complaint, fears, longings for freedom, desire for reunion with family, angry expressions of living conditions and treatment—Sharif transposed complaints into high praise for everything from the food to individuals in charge of their care. In one letter, Sharif chose to single out Mullah Usaf for special recognition, which brought an uncharacteristic flicker of surprise and appreciation in his face as he listened intently to each false word Sharif read. However, Sharif saved his best linguistic magic for Georg's letter, written in German (a language that could as well have been ancient cuneiform in his eyes) for the German diplomats in Pakistan. Here followed a gift of true improvisation as he read of Georg's articulation of his love for his family, of the improved living conditions since his last correspondence, of friendships developed in prison, and the nice treatment they were receiving at the hands of their hosts. When Sharif came to the section in Georg's letter where he described and drew a picture of the prison, he took it upon himself to offer the same rationalization Georg had given to explain Heather's drawing. It was natural to link the two, and Mullah Usaf took it at face value. Perhaps the kind treatment he received in Sharif's bogus translations had softened him. Whatever his reasons, he ordered his secretary to stamp the letters and gave them to Atif. The SNI eight looked at Sharif in wonder when he finished his performance; he had literally risked his life for the sake of these Westerners.

Atif took with him the final written communication the hostages composed for their loved ones. With Atif's departure, the outside world lost all contact with the SNI eight. In Georg's last letter to Udo, written in English, he tried to keep a brave face but could not completely hide his deep despair and feeling of helplessness.

October 20, 2001
Dear Udo,

So far we've managed to survive all the air raids with our nerves still intact. Since yesterday, everything has been quiet . . .

The atmosphere is growing increasingly tense. More and more we find ourselves having to really focus on God and His promises; we wouldn't cope otherwise. Humanly speaking, our prospects are now extremely bleak. The court proceedings have no doubt been thrown overboard. There are hardly any high-level Taliban left here now. Most of them have fled south. Only the less important people have stayed behind . . .

We don't receive any faxes or other messages anymore: all the staff at the foreign ministry who used to bring us the faxes appear to have fled. It's very discouraging. The incessant bombing, the tension, and the uncertainty of everything are an incredible challenge. It's now perfectly clear to us that we're being held here as hostages—by people who hate us . . .

Georg

CHAPTER EIGHT

HIGHWAY TO KANDAHAR

G eorg compared the Taliban to wounded animals whose behavior became more unpredictable with each day of bombing. Some of the less friendly guards would refer to Georg as "George Bush"; they pointed to the sky as the American planes flew overhead and said things like, "Here are your friends coming again," and "If we must flee the city, all the foreigners will be the first to die." Since the SNI workers were the only foreigners left in Kabul, the chances of their survival looked bleak. Georg and Peter kept to themselves as much as possible, foregoing even the daily walks in the compound for fear of drawing undue attention from trigger-happy guards overwrought by the constant bombing.

The hostages had allowed themselves the luxury of dreaming that when the invasion began, the Northern Alliance and the

Americans would march into Kabul and liberate the city. They imagined themselves celebrating with the rest of the citizens of Kabul, much like Europeans celebrated when the Americans liberated them from Nazi occupation in World War II. They hoped they could quickly get back to work rebuilding the Shelter Now organization and facilities, helping the Afghans restore their lives. They did not even want to return to their home countries, but rather remain in Afghanistan. Nevertheless, with each successful bombing raid in the city and against the Taliban defensive lines north of the city in the region of Shamali, the fear and helplessness grew among the Taliban . . . and so grew the helplessness and fear among the hostages. The liberation of Kabul appeared imminent, but would they live to see that day?

Mullah Hamid was particularly worried about keeping them safe. He was certainly a loyalist of the Taliban regime and a devout Muslim, but he had grown fond of his charges and wanted to do all he could to protect them. While escorting Georg to the office of the prison director, Mullah Usaf, Hamid expressed his anxiety about his ability to keep them out of harm's way.

"I am worried the Taliban in Kandahar and al-Qaeda fighters might abduct you or kill you for revenge," he said to Georg as he escorted him to Mullah Usaf's office—unsettling news for Georg, who was already unsettled by this summons. "I don't know how I can protect you."

Even before Mullah Hamid brought Georg into the room, Georg sensed he was about to experience something peculiar; based on Hamid's nervousness, he concluded it was not going to be pleasant. Mullah Usaf sat next to a man supporting a turban so large it appeared like an imposing, black storm cloud rising out of his head;

Georg half expected to see lightening and hear thunder each time he moved his head. Five other men, their skulls wrapped with less imposing amounts of cloth, flanked the storm cloud. If size mattered, then the size of this turban made him the alpha male in this group, and if intimidation was the desired effect, then that, too, succeeded. Hamid stepped into a corner, his downcast eyes and sealed lips indicating to Georg that any hope for support from him was misplaced. After a few innocuous questions regarding identity, the storm cloud rose out of its seat. A short discussion ensued spoken in Dari—unintelligible to Georg and deliberately chosen by the group to bewilder him—and then the black storm turban led the lesser clouds out of the room like obedient children. Georg turned to Hamid.

"A delegation from Kandahar?" he asked, knowing the answer before he heard it.

Hamid simply nodded, and a deep sense of fear found a home in Georg's heart.

The few times the Taliban allowed the hostages to receive letters from friends and family were a lifeline that proved a profound blessing. As any hostage would say, it is impossible to overstate the importance of receiving word from the outside world, to see handwritten thoughts and feelings expressed to you by the people you know and love; to know that these people think of you, harbor you in their hearts, utter your name before God, speak of you to strangers, and petition them for their prayers on your behalf. To say the letters received by the SNI hostages were comparable to reading Scripture would be an exaggeration, but they were very dear, read and reread, personal news shared with their fellow hostages, the connection to the outside world as important as food and water.

Atif's last delivery of correspondence was the day he returned to Pakistan. Georg had three letters from Marianne he wanted to savor in private, but privacy was difficult to come by. Between the failure of Atif to secure their release or even move the legal process forward to a conclusion, his subsequent departure, and the constant bombing, Georg was looking forward to reading the comforting words from his wife. He would read the letters after his dinner of potato soup . . . but before he could take the first bite, he received another summons to come to Mullah Usaf's office.

In typical fashion Usaf was antagonistic and demanding.

"Pack your belongings immediately!" he shouted. "You are being moved."

He waved his arms about, causing Mullah Hamid and the guards to shuffle and stiffen in preparation for a rapid response the second Mullah Usaf was ready to exit, but Georg was not in a compliant frame of mind.

"Why must we leave? It is good here. We like it here."

"We are taking you to a better place."

This taking-you-to-a-better-place business was such a familiar refrain that it was becoming a cliché.

"You say this and you do not keep your word. We need to stay here." Georg's reaction was inspired more from an annoyance that Mullah Usaf would once again use these frantic surprise tactics to agitate and demoralize the hostages than from any real negotiating power. He chose to stand up to bullying, even if it proved futile.

"It is for your safety," Mullah Usaf explained. "You need to be in a safer place during the bombing."

Georg was not buying the argument. The Afghan Angel had informed him that he was in regular contact with the U.S. forces via satellite phone, giving them the exact coordinates of their location. Moreover, Georg received routine scraps of news from Sharif, updating him on the bombing campaign. He knew the bombing was decimating the Taliban forces and that a number of Afghan cities had fallen to the advancing Northern Alliance, which was even now just miles from the outskirts of Kabul. After the recent meeting with the delegation from Kandahar, Georg suspected Mullah Usaf had orders to keep the hostages safe at all costs—and that Usaf feared there would be a commando raid upon the prison to free the hostages.

"We don't need to go to a safer place. We are safe here. We want to stay."

"Who is the warden of this place?" cried Mullah Usaf, his rage bordering on physical eruption. "Who gives the orders?"

Georg saw that defiance was not an option. In this wartime pressure cooker, Usaf's aggressive nature could turn ugly. In an instant the situation could change dramatically for better or worse; it was best to be cautious.

So he returned to his cell with the guards to tell Peter the disquieting news. Peter was about to devour a bowl of the potato soup brought for their supper when Georg and the guards burst into the cell. The guards told Peter he could take the pot, so they hurriedly packed and left their cell, Peter clutching the pot of soup as if it were a culinary delight prepared for a royal table.

Among their many friends within the prison, no one was able to help them, not even Mohammed Sharif. When Sharif saw Peter and Georg heading down the corridor and discovered the reason for their removal, he was despondent. He could do nothing, and he watched his friends leave, wondering whether he would ever see them again.

Neither Peter nor Georg could shake off a profound sense of trepidation. Where were they being taken? How safe was this new place? Would their Afghan Angel know Mullah Usaf had ordered the hostages taken there? Could he get word to the Americans of their new location and this sudden change of strategy before the next round of bombing? They had no rights. They had no power or support. They were foreigners held captive by people who hated them and were prepared to use them in whatever way necessary to advance their cause. It was a dangerous, uncertain future.

The only bright spot of this march into the dark unknown was that they were to share it with the women. The six of them sat in the van waiting for the two men, their meager possessions pressed into their laps by the weight of their protective arms, their glum, exhausted faces revealing the same sentiment of foreboding felt by Peter and Georg. Like the men, they did not believe they were going to a better place, or that they would be back in the morning. They had lugged all their worldly goods with them, refusing to leave anything behind.

The journey gave them no clues as to their destination. The heavily armed caravan raced through the city center, past deserted foreign embassies, and finally drove into the entrance of the intelligence service's highest security prison—Riasat 3. From one prison location to another, each site they were taken to was a plunge into a lower circle of hell. Riasat 3 was a step back into the Dark Ages, a prison that inspired horror stories of those who entered and never returned to society. As soon as the hostages stepped out of the van, the guards herded them toward an imposing building, then separated them at the doorway, depositing the women on the first floor and hustling the two men down the basement stairs. There was not even enough time given to say good-bye.

Georg points out drawings on the walls of the cell in which he was held at the Vice and Virtue Prison.

The passageway was long and shadowy. The high-pitched squeals of rats punctuated the stifling air as they shuffled down the corridor. Visibility was barely an arm's length, yet they kept moving forward at a pace set by the guards as if some sinister creature were in pursuit. At the end of the corridor, they paused before a large metal door. The lead guard unlocked the lock and slowly pushed the heavy door open, its rusted hinges releasing a grinding screech, until it banged against the stone wall with a loud crash. One could only imagine Dante about to enter the Inferno: "Abandon all hope, ye who enter here." The guard pointed to the basement steps and ordered them to descend into darkness. The guard refused to lead the way, and there was no light to illuminate their faltering steps. Georg and Peter leaned into the wall, their outstretched arms feeling the way down the murky staircase.

The lack of vision intensified the other senses, the sense of smell having the quickest reaction to the darkness; the dank, verminous smell of decades of human and animal squalor unable to reach the sanitized air above. The odor almost brought Georg to his knees as he felt his way through the blackness.

They paused when they reached the bottom step, gasping, their lungs trying to filter the stench and adapt to the rancid atmosphere. Their eyes began adjusting to the shadows cast about the basement like black spirits. The few low-wattage bulbs exuded a bare, Tinker Bell glow. Flesh-and-blood forms began to take shape as they surveyed the primitive dungeon, a place inhabited by the damned. The two men shuffled past woeful prisoners, competitive in their degraded state of misery: mournful faces, racking spasms of coughing fits, wild expressions of shock, spastic twitches of limbs—a haphazard choreography—strands of beard and hair a tattered weave around vacant eyes, dripping noses and drooling mouths greeted them. Those long gone from mental reasoning barked or growled a new traumatized language, its meaning understood only by the one who uttered it. If not chained to the wall, prisoners wore chains connecting their arms or legs, and any movement came with the heavy clank of metal echoing through the dense, medieval darkness. This was the final stopping point for those destined for amputation or execution for crimes most of them never committed. Where was Georg and Peter's place in this new world? Where was God? If the stench had not taken their breath away, entering this nightmare did.

The men stumbled into their underground cell: scabby walls, an insect-ridden couch and mattress, a candle, and a sliver of a window on the far wall. If you stood on tiptoe, you could see a half-picture frame width of the outside world. The Taliban had dropped Georg and Peter into a tomb. A sudden attack of panic filled Georg. The walls closed in, and an overwhelming fear of this being their final destination, of he and Peter becoming like these deranged inhabitants, filling the air with their insane howls, was too much to bear. All thoughts of having a nice potato soup dinner and reading his letters from Marianne vanished. He sat down on the couch, devastated and mute, trying to catch and control his breath.

The women fared little better. Riasat 3 was an all-male prison, so *sharia* law forbade any women on the premises—which meant no female guards to protect them. Although Mullah Omar had disapproved of this same scenario for Yvonne Ridley, apparently he had adjusted his legalistic thinking in this case.

The Taliban were everywhere, and guards kept coming in and out of their cell. This certainly did not feel like the safer place promised by Mullah Usaf, with the steady flow of men glaring at them with menacing eyes or hurling verbal abuse at them. In order to protect themselves, they stacked their suitcases against the door, forming a temporary blockade between them and any potential danger. If any of the women needed to visit the bathroom, they went in pairs, never alone. It was too dangerous. But when the bombing began, they all remained in one place, huddled in a corner away from the window. The bombing was horrible, but at least it distracted the guards and kept them from entering their cell—a small blessing, but one for which they were grateful.

Through the night, with bombs falling all around them, they worshipped and read Scripture by candlelight. To bolster and encourage their faith, Diana reminded them that they were in this predicament for a reason. God had asked them if they were willing to pay a price to help an oppressed nation, and this was the price exacted. Even if being in this dilemma was against their will, it was her opinion that God had handpicked these eight individuals to stay in Afghanistan and pray for her people. It was a rare calling, but with the constant bombing throughout the city and the hostile Taliban guards lurking just outside their cell door, the privilege of standing in this gap for Afghanistan seemed to test a strength they were not sure they possessed.

When the bombing began, it set off a dissonance of rattling chains, vocal howls, and whimpers, sounds of terror and bedlam that brought Georg out of his stupor. A man stood in the doorway, an emaciated wisp of hair and beard and tattered clothing—but a face that appeared to have a strand of sanity. Peter and Georg were too shell-shocked to know how to respond. Locked in their despair, they stared at the man, so he invited himself in and sat down. He looked about the room as if inspecting it to be sure it met the approval of the new arrivals. He smiled. It was strained, even painful in its crooked shape, but nonetheless a smile. How was it possible to smile in this place? Perhaps the appearance of sanity was a deception. Perhaps the smile masked the leap over the edge.

"I am Mustafa. I tell my story to the new ones," he said in Pashto. "It helps the new ones adjust. It helps remind me that I have a history."

His voice was a cracked whisper, as if half his vocal cords had hardened. It was the voice of an old man, though it was impossible to determine his exact age.

"My neighbor had a grudge against me, a grudge I have paid for with seven years of my life. The grudge, I have forgotten. The cost of the grudge remains locked in my memory," Mustafa said, pointing a twisted finger to the middle of his smudged forehead.

"I could do nothing to prove my innocence, so I was sent to the infamous Pul-e-Charkhi prison—the worst of the worst, a chamber of horrors that makes this place look like a street fair."

Looking about him, Georg could not believe that was possible, yet he knew the infamous Pul-e-Charkhi was where the sixteen Afghan SNI employees were currently incarcerated. He bowed his head, remembering the torment they had already experienced and imagining what misery these dear friends must be going through now. But another man's story distracted him.

"For seven years I called Pul-e-Charkhi my home, three of those years spent in chains in an underground cell, much like this one only no window, no outside light."

Mustafa held out his arms to show the lumps of scarring on his wrists.

"I could not cut my hair," he said, running his fingers through the greasy strands of hair and pulling the loose tresses behind his ears. "I could not cut my fingernails. And the toilet . . . ah, the toilet was where I lay. Imagine that."

Georg did not want to imagine that. Their own recent

experience with the filthy conditions of a lavatory was pristine by comparison.

"I lost all contact with my family. Did the authorities tell them where I was? Did they let them come to see me? Did they tell them I was still alive? No word came from them, no letter, no visit. I was dead to them. I was dead to everyone."

Mustafa bowed his head, a brooding nod to his own demise.

"No one came to me during that whole time . . . no one came. The despair, the loneliness . . . I cannot describe that horror of isolation. I allowed myself to go mad in order to survive, let myself become insane to hold on to a thread of sanity."

This amused him. Only someone who has belly-crawled across that razor-edge of sanity could understand the concept.

"I made friends. We were an exclusive group, but one by one, they all left. A few, they released, a very few. Most they executed. I envied them. Yes, I envied even more the ones they hanged, or shot, or beheaded. They were free, welcomed into the bosom of paradise, and I . . . I idled away the hours alone in chains, wallowing in my own filth, wondering why Allah had abandoned me."

Georg responded to the sense of abandonment expressed by this stranger, a feeling so familiar, so real. He looked into the craggy face of the storyteller, listening now to every word with deliberate intent.

"When the day came for them to unlock my chains, take me from the hole that had been my home for seven years, and set me free, you would have expected it to be a day of rejoicing, but I did not rejoice. I was confused, terrified. They pushed me out the door like an unwanted dog, shooing me into the streets, yelling at me to go home. Home, if only I could find home; if only I could remember where I left it."

He stood looking about the room as if in search of a lost object, then sat again.

"I wandered the streets, lost, my mind unhinged in a new madness. I was out in the world, detached from the safety of my cell. I could not find my home. I searched and searched for days. A kindhearted *imam* let me sleep in his mosque at night, fed me, prayed for me. I have forgotten much of my life, but I remember the rare kindness.

"Eventually, I stumbled out of my mental fog like a traveler emerging from a long pilgrimage, and I stood before my house. At least I thought it was my house. Seven years is a long time and much had changed. The door opened, and the family members who stood in the doorway recoiled in horror. Who could blame them? I was back from the grave, looking as if I had been dead for seven years. They told me my father and brother had died, and when my young wife saw me, she clutched her heart and fell in a heap on the floor. She never recovered. She died, a trauma to the heart, they said. Me, I was her trauma. Imagine dying of shock. I did not believe that was possible. And though I'm not exactly sure how or when I got here, I returned to the only thing I knew . . . the grave."

Mustafa stood, tottering a bit before finding his balance, and then scuffed his feet across the floor toward the cell door, his legs shuffling as though linked together by imaginary chains. He turned around and faced Peter and Georg.

"You and the others have come to us innocent of what they accuse you. I understand that. You are known and loved by many."

"But how did you know? How do you know us?" Georg asked.

"If you listen, the news can find its way even into the grave," he said, tapping an ear, his smile returning, his parted lips revealing a near-toothless mouth. "It will be a pleasure to help you in any way I am able."

He vanished, a sympathetic ghost who touched their fearful hearts with kindness.

No matter the dark corners in which they found themselves, no matter the feeling of despair, even in the depths of the grave, God brought to Georg and Peter people who were kind to them, people who had suffered far worse unjust punishment and were still able to offer a caring smile. The goodwill of a stranger humbled them.

After Georg translated Mustafa's story to Peter, there was not much else to say, so Georg pulled out the letters from Marianne and settled into reading, while Peter stretched out on the mattress to read the correspondence from his own family.

In the first letter from Marianne, Georg was stunned to learn that she and the boys were now in Germany. The situation in Pakistan had become too volatile. It was no longer safe, and they'd had to flee, so now they were even farther away than before. All this time, it had been a small comfort for Georg to know that just across the border in Peshawar, his family had been waiting for him. If by some chance he and the others were able to escape, they could enjoy a happy reunion within a few hours. Now the distance between them had become a great gulf, deep and wide, and in his wretched state, he imagined the improbabilities of ever crossing it.

To add to the pain, he also learned in that first letter that Marianne's father was deathly ill. In the second letter her father had drifted into a coma, and by the third letter Marianne recounted the sorrow of her father's death and the details of the funeral. He was absent for it all, a most important and critical transition in the life of his family, while he rotted away in a prison cell that was a throwback to the first century. The agony he felt now expanded to a point beyond his imagination. He and his family were so far apart. How did Marianne cope with the death of her father? In his absence she had to comfort her mother. She had to comfort their children. How did his boys have a full appreciation of what was happening when they could have no communication with their own father? As far as they knew, their father, her husband, could be dead as well. Who would comfort Marianne? Who would comfort his sons? Who would comfort him? In his desperation, Georg opened his Bible to Psalm 91 and began to read:

> He who dwells in the secret place of the Most High
>> Shall abide under the shadow of the Almighty.
> I will say of the LORD, "He is my refuge and my fortress;
>> My God, in Him I will trust."
> Surely He shall deliver you from the snare of the fowler
>> And from the perilous pestilence.
> He shall cover you with His feathers,
>> And under His wings you shall take refuge;
>> His truth shall be your shield and buckler.
> You shall not be afraid of the terror by night,
>> Nor of the the arrow that flies by day,
> Nor of the pestilence that walks in darkness,
>> Nor of the destruction that lays waste at noonday.
> A thousand may fall at your side,
>> And ten thousand at your right hand;

But it shall not come near you.

Only with your eyes shall you look,

And see the reward of the wicked.

Because you have made the LORD, who is my refuge,

Even the Most High, your dwelling place,

No evil shall befall you,

Nor shall any plague come near your dwelling;

For He shall give His angels charge over you,

To keep you in all your ways.

In their hands they shall bear you up,

Lest you dash your foot against a stone.

You shall tread upon the lion and the cobra,

The young lion and the serpent you shall trample underfoot.

"Because he has set his love upon Me, therefore I will deliver him;

I will set him on high, because he has known My name.

He shall call upon Me, and I will answer him;

I will be with him in trouble;

I will deliver him and honor him.

With long life will I satisfy him,

And show him My salvation." (vv. 1–16)

Georg read, reread, and read again these words of the psalmist. It was all he had to cling to, the only comfort he could grasp. Buried alive in an underground cell, bombs exploding all around his prison, surrounded by the stench, the sounds, and visions of torture and madness, letters from his wife telling him of death and sorrow within his own family . . . these words from Holy Scripture were all he had to comfort him, so he drank deeply from their inspiration, like a man dying of thirst. Then he and Peter began to pray together, pacing within the confines of their cell, pouring out their anguish to God, much as they had done the first day of their imprisonment when their lives plummeted into chaos.

For Georg there was no rest, despite having taken two sleeping pills. It was the longest and darkest night of his confinement. He lay awake wondering if he, too, would lose his sanity listening to the shrieks of lunacy coming from the other cells, the exploding bombs outside his window, and the pounding of his own heart—which seemed at the point of splintering.

The next day brought some temporary relief when Mullah Hamid came to pick them up. The women were waiting in the vehicle when the guards escorted Georg and Peter into the compound. Georg noticed Mullah Hamid in an animated quarrel with Mullah Hasan, who had risen to the position of warden of Riasat 3 because of his interrogation skills. Nicknamed "Mullah Cable," his torture instrument of choice was a short-handled whip with steel cables an inch thick wrapped in plastic. When other forms of persuasion failed to break a victim, Mullah Cable would instruct his guards to lash the victim with the whip until he provided the sought-after confession. The sight of the two *mullahs* in heated debate brought on instant worry. Incarceration in Riasat 3 was bad enough, but discovering who was in charge of the prison made it even more alarming. Georg was sure that the conversation between Hamid and Hasan was about them, and as he and Peter got into the vehicle, he sensed Hamid had succeeded in dissuading Hasan of some heinous inclination toward them, or had stopped him from carrying out an order given from their superiors in Kandahar. He was relieved when Hamid got into the vehicle with the SNI eight and Hasan got into the Land Cruiser carrying the Taliban soldiers to escort them back to the intelligence prison. The eight of them could not have been happier when the gates of the Hamid Hotel opened for them. It almost felt like a sweet taste of freedom.

However, the taste did not last too long. Georg never learned the subject of their dispute. Perhaps Hasan wanted to keep the prisoners all the time and Hamid successfully argued for their return during the day (when there was no bombing). Whatever it was, a new routine had started. At night, Hasan came and personally drove the prisoners to Riasat 3, always with heavy-armed escort. For some reason, he did not entrust this task to anyone and needed to verify the safety of the prisoners with his own eyes. Then the next morning, Hamid picked them up and returned the eight to the intelligence prison. He, too, it seemed, wanted to verify that nothing had happened to the eight during the night. It appeared that neither *mullah* trusted the other one.

Unbeknownst to the SNI eight, during this time of traveling back and forth between the different prisons, their Afghan Angel was in regular contact with the U.S. forces by satellite phone. He was able to keep track of their locations by GPS and would inform the Americans of their exact position at any given time. If they had only known, it might have eased some of their panic. Their captivity was nearing the one hundredth day, and the turmoil among the Taliban and in the prisons could not help but affect their own minds. There was nothing and no one they could count on except the persistent disruption to any normalcy. Then Margrit felt God was impressing on her heart particular words of inspiration and hope for everyone.

"Tea time is over," she said to the others in one of their trips to and from the two prisons, a code phrase they often used among themselves to mean that the days of the Taliban regime were numbered. All the women felt this was true. The custom of serving tea to guests was the metaphor; *tea* was their code for Taliban. They all felt that when the Taliban was kicked out of Kabul and Afghanistan, then they, too, would be freed, that both events would happen simultaneously.

Diana also had her own thoughts on the matter. "We have relied on diplomats, the Red Cross, lawyers, our Afghan Angel, a few prison guards, and though they have provided some help along the way, in the end it is only God we can turn to and trust," she said.

Then Diana began to quote some verses from the prophet Isaiah that proved to have poignant insight to their specific situation.

I, even I, am He who comforts you.
Who are you that you should be afraid
Of a man who will die,
And of the son of a man who will be made like grass?
And you forget the LORD your Maker,
Who stretched out the heavens
And laid the foundations of the earth;
You have feared continually every day
Because of the fury of the oppressor,
When he has prepared to destroy.
And where is the fury of the oppressor?
The captive exile hastens, that he may be loosed,
That he should not die in the pit,
And that his bread should not fail.

> But I am the LORD your God,
> Who divided the sea whose waves roared—
> The LORD of hosts is His name.
> And I have put My words in your mouth;
> I have covered you with the shadow of My hand,
> That I may plant the heavens,
> Lay the foundations of the earth,
> And say to Zion, "You are My people." (Isaiah 51:12–16)

If only for the moment, these words buoyed the spirits of the prisoners. In the randomness of their situation—the constant threats and harassment from agitated guards who took their own fears and frustration out on the prisoners, the hours of bombing at night, locked up in a medieval prison—they had to try and not be distracted by the turmoil around them. They had to focus on God and place their lives completely in His hands. It was frightening to feel so vulnerable, but they had little choice. God would have to supply them with His strength.

One evening when Georg and Peter arrived at their cell in Riasat 3, Mustafa introduced them to a man who hobbled into their cell, supported by a crutch. He had a long beard, wore a prayer shawl, and in his free hand he held a string of prayer beads. To Georg, he looked like some vagabond holy man fresh in from a desert quest, so it came as a shock to find out that he was a captured fighter pilot for the Northern Alliance.

"I am Mashuq. I know your story, and I can help you," he said with a bow of his head, the prayer beads snaked through his fingers as he tapped his heart with his hand.

A lifelong bond of friendship was formed between Georg and Mashuq while they were in prison.

Mashuq had spent the last eight months in jail, three of them in solitary, with the first thirteen days spent in Mullah Cable's special torture chamber. He hobbled about on his crutch because his torturers had suspended him upside-down from the ceiling, his ankles locked in chains, the soles of his feet beaten to shreds with the steel-cabled whip.

"I was a pilot during the times of the *mujahideen*, but when the Taliban came to power, I did everything I could to stop them. I made secret films of some of the executions carried out by the

Taliban in the stadiums and smuggled them to the media in the outside world. I am a member of the Panjiri tribe of Ahmad Shah Masood. That alone is enough to hang me in the square. I was a member of a tribe they despised. They did everything they could to destroy me, but they never broke me," Mashuq said, clenching the beads in his fist. "They could not break me."

Mashuq's appearance belied his audacious speech. How could this crippled, bearded man wrapped in a tattered prayer shawl be a former fighter pilot, endure days of brutal torture, and months of solitary confinement, and how in the world could he help them? Surely, his mental state had deteriorated in this hellish place and given him delusions of grandeur.

Mashuq ordered those prisoners out of the cell that had come to listen to his story, and they obeyed. He instructed Mustafa to prepare tea, and he obeyed. He handed a guard some cash and told him he wanted a lock for Georg and Peter's door, and he went to fetch one—and just like that, Peter and Georg had a new routine, made bearable by Mashuq and Mustafa. The pair greeted Georg and Peter with tea each night when they arrived, and once Mustafa had filled their cups with the fresh brewed tea, cleared the cell, and attached the newly purchased lock on the door, Mashuq dug into the prayer shawl wrapped around his waist and, with a magician's hand, pulled out a radio.

Night after night, the small group huddled around the radio, listening to the continual updates from foreign news organizations on the progress of the war, stopping and hiding the radio under the bed only when an unsympathetic guard made the rounds. Since Mashuq was a fighter pilot, he was familiar with the geography of Afghanistan. He drew a map of the country, and based on the reports, he was able to sketch the location of each city and explain in detail what was occurring on the ground in regard to the fighting and what cities had fallen to the advancing Northern Alliance army. With the help of the U.S. bombing campaign, that advance was happening at a rapid pace. After the fall of the northern city of Mazari Sharif on November 9, Mashuq said that it could be only a matter of days before the Northern Alliance would arrive to liberate Kabul. Georg took it upon himself to write out in as much detail as possible the information from the nightly radio broadcasts along with Mashuq's "color" commentary and slip these notes to the women on their trip back to the intelligence prison the next morning. This way everyone knew what was going on and could prepare themselves for their much-anticipated liberation. Though they had to be cautious as to when to listen to the radio, it was exciting to have direct access to news from the outside world and not depend on irregular news briefings from sympathetic guards.

One particular night when Georg and Peter arrived, after they had secured the cell and drunk their first round of tea, Mashuq produced five saw blades and set them on the floor beside the radio.

"I have an escape plan," he whispered, and he waited, refilling the empty teacups with hot water while Mustafa checked the door to see if anyone was nearby and listening.

"How did you get these?" Georg asked, amazed at the sight of the saw blades.

"The Taliban has no money to pay their guards. There are those whose ideology is not as strong as their hunger," he said, his smile revealing obvious pride in his accomplishment.

"What is your plan?" Georg asked. At this point in their

captivity, Georg would entertain any option to gain their freedom. He would rule out nothing.

Mashuq waved him into the hallway, where he pointed to a window in an empty cell across from Georg and Peter's cell.

"We saw through the bars in the window," he said. If they could remove the bars, Mashuq was the right size to slip through the opening. "After I take a Kalashnikov from one of the guards, I will come back down for you, and then we will release the women."

"How will you do that?" Georg asked, more from wonder at this feat than from concern for the guard's safety. "How will you get the Kalashnikov?"

"Some of the guards may have to die."

Mashuq did not explain the "how." He spoke his answer in the flat tone of a veteran soldier who had seen death and who had initiated it. He was a professional.

Up until that moment, Georg thought he could support the attempted escape. Who could rule out that it was not God's plan for them to take matters into their own hands? However, this was different. He had not considered someone actually dying for their longed-for freedom. The conviction came quickly.

"I cannot support this, Mashuq," Georg said, shaking his head.

"This is war, Georg. People die."

"But not in this way, not to save us."

Mashuq looked perplexed. This soldier did not understand the concept of respect for one's enemies, so Georg had to explain.

"It has been our prayer all along that no one should die so we might be free. We don't want to kill anyone. When this war is over and the Taliban are no longer in power, we want to set up our operations again and rebuild our projects. God has given us a heart for

Afghanistan and her people, which includes the Taliban. How can we continue to work and serve in this country if we are responsible for anyone's death, no matter how he might have treated us?"

Mashuq looked at Peter. He nodded his head, approving what Georg had said, and one by one, Mashuq picked up the saw blades and returned them into the folds of his garment. He squatted down on his haunches and stared at the floor, his soldier's mind grappling with this interjection of Christian pacifism.

"I'm sorry, Mashuq, and I thank you for the risk you've taken on our behalf."

Mashuq kept staring at the floor. He scraped his finger in a jagged line through the dirt and grime, his eyes staring at a point beyond the finger scratching.

"Georg, I want you to write me a letter of introduction," he said, which Georg could not help but find amusing. Was Mashuq now thinking of future employment, that he needed Georg to write him a letter of recommendation? "Do it now, because I do not know how much time we have left."

"Yes, of course, but why do you need this letter?"

"Before they brought you to this prison, I pretended to be deathly ill so they would have to send me to the hospital. I was there for a few days and found people who would help me escape . . . for a price, of course. I will make my way out of the city and get back to my army or maybe all the way to the American embassy in Pakistan. I need your letter so that they will believe me when I tell them about you. Then we can plan a rescue when they are transporting you from one prison to another."

Georg sat down immediately and wrote out the letter. This was a plan he could endorse. This was a plan that on its surface seemed plausible and gave both him and Peter a renewed hope. Mashuq advised Georg not to share this with the women until he was safely out of the prison and at the hospital. If he did not return to the prison within twenty-four hours, then that would be a good sign he had made his escape. There was no reason for anyone outside this cell to know about the escape plan until the last moment, no reason to raise hope or alarm when any number of things could go wrong.

Yet however good this plan might have been, it did not happen. Circumstances went into freefall instead. The next afternoon, long before the normal time for the eight hostages to return to Riasat 3 for the night, both Hamid and Usaf came to fetch them. Georg had never seen them both so agitated, and the guards reflected their high level of anxiety, waving their weapons and shouting for the hostages to hurry.

When the company arrived at the waiting vehicles, the hostages were shocked to see a group of Taliban standing between them and their transportation back to Riasat 3. Hamid immediately went into action, facing down the Taliban, who demanded the hostages released into their custody. That would be certain death. The intensity of the disagreement grew, as Hamid refused to give up the prisoners, and Usaf quickly got the hostages into the Land Cruiser. They were still arguing as Hamid got into the Land Cruiser and ordered the driver to move over to the passenger side of the vehicle. He jerked the transmission into gear, mashed down on the gas pedal, and he and the rest of the caravan sped out of the compound.

There must not have been driver's education courses offered in Kabul, nor any sort of training for driving through city streets at high rates of speed. Mullah Hamid would have failed either course. Several times, he came within inches of sideswiping another vehicle or upending the Land Cruiser when he took a curve too fast. Fortunately, the other drivers on the road drove defensively and swerved out of his way. The irony was not lost on Georg that while they had thus far survived all kinds of life-threatening adversity, they might die in a traffic accident at the hands of someone who was really trying to help them. He was just thankful that the U.S. bombs were not raining down on them at the same time.

Mullah Hamid slammed on his brakes in front of the Riasat 3, trying to avoid the traffic congestion in front of the prison. Armored vehicles, trucks, Land Cruisers, and tanks were streaming in and out of the entrance, drivers blowing their horns, guards yelling, trying to establish some order to the chaotic flow of vehicles. When Hamid saw a gap in the traffic flow, he floored the accelerator, and the Land Cruiser sped into the compound. Mullah Hasan had a team of guards surround the Land Cruiser vehicle and ordered the hostages out of the vehicle. Georg looked back at Hamid as the guards herded him and the others toward their night cells, and saw him talking with Hasan. He could only wonder about their discussion, but he felt that the odds of ever seeing Mullah Hamid again were rare.

Peter and Georg lurched down the steps, with the guards at the head of the stairs shouting for them to hurry before slamming the door behind them. There was too much commotion going on in the prison to worry about whether or not the two of them made it safely to their cell. At the bottom of the steps, Mashuq waited for them, barely able to contain his excitement.

"It is happening," Mashuq said, grabbing Georg and Peter by

their arms and leading them in the direction of their cell. "Cities are falling. I've heard it on the radio."

They stumbled into their cell, where Mustafa had tea waiting. All hell might have been breaking loose above them, but there was always time for tea.

"Turn on the radio, Mustafa," Mashuq whispered, before closing the cell door and locking it with the padlock. "The Northern Alliance troops have begun their attack and are shattering the front lines at Shamali. They are only about six miles away from the outskirts of Kabul."

"It can't be long now," Mustafa said, and pointed to their teacups. "So sit and drink. The army is headed for Kabul. Soon we will be free."

It was an impossible thought to consider. Freedom. It appeared to be just at the door. All they had to do was sit tight, wait for their liberators to unlock the prison doors, and set them free. But was it that simple? There were too many variables to this equation. Too many things could go wrong before the liberators knocked on their door.

"It could happen tonight, Georg," Mashuq said. "We are scrubbing my plan to escape from the hospital. I want to stay with you . . . help protect you."

That was one thing in their favor. Once the Northern Alliance invaded the city, there would be street fighting added to the current level of pandemonium. Mashuq's military training might well come in handy were those circumstances to come about.

"I must tell the women," Georg said. "They must know what is happening."

"Tell them to stay together and not to open the door until they hear your voice."

Georg took a page out of Mashuq's playbook. He approached the guards holding his stomach, and in anguished tones told them he was very sick and needed to see Diana. She was a nurse and he desperately needed some medicine. The guards rushed him upstairs to the women's cell; their need for haste was not for any concern they had for Georg's health, but to get this task done quickly and the prisoner back in his cell.

Georg gave a light rap on the door and calmly spoke Diana's name. He did not want to alarm the women with his unexpected appearance or tip off the guards that he had inside information regarding the advancing Northern Alliance Army. He remained in character, maintaining his deathly ill performance and speaking in English as Diana fetched the medicine. He told the women the true nature of his visit.

"Be ready for anything tonight. Mashuq says the Northern Alliance is breaking through the front lines at Shamali and is coming to Kabul."

The women knew better than to show any excitement at this news. In spite of the fact that the guards understood no English, it would arouse suspicion were they to react with a joyful expectancy at the idea of Georg being sick. It could be easily misinterpreted.

"Pray. Pray nonstop, and be prepared. Anything can happen. There could be intense street fighting once the army arrives. Give the Taliban no reason to turn on us. The guards are very agitated, so lock yourselves in your cell and do not open the door again unless you hear my voice. Under no circumstances should we be separated, no matter what happens."

Diana handed Georg the medicine. He turned to leave, and before Diana closed the door, he looked back at her.

"Pray," he whispered urgently. "Pray." And Diana nodded in understanding.

Georg waved the medicine packet in front of the guards—mission accomplished—and stumbled down the corridor back to the stairs, his performance worthy of critical acclaim.

The bombing started shortly after dark, and the officials never turned on the prison lights for fear of attracting attention. All was darkness except when a bomb exploded, giving off its brief, fireball flash. Like the sin-eaters of old, Georg took on the fears and anxieties for all the hostages, and once back in his own underground chambers, he took refuge in a small storage closet and poured out his heart to God. He took it upon himself to intercede for them all. The pressure was enormous. An errant bomb could fall on them. The Taliban could decide to kill all the prisoners before fleeing. Al-Qaeda could return, and in the confusion, steal them away. The Northern Alliance could accidentally kill them by friendly fire. Any number of scenarios could have a tragic end, and Georg prayed fervently that God would protect them and provide safe passage through every life-threatening set of circumstances. His specific prayer was the hope that the Taliban would flee the city, and in their panic, forget about the hostages, leaving them all safely in their cells; that there would be no more killing; and that the Northern Alliance would liberate them by the next day and they could reunite with their families.

It was not long after he left his prayer closet and rejoined the others in his cell to listen to the radio that the guards returned. However, these were different guards; not the regular prison guards they'd grown accustomed to over the last few weeks. They were not even the same guards that had earlier escorted Georg to the women's cell. They burst into the room, indifferent to the contraband radio, indifferent even to the other prisoners in the entire underground chamber. They had come for these four men alone. These were professional soldiers, fierce-looking, dressed for war, and in no frame of mind to tolerate a hint of insubordination from the hostages. They did not speak. They grabbed Peter, Mustafa, Mashuq, and Georg and pushed them out the door. Georg spoke in Pashto that they needed to get the women, but he received no response from any of the soldiers.

To his relief, a couple of the soldiers took Georg up the stairs to the women's floor while the other three waited in the hallway. When Georg approached the women's cell, a soldier was beating on the door with the butt of his AK-47 and shouting for the women to open the door. Georg arrived just in time—as another of the soldiers was about to shoot the lock off the door. Georg's escort ordered the others to stop pounding on the door and to step away.

"Ladies, it's Georg," he said, knocking gently on the door. Georg wanted them to have confidence that it really was him and that they were not being set up to die right there in the corridor. "They have come for us. They are not the normal guards. They are very nervous and ready to shoot. So come out. We have to go."

In case the women were hesitant at all, the soldier in command of the group shouted an order at the women on the other side of the door, and it opened within seconds.

"Hurry," Georg said, waving his arm in the direction of the exit. "We must go."

When the soldiers marched the captives out of the building toward the waiting vehicles, Georg had to reconcile the fact that the Taliban had not forgotten about them after all. God must have had a different way of escape in mind than the one Georg had prescribed in his prayer closet; he was thankful the soldiers had not killed them right on the spot. They were certainly not yet out of harm's way, but they had successfully gotten out of one tight situation. What would God do now?

There were two vehicles waiting to transport them to God knows where. When the soldier in charge began to divide them up—women in one vehicle, men in the other—Georg resisted with a boldness he did not know he had. Then the whole group joined in, backing up their leader, all of them insisting they would not allow the soldiers to separate them. Instead the soldiers shoved Mustafa and Mashuq in one vehicle and ordered the SNI eight to get inside the Land Cruiser. There were vehicles racing out of the compound, soldiers running about. None of the vehicles had their headlights on. Visibility was little more than a few yards in front of them. None of their former guards was around. Mullah Hasan was nowhere in sight. They were now in the hands of a new breed, the hard-core soldier, and even though these soldiers might be fleeing the advancing Northern Alliance, it did not mean they were not prepared to fight, die, and kill for the sake of the Taliban regime.

The eight sat crammed inside the Land Cruiser, one on top of the other. Silke suffered from claustrophobia and began to get panicky and hyperventilate. A few immediately started to pray for Silke, and soon she began to calm down.

They had barely driven out of the prison compound before someone realized that a rocket launcher lay beneath the bench where half of them sat. They were definitely now in the hands of a higher level of military custody. They should not expect a Mullah Hamid, an Afghan Angel, or a Mohammed Sharif to rise up from the midst of these strangers. Georg had not seen Sharif before the Taliban rushed them away to Riasat 3. There had been no word from their Afghan Angel. Mullah Hamid had succeeded in keeping them out of the clutches of al-Qaeda, but he could do little for them now.

The few people on the street rushed about in search of shelter. The city was in blackout. All vehicles commandeered for military use raced southwest out of Kabul, their headlights turned off to keep from becoming targets for bombs. It was a mass exodus, everyone headed in one direction at a breakneck rate of speed, every vehicle packed with armed Taliban and al-Qaeda. No one was willing to stay in Kabul and defend the capital. The incessant bombing missions had worn down the Taliban to such an extent that they had no alternative but to flee.

Once the Land Cruiser got onto the main road, one of the women asked Georg where he thought they were taking them. In his heart he knew, and it was the last place on earth he wanted to go. They were on the road to Kandahar, the stronghold of Mullah Omar—with the highest concentration of Taliban soldiers and al-Qaeda operatives in the country. The Taliban stationed in Kandahar were known for their exceptional cruelty; they had a reputation for brutality against anyone accused of breaking the law, and for extending no mercy toward the infidel. Georg believed that if God did not intervene to deliver them and they were to make it all the way to Kandahar, none of them would ever come out alive. So he lied and told them they were probably on their way to a Taliban safe haven or outpost somewhere in the desert. He could not tell them where he believed they were going. He could not tell them that he believed they were facing certain death. He could not tell them that in his own heart he had sunk to a new level of fear.

Not long after they were on the highway to Kandahar, the two-way radio in the cab sputtered to life: Kabul had fallen to the Northern Alliance. Immediately the Taliban riders in the front seat began to communicate their dismay to one another and on the radio with those in the other vehicle. The eight sat in stunned disbelief, absorbing the news, no outbursts of joy coming from their mouths. Had they just missed their chance at freedom by a few minutes? Before their departure it seemed as if Kabul was about to be liberated; they'd been anticipating release from this hell. But it was not to be. *God must have another plan*, Georg thought. And God was their only hope, but at that moment, as they sped past darkened villages deeper into Taliban territory, it was difficult to feel any hope about this excruciating situation.

CHAPTER NINE

LIFE OR DEATH

F ive million U.S. dollars," Mullah Hasan said to Georg, his face dead of expression, a poker face with no tells. "That is the price of your freedom." Both pairs of eyes locked. It was almost like a childhood game of dare between two boys, but this was high stakes, with life or death hanging in the balance.

After an hour on the road, the two vehicles—one carrying the SNI eight and the other carrying Mashuq and Mustafa—turned off the main highway to Kandahar and descended a steep, one-lane dirt road. They stopped at a checkpoint on the outskirts of a village, the outlines of its houses barely visible in the imposed blackout. Out of the darkness appeared Mullah Hasan, the warden of Riasat 3. No wonder they had not seen him when they'd arrived at the prison that afternoon or when the soldiers transported them out of the prison that evening—he had fled like the others. Hasan walked up to the driver of the Land Cruiser and asked if all eight of the Westerners were in the vehicle. He must not have trusted the answer, because he stuck his head through the window and counted them. Satisfied with his math and the news that Mashuq and Mustafa were in the second vehicle, he ordered them to get back on the main road and continue driving toward Kandahar. Then he climbed in the front seat of the second Land Cruiser, and the two-vehicle convoy got back on the road.

With Hasan taking charge, the tension increased among the SNI eight. Of all the wardens who had been in charge of the hostages, he was the cruelest. His reputation inspired fear, and his presence now traumatized Georg and the others. Mashuq physically walked with difficulty because of the results of Hasan's brutal torture. Why should they trust him, given the unpredictability of his hot-blooded nature and the volatility of the situation?

At one point during the journey, Hasan ordered the convoy to stop at a checkpoint where other vehicles of the Taliban had gathered to reconnoiter. Here he tried to convince his comrades to mount, if not a counteroffensive of Kabul, at least a defense against any further Northern Alliance incursion. Given the effectiveness of the U.S. bombing, none of the other *mullahs* seemed inclined to throw their turbans behind the idea of sacrificing themselves or their men for so fruitless an effort, so Hasan tabled the debate and the group pressed on.

They passed checkpoint after checkpoint on their journey to Kandahar, each stop giving the hostages a flicker of hope that they might meet up with Afghans aware of who they were and who might be willing to help them. However, the convoy passed through each checkpoint with ease, no questions asked, no hint of liberation.

The hostages could barely move due to the cramped seating in the back of the Land Cruiser. The driver veered back and forth across the highway, given the Third World road conditions; the hostages felt like they were on a dreadful, never-ending carnival ride. However, this was the price paid for their insistence on being together.

No one ventured to express the fears filling the vehicle. Why raise them? If God had indeed asked them to intercede for Kabul, then with the liberation of the city, it appeared their mission was complete. So what was their mission now? Bombs were falling in the immediate area. No one knew of their whereabouts. At any moment they could find themselves caught in a firefight between opposing forces. They were speeding down a pockmarked highway in the dark with no headlights on, careening back and forth in a top-heavy vehicle, wondering why God had kept them alive for three and a half months in prison only to let them die on the road to Kandahar. Despair settled in and, except for the rattling of the Land Cruiser on the gritty road, silence engulfed the hostages.

It was Heather who took the initiative to turn things around. The one who had reacted with such fear and terror in prison during the bombing raids now took it upon herself to call out to God and encourage her companions to turn their panic into peace. She pulled a flashlight from her purse and opened her Bible. She returned to verses from Psalm 118 that had been a special comfort to her in prison and began reading them aloud.

Oh, give thanks to the LORD, for He is good!
For His mercy endures forever . . .
I called on the LORD in distress;

The LORD answered me and set me in a broad place.
The LORD is on my side;

    I will not fear.

    What can man do to me?

The Lord is for me among those who help me;

    Therefore I shall see my desire on those who hate me.

It is better to trust in the LORD

    Than to put confidence in man.

It is better to trust in the LORD

    Than to put confidence in princes.

All nations surrounded me,

    But in the name of the LORD I will destroy them . . .

They surrounded me like bees;

    They were quenched like a fire of thorns;

    For in the name of the LORD I will destroy them.

You pushed me violently, that I might fall,

    But the LORD helped me.

The LORD is my strength and song,

    And He has become my salvation.

The voice of rejoicing and salvation

    Is in the tents of the righteous;

    The right hand of the LORD does valiantly.

The right hand of the LORD is exalted;

    The right hand of the LORD does valiantly.

I shall not die, but live,

    And declare the works of the LORD.

The LORD has chastened me severely,

    But He has not given me over to death.

Open to me the gates of righteousness;

I will go through them,

And I will praise the LORD.

This is the gate of the LORD,

Through which the righteous shall enter.

I will praise You,

For You have answered me,

And have become my salvation.

The stone which the builders rejected

Has become the chief cornerstone.

This was the LORD's doing;

It is marvelous in our eyes.

This is the day the LORD has made;

We will rejoice and be glad in it. (vv. 1, 5–10, 12–24)

The holy words sank into their hearts, exorcising the foreboding and despondency that had overtaken their souls. A sense of peace began to fill the mobile prison. When someone began to sing one of the spiritual songs composed in prison, they all gradually joined in, their hearts dispelling the last vestiges of despair, replacing it with a peace that transcends all human understanding—the peace written about by the apostle Paul, a man who could relate to being persecuted for his faith. Peace may have come in that spontaneous moment of praise, but the hostages' life-and-death struggle had not ended.

In the middle of the night, the convoy turned off the highway and rolled into a village. The hostages hoped they were at least going to have a chance to stretch their legs, or perhaps stay the rest of the night in one of the houses in the village. But the driver eased past the houses and pulled up to an abandoned, empty steel container the size of a crate used to transport goods overseas. Once everyone had peeled themselves out of the vehicles, Georg and Hasan had a face-off in front of the enormous steel crate.

"Five million dollars," Mullah Hasan repeated, raising his voice to be sure Georg was clear on the amount. "I will get you a satellite phone. You will call your embassy."

This twist of circumstances did not surprise Georg. Mullah Hasan was a devious man and an opportunist. So this was the reason the hostages had been whisked out of Kabul—Hasan saw a chance to extort some money. Why not? Stranger things had happened to them. Why should they not add "kidnapping victims" to the list of atrocities they had endured over the last 103 days?

Georg was the first to blink. Fatigue and the fear of a return to prison or worse had gotten the better of his judgment. By that time he did not care how they got out of the country, even through the paying of a ransom; however, he did try to lower Hasan's expectations of a windfall profit.

"That is too much," Georg said. "Our embassies do not normally pay in these types of situations, and our families are poor, humble people. They do not have that kind of money. You should not expect so high a price."

Hasan stepped away from Georg, presumably to get the satellite phone in the other vehicle. When Diana heard what Hasan was up to, she was furious.

"No, Georg. I want to be free as much as you," she said, trying to control her anger so that Mullah Hasan would not see her talking aggressively to a man. "I would rather die than give this guy money. I don't believe God wants to rescue us this way."

In the meantime, Hasan was having his own debate with his

Taliban companions. Many of them wanted to kill the hostages and rid themselves of the hassle of keeping up with them. The Westerners were infidels; if these Taliban killed them, they would gain a unique title: *ghazi*, which means "warrior for the faith" and is a revered tribute for a Muslim. Hasan was not so much interested in religious glory; he just wanted to rid himself of the burden, preferably for a cash reward, although that now seemed unlikely, given the validity of Georg's line of reasoning. He would consider a compromise. They could kill the two men, get the *ghazi* title, and then divide the women among them as *ghanima*: holy spoils gotten during a holy war. That way everyone would win: they'd have religious recognition for killing infidels and holy loot.

Hasan returned to Georg and the others and did not even pursue the demand for ransom money. He ordered his men to lock the prisoners in the steel container, then marched off toward the village.

Mashuq and Mustafa were not in the same category as the SNI eight—they were neither valuable for ransom nor worth anything dead—so they were not given much attention. While the guards were examining and preparing the container for its occupants, Mashuq and Mustafa saw an opportunity to slip away; Mashuq gave Georg a blanket and a small flashlight before he and Mustafa vanished. It was the last he and the others saw of the pair.

In the darkness the hostages stared at the empty steel container. In the days of the *mujahideen*, it had been standard procedure to herd their enemies into these containers and execute them. The practice caught on with the Taliban and they, in turn, perfected it into a sadistic science with variations. Sometimes they attached

wire cables to the container and electrocuted their victims; sometimes they tossed hand grenades into the container once the victims
were inside. During the summer they might seal the victims inside
and let them suffocate; or they simply fired their weapons into the
container, killing all inside.

Two guards walked around to the back of the container to close
the rear doors. The SNI eight could not move; these common execution practices had been shown on television, and they were afraid.
Georg attempted to negotiate a compromise, allowing them to stay
in a home in the village. When that did not work, he pleaded with
them, begging for mercy, but nothing he said could change their
minds. Georg did not want to press the issue too far. These men
were under duress and in no mood to extend any compassion.
Many of them were more inclined to kill the hostages outright.
They panicked easily and were unsure what to do without direct
orders. A simple misunderstanding or an unintended provocation
could send them over the edge.

The ladies asked if they could go to a home to use the bathroom
before entering the giant crate. It was a tactic to delay the inevitable,
but the guards were impatient and humiliated the women by order-
ing them to go behind the container while the guards watched. Once
the women were finished, the guards waved their weapons in the
direction of the container and the hostages began to inch their way
inside. This container had no bullet holes or any marks caused by
exploding hand grenades. Could this be a sign that this undam-
aged container might be a safe haven? Or would it be an opportunity
for the Taliban to vent their frustration on an unspoiled container?

"Oh God, if I have to die, please let it be quick," Diana whispered as she crept toward the back of the container.

It was the middle of November, and the temperature had dropped below freezing. At the far end of the container were a mattress and a few blankets. The group had begun to divide the raggedy blankets when they heard Heather crying and arguing with one of the guards. She refused to go inside and had positioned herself at the entrance, making it impossible for them to close the door. The guard threatened to beat Heather, a consequence she agreed to accept in order to keep him from closing the door. Then he complained to Georg that Heather was posing a problem; she was behaving like a "very bad woman." Of course, Georg could have responded in kind, reminding the guard that putting men and women in this one crate to spend the night together was contrary to Muslim law and Afghan culture—but now was not the time to get into a theological debate. Instead, he first tried to convince Heather she should come inside. When he failed at that, he explained to the guard that she was a young woman, far from home, terribly frightened; could they reach some kind of compromise? Perhaps to bring a little peace to everyone's frayed nerves, the guard agreed to keep the door open as long as Heather remained right at the entrance. It was a happy arrangement and a great relief—especially to the hostages. Heather's assertiveness, inspired by a combination of courage and desperation, could very well have saved their lives one more time.

The other women lay huddled together on the mattress in the back of the container, sharing two blankets and trying to combine their deficient body heat to keep from suffering frostbite from the stinging cold. Georg and Peter shared the remaining blankets and sat closer to the entrance, while Heather spent the night sitting with the guard. Once everyone had calmed down, Heather tried to converse with the guard in her broken Pashto. When he saw that

Heather was not going to try to escape or do anything that could put him in a bad light with Mullah Hasan or the other Taliban, he began to come around. When they brought him tea, he shared a cup with Heather. When he noticed Heather unable to control the tremors in her body from the bitter air, he gave her his blanket, and when that did little to stop her shivering, he prepared for her a bowl of hot coals and demonstrated how she should place it between her feet to keep warm. The primitive heating method was an act of unexpected kindness from the enemy.

When Mullah Hasan returned in the morning, he renewed the to-fight-or-not-to-fight debate with his fellow combatants. When Hasan saw none of his comrades were interested in taking a stand against the Northern Alliance, he gave it up and ordered the hostages taken out of the container. When he discovered two of his prisoners had escaped, he was infuriated, but wasted little time searching for them. He'd lost the argument to mount a defense, he'd lost two prisoners, and now he was losing time. He had the high-value cargo still in his possession, and he ordered the Land Cruisers back on the highway. Hasan did not allow the hostages the opportunity to go to the bathroom, nor did he offer them any food or drink. Regardless of the lack of these common social graces, the SNI eight were thankful that Hasan had chosen not to kill them in the container.

Hasan took over driving the Land Cruiser with the hostages inside, and Georg took the opportunity to inquire where he might be taking them.

"To Ghazni," Hasan said, his eyes focused on the road. "I will take you to a nice place, a nice house. You will eat and get warm. Get a satellite phone and call embassy."

It appeared Mullah Hasan still intended to play the ransom-for-hostages card, and this gave Georg some relief . . . and pause. Hasan would keep them alive a little longer, but what would happen to them if he failed to secure any ransom money from the embassies? What would Hasan do with them once he realized he would get no money for his trouble?

As the day before, they passed checkpoint after checkpoint on their journey; with each stop the hostages wondered if Mashuq and Mustafa had met up with the Northern Alliance yet to organize a rescue attempt. But they passed through each checkpoint without delay, no one acknowledging who they were or giving them the least bit of hope for liberation. And it was just as well. Such an attempt could have resulted in multiple deaths, and the hostages had prayed fervently that no one would die for the sake of their freedom.

Ghazni lay between Kabul and Kandahar. Georg knew this was Hasan's home city, and though it was a good thing that they were not going to Kandahar for the moment, he realized the chances of the Northern Alliance finding them had diminished. After three hours on the highway, they arrived in Ghazni in the middle of a gun battle. It could not be the Northern Alliance—that army had just barely liberated Kabul. So who was fighting whom?

Hasan took a turn off the main road away from the fighting and drove down a side street. In front of them, the hostages could see a large, unsightly building with high walls, barred windows, and razor wire along the tops of the walls. Their hearts sank. This was prison number four in their marathon incarceration. Hasan pulled into the front entrance, and straightaway Taliban guards, Kalashnikovs in hand, surrounded the Land Cruiser.

"Mullah Hasan, you said you were taking us to a nice house. This is a prison!" Georg protested, stating the obvious.

Hasan ordered them out of the vehicle, and as he backed away from the entrance, he informed the guard who looked to have the highest rank in the group that he would return soon. With explosions going off nearby, Hasan sped away.

The guard in charge wasted no time; he hustled the hostages up a flight of steps in the front of the prison and put them into two rooms with a connecting door. The windows in each cell looked out upon the street below. The cells were a disaster of clutter, as if a camp of bandits had dispersed in a hurry, leaving behind its refuse. The shared toilet was a torrid cauldron of excrement. They stood in horror before the worst bathroom conditions of their entire imprisonment.

"This is unacceptable," Georg said. "We'll get sick if we have to use this toilet."

"You are in Afghanistan," said the ranking guard. "This is the toilet you use."

"We have worked in this country for nineteen years," Georg said, his heart at a breaking point, his anger at a boiling point. "We have done so much for the people of Afghanistan, and this is the reward we get?" he said, pointing to a disgusting Exhibit A.

"You are evil people," the guard said, pointing to Georg, his own disgust as evident as Georg's when he had pointed to the filthy toilet. "You are very evil people."

The sound of explosions came again. This time it was much closer, and the building shook, sending the Taliban guards scurrying out of the room. When they tried to lock the door behind them, once again Heather protested. She would not back down, and when

Georg stepped in to intervene, the ranking guard did not put up much of a fight. He threw up his hands and left with the others.

The hostages were amazed that the Taliban had left them all together in adjoining cells. This lapse was due to the frantic and confused spirit that dominated all the Taliban. Their world was literally blowing up all around them, so the improper gender integration of a prison cell was the least of their concerns. The hostages, as they looked at the appalling bathroom and listened to the battle just outside the rattling walls of their fourth prison, thought things could not get any worse.

There was nothing to do but try to make the best of an awful situation, so they began to straighten up the rooms. To their surprise, it was not long before some of the guards brought them tea and a basket of the traditional Afghan *naan* bread. Some of the women unpacked the last of the food they'd brought with them from the intelligence prison. They thanked God for their continuing survival and ate their meager rations as the sun began to shine brightly through the dingy windows.

There was a hiatus in the gunfire, so the hostages began to worship and read Scripture once they'd finished their meal. Worship was their only source of strength and peace. Whom else could they turn to but God? They also prayed for one another. A few were suffering from intestinal bugs and needed relief from the debilitating discomfort. Georg requested prayers so that he might be able to remain calm and make sound decisions as he tried to keep everyone safe. Although the Taliban had kept the hostages segregated for weeks, for the last forty-eight hours they'd been inseparable, and it looked as though this would be their new reality given the chaotic circumstances. The group naturally looked to Georg for leadership.

In the middle of their prayers, the shooting erupted once more, but this time they could tell the gun battle was in the distance and not close to the prison. One of the women dashed to the windows and saw the prison guards and other Taliban soldiers in full retreat, fleeing the compound and heading south. When the others crowded around the window, they could see that there was no one firing at the soldiers and prison guards—their enemies were giving ground with no one in pursuit.

Once the Taliban were gone, all was silent. The street in front of the prison was empty. In the hour that followed, no one came to their cell, nor was there any activity outside the prison. The hostages filled the time with singing and praying while they waited. Then, suddenly, fighters began to appear from street corners and buildings, some of them firing their weapons into the air. These heavily armed men wore turbans and long beards exactly like the Taliban.

They moved to the main gate of the prison and began to break down the doors. These men did not appear to be liberators to Georg, and his anxiety level began to grow. He was convinced that the Taliban had returned and, for all he knew, these warriors would exact their revenge, kill him and Peter, and rape and kill the women. A sense of helplessness began to overwhelm all of them. Perhaps now Heather regretted her firm resolve not to have their doors locked—but even locked doors would only be a temporary stopgap for this hostile-looking crowd.

Once the fighters had breached the main gate of the prison, Georg gathered all eight of them into one cluster and they began to pray, as the sounds of the combatants got closer and closer to their cell. Even though the hostages uttered their prayers for God to protect them, in his private terror, Georg secretly hoped that if this were the end, the Taliban would just shoot him and get it over with quickly. He did not want them to be beaten to death or the women raped before they were killed. In Pakistan and Afghanistan, he'd witnessed a number of executions; he personally harbored an abnormal fear of abduction and execution. As he spoke his prayers to God, these competing wild thoughts raced through his frazzled mind.

With a loud crash, the door to their floor burst open and they could hear trampling feet and voices headed in their direction. The prayers stopped when their cell door opened with a loud crash. They waited, paralyzed with fear, unable to speak a word or move.

A gigantic man with cartridge belts draped over his chest, dust covering his bearded face, his clothes soaked with sweat, burst into their cell. He held a machine gun in one hand, and his eyes bulged out of their sockets. Behind him were other men with weapons, rushing about up and down the corridor, breaking open the doors of other cells and setting prisoners free. Here was the moment of truth. They were face-to-face with death or liberty. The eight hostages waited as the armed man stared at them in disbelief. He was completely surprised to see the hostages. What were these foreigners doing in this prison? He had expected to find just Afghanis locked in these cells.

Georg realized it might be possible that this man was not a Taliban after all. He spoke to the bewildered-looking man in Pashtu.

"Are you with Massoud?" he asked. "Are you part of the opposition?"

"Yes," the man replied. Now two or three more fighters had joined this giant at the entrance of their cell.

Georg could not believe his ears.

"Are you sure?" Georg asked, with a twinge of hope pinching his heart.

"Yes," said the giant. "We fight with Massoud."

His pent-up hope burst into elation, and Georg shouted. "It is the opposition! We are free! We are free!"

A local militia—many of whom had connection with Massoud, the assassinated leader of the Northern Alliance—had staged a coup and driven out the Taliban from the city, the soldier told them. Now they were setting the prisoners free. But were they dreaming? How could the Westerners trust what this stranger told them, someone who looked like the very ones who had held them captive? This man had enough armaments on his person to kill them all within seconds.

"You are not the Taliban?" Georg asked again, unable to believe what he saw with his eyes and heard with his ears.

"We have driven them out," the soldier said, raising his machine gun in the air, a gesture of triumph. "They are gone."

Georg could not contain himself. He dashed over and embraced his liberator, kissing him on his sweaty, dusty, bearded cheek. He was not a mirage! Freedom tasted of salt and grime, and it was the sweetest taste Georg could ever remember.

Multiple faces stood in the doorway of the cell, and a chorus of voices kept repeating the phrase, "Come out! Come out! You are free!" It was as melodic to the ear as any chorus sung by an angelic host.

One minute they thought they were dead. The next minute they heard they were free. It was like a dream happening at hyperspeed. They began to embrace one another. Tears of joy flowed down their faces. Word had spread among the locals that the foreigners from Kabul were in the prison, and Ghaznians flowed in and out of the cell, staring in wonder at these Western captives they had heard about.

The SNI eight grabbed their belongings and rushed downstairs to the main entrance of the prison. Just as they were about to dash into the street, their liberator stopped them. There was still some residual gunfire, and he did not want them to pass through the gate, so they hid in a guard shack. He had to be sure it was not a counterattack from the Taliban. It was only a minor setback, and once the soldier determined there was no danger, the SNI eight exited the building.

They ran across an open field adjacent to the prison with a cadre of the militia who had liberated them, dashed into the protective cover of the nearest neighborhood, and began walking through the streets. It was a *Twilight Zone* experience. Just freed from 103 days of nightmarish captivity—the last forty-eight hours of which could have ended in their deaths on several occasions— the eight now stumbled into a street-festival atmosphere. People were streaming out of their houses, laughing, singing, and cheering. Women threw off the hoods of their *burkas*, exposing their faces in public for the first time in years. Music blared out of houses. Children danced in the street to the music their families had not been allowed to play in public or in the privacy of their homes under the Taliban.

The SNI eight were certainly a curiosity stumbling through the neighborhood in the middle of this ecstatic throng, but when news spread that these were the foreigners held captive by the Taliban, people ran up to them just to touch them, shake their hands, sling an arm over a shoulder, embrace them, and offered to help carry their belongings. It was the end of a very dark time, and no one could stop the celebrations. The very experience the hostages had hoped to have in Kabul, they were now able to have in Ghazni. The exhaustion the eight of them felt lifted from their shoulders, displaced by the exhilaration of freedom. They ambled through the streets as though under a spell, unsure of where they were going, the giddy noises of independence ringing in the air—but were they completely out of danger?

The militia leader took the eight to the offices of Mohammed Saleem, the chief intelligence official of Ghazni. Saleem had been one of the underground leaders in the uprising against the Taliban, and his office was a central location for people to gather. He was kind to the hostages, allowing them to clean up in the bathroom and generally providing a welcoming atmosphere for them to relax in . . . but that was more difficult than expected. The problem was not the average citizens, flowing in and out of the office trying to sneak a look at the foreigners as if they were international celebrities. The biggest problem for Saleem was coordinating and dispersing the different groups of heavily armed men that kept coming to the office, wondering what was happening and trying to find out who was now in charge of the city.

There were three different ethnic groups in Ghazni: Pashtuns, Tajiks, and Hazaras, all fiercely tribal and all bearing some level of animosity toward each other. Since the Taliban were primarily Pashtun, they were the ethnic group currently out of power and certainly out of favor with the majority of the population. Even though the local militia had effectively expelled the Taliban from the city, thousands of Taliban and al-Qaeda fighters were scattered all over the countryside and could at any time stage a counterattack. Ghazni was no safe haven for anyone, least of all the foreigners.

It was soon evident to Georg that ethnic groups, each with their own commanders, were vying for control of the city. Arguments broke out in the office between some of these posses. One group of fighters demanded to speak with the foreigners and take charge of them, but Saleem refused to let them go. Georg was not sure whether to be flattered by all this attention—or wary. Once the disputing bands of soldiers had left the office, some level of calm settled in, and Saleem was able to serve his guests something to eat and drink. The eight foreigners thought it was the most delicious meal they had eaten in months.

It was nice to be able to relax and enjoy a good meal, but Georg was restless. He wanted to get in contact with the German embassy in Pakistan, so he began to press Saleem for a phone or some way to get in touch with someone. But Saleem had no way to communicate with the outside world from his office, so while the rest of the SNI team remained at the office, Saleem and Georg, accompanied by well-armed bodyguards, went out into the city in search of a phone. There were only a few communication centers in Ghazni equipped for international communications, and when the party arrived at each center, they found it closed, looted, or destroyed. Saleem could see the dismay on Georg's face and tried to encourage him, but it was hard to be encouraged as they drove back to Saleem's office. Tribal groups had thrown up roadblocks throughout the city. Even Saleem could not conceal his own concern as they passed through each roadblock in the clannish neighborhoods. Many of the shops and businesses they passed had been plundered or destroyed. They could hear shots fired from time to time. No one was truly in charge of the city, and unless there was a coordinated effort by ethnically diverse city leaders, it seemed as though Ghazni could fall into chaos or, worse, al-Qaeda and the Taliban could retake the city.

When the party returned to the office, Georg remembered that he had visited the local Red Cross office in Ghazni on a stopover to Kandahar the year before. Saleem suggested that they first take the SNI team to the home of his relative—it would be a nice, comfortable place and safer for the others—and from there, he and Georg could go to the Red Cross office. The rest of the team could bathe and sleep while he and Georg tried to contact the German embassy.

Saleem took the SNI team to the home of Hamisha Zareef, a wealthy man who had a number of buildings within his compound, all surrounded by high walls. It certainly felt more secure than the office, and when the team were shown to their spacious rooms with actual beds and vermin-free mattresses, carpeted floors, clean bathrooms with showers, and trays of food, they could finally believe "going to a nice place, a better place, a safe place" was, in fact, a reality after countless lies. Their host also brought in a doctor to care for those in the team who were sick. The physical, emotional, and psychological healing began to occur.

After enduring deprivation for so long, the standard Afghan custom of hospitality felt like luxuries only royalty would enjoy. Georg and the others could join Hamisha Zareef's family and listen to the radio without fear of guards bursting into the room and punishing them; it was a mental adjustment to the new "normal" of hearing radio broadcasts without fear. The group listened to the description of the liberation of Kabul, and the SNI team longed to be there, reunited with family and friends who were celebrating the Northern Alliance victory.

Nevertheless, in spite of this new and hospitable environment, Georg was still in a hostage frame of mind. He was ready to leave very soon after their arrival, but Saleem did not appear to be in any hurry to get Georg to the Red Cross office. This reluctance seemed like a red flag, and Georg grew suspicious of Saleem. Georg left the group and went outside to be alone in the compound to think and pray. While strolling through the garden, he got the surprise of his life. A young boy of twelve or thirteen, one of Hamisha Zareef's sons, approached him.

"I have seen you before," the young boy said. "I recognize you from the vice and virtue prison in Kabul. I used to see you and the other man through the bars of the window in the reform school when they let you walk outside in the courtyard."

This news stunned Georg. What a small world—but what was this boy doing in the vice and virtue reform school? Why would such a wealthy man send his son to such an awful place? The boy shrugged his shoulders and gave an elusive answer: he had annoyed his father and had been sent to this reform school to learn to become a good Muslim. This was not like sending a child to boarding school. This subsidiary of the vice and virtue police prided itself for its strict religious instruction and corporal punishment; by Western standards it was a cruel and inhumane place for young boys. This indicated a certain fanaticism that disturbed Georg. Perhaps Hamisha Zareef was not the kind and generous host he portrayed himself to be.

Finally Saleem was persuaded to continue on to the Red Cross. On the way, Georg asked Saleem delicate questions about his relative. He was shocked to learn that Hamisha Zareef not only had close connections with the Taliban—the reform school intelligence chief was a good friend—but that he was also a secret member of the Taliban himself! He'd abandoned his Talib credentials once he saw the tide turning and was now contending for position in the city's new power structure. Georg could hardly believe what he was hearing. They had just escaped the clutches of the Taliban, only to find themselves hosted by a former member of the Taliban with close ties to the regime's intelligence division—a man who was cruel enough to send his mischievous son for reeducation at the vice and virtue reform school. Out of the frying pan and into the fire. They could not get out of Afghanistan fast enough.

Once at the offices of the Red Cross, Georg was immediately able to establish contact with the Red Cross office in Islamabad, which in turn contacted the German embassy, which then contacted the American embassy. A plan to get the foreigners out of Ghazni was put into motion. Georg began to feel hopeful after this initial contact, and he returned to Hamisha Zareef's compound to share the news with the others. They spent the night under heavy guard, but for the first time in 103 days, it was not the Taliban guarding them, nor were they treated like prisoners. Or were they? There was certainly the threat of rival ethnic groups storming the compound and stealing the SNI team for their own nefarious purposes . . . or the Taliban coming back to town. What scenario would play out? Georg spent a restless night wondering how many times they could cheat death and get away with it.

Georg returned to the Red Cross the following morning with Saleem and his bodyguards. Because Afghanistan was a country at war and the Taliban still surrounded Ghazni, it was impossible for the Red Cross to risk sending in one of their own helicopters to extract the Westerners. In addition, it was not within their mandate to participate in any way with a military operation. They did offer to drive the SNI team back to Kabul, but after further discussion, they concluded this plan was too risky, given the fact that the Taliban and al-Qaeda still roamed the countryside and had checkpoints all along the highway. When a message came in from the U.S. embassy that a team of Special Forces would come to Ghazni to rescue the SNI eight once they'd chosen a site where the helicopters could land, the Red Cross insisted that Georg sign a release form stating that the international organization had no responsibility in facilitating this event. The Red Cross could ill afford a perception that it had a role in a military operation—especially if harm came to anyone in the process. Georg signed the papers without hesitating.

Saleem's office became a gathering place for many of the ethnic leaders of the city. And once Georg had signed the official papers clearing the Red Cross of any involvement in a rescue, a heated debate broke out among factional groups as to which location would be best to stage it. Everyone, it seemed, wanted to be involved in this event except the Red Cross. While individuals argued, Georg received a message from Hamisha Zareef, who feared he would not be able to protect the SNI team in their current location. The probability of a mob attack by the Hazara ethnic group seemed a tangible threat. Zareef wanted permission from Georg to move the team to another house he owned nearer the city, but the SNI team refused to leave without Georg's authorization. Georg jotted down a quick note giving his consent for the team to move. "I will join you at the new location," he wrote. "Things are proceeding well."

And so it seemed. The gathering in Saleem's office came to a consensus regarding the rescue location, and the Red Cross official sent the computer transmission of the location on to the office in Islamabad. A short time later, they received word that the American Army knew the location, that they would arrive at midnight, and that the SNI team members could not take any bags with them, just what they wore. With a renewed sense of optimism, Georg rode in the vehicle with Saleem and his men back to the new safe house to rejoin the rest of the team. The house was smaller than the previous one, but still with a high protective wall around it and plenty of guards.

Over lunch, the eight foreigners were like children, talking excitedly about a Hollywood-style rescue, courtesy of the U.S. Special Forces. The biggest decision for them now was what bits and pieces of their lives they would take and which ones they must leave behind. They dressed in layers and stuffed personal items into the folds of material, chatting happily about what they would do once they got back home.

Later that afternoon, Georg got word from the Red Cross that someone had arrived at the office and needed to speak with him. This was unexpected, but the message had an air of urgency, and he could not take any chances, so he returned to the Red Cross office. Once he arrived, the Red Cross official pulled Georg aside, away from the warlords and their entourages. Someone was waiting for him in the men's room, Georg was told; he should make his way there without drawing attention to himself. The subterfuge and intrigue all felt as though it were out of a spy novel.

Inside the men's room, a person waited for him, covered head to toe with dirty clothes, only his eyes exposed. The man removed the cloth masking his identity, and Georg looked into the face of the

Afghan Angel. He could not believe it. The U.S. Army had informed him that Georg was at the Red Cross office in Ghazni; he now presented Georg with a satellite phone he had smuggled in from Pakistan. The two men had no time for idle chatter, just a quick embrace, a thank-you, and Georg left the men's room first, before the Angel slipped out the back moments later. Georg now held in his hand the ability for direct communication with the American forces. He no longer needed the services of the Red Cross or second- and third-party computer transmissions.

Once Georg established contact, the colonel in charge of the rescue operation requested permission to speak to the two American girls. It was a simple way to confirm that Georg was who he said he was and that this was not some devious ploy to put American soldiers in danger. Saleem ordered his men to rush Heather and Dayna to the Red Cross office, and both of them spoke to the colonel. The bona fides established, Georg was instructed to get to the rescue site before 3:00 p.m. to put a sign up for the pilots in the surveillance plane. This way both parties would know the exact location for the rescue.

Unfortunately, Georg never made it to the site. After their brief conversation with the colonel, Heather and Dayna returned to the safe house, and Georg found himself in a maelstrom of opposing arguments among tribal/faction leaders about the feasibility and danger of the rescue plan everyone had agreed upon earlier that day. Some wanted to discuss the plan with the new leaders of Ghazni, but others argued against it, for fear of secret Taliban followers among the new leadership. Others thought that if they helped the Westerners (such as taking them to the rescue site), they could become targets of reprisals. In addition, there was a dusk-to-dawn curfew in place, and dozens of checkpoints. Still others thought the whole plan was too dangerous to pull off, that the pickup point, being beyond the city limits, had too many possibilities for ambush. Ultimately, they all refused to be of any help. When the three o'clock deadline came and went and he was still in debate class with people who no longer seemed concerned about helping them, Georg began to have a sinking feeling. Murphy's Law was in effect.

It did not take a genius to speculate that some of these Ghazni warlords might benefit from taking custody of the foreigners. There was economic incentive, as well as political power to gain should the Taliban retake the city. Georg could see rival groups vying for political and economic advantage and the SNI team suffering the consequences. He felt as though he and the others were on an island surrounded by Taliban and al-Qaeda—and now the island was rapidly becoming hostile toward them. Even Saleem seemed to be pulling away from Georg, sensing that helping the foreigners was more trouble than it was worth. Georg called the colonel to explain and suggested the Americans come the next day. He was told that was impossible; it had to be at midnight that night—they had to act fast before the city deteriorated into a war zone of factions fighting for power.

Minute by minute, the reality on the ground was changing; Georg struggled to keep his calm as he went round and round with people who were looking more and more like the ones who had captured them more than one hundred days ago. That old feeling of despair descended like a familiar blanket. It was already after dark, the curfew was in place, and there was no one in the streets. Saleem ordered his men to take Georg back to the safe house, and at one point on his drive back, his armed entourage had to stop at a checkpoint. Guns were drawn and threats made, but fortunately, no weapons were fired. It was all Georg could do to hold it together, and he returned to his team a defeated leader. He had nothing left to spin their circumstances in a positive light: he told them the truth, gave them the facts as he understood them, said the situation was dire, and urged them to pray—for him especially. Georg did not have the heart to tell them that he had reached his wit's end, and decided he would wait until the guards in the house had settled down and were asleep before he tried to call the colonel to ask what to do next.

When the guards had gone to sleep, Georg slipped outside into the courtyard and called; it had been several hours since their last contact, and the colonel expressed his concern about not hearing from Georg. He'd been fearful that the worst had happened but was relieved to be speaking with Georg now. The colonel asked about their location, but Georg could not tell him exactly where they were. The satellite phone was capable of giving a GPS reading, but Georg's knowledge of this technology was limited, so the colonel gave him a quick and simple tutorial on how to take a reading. To add to the drama, the phone's battery was beginning to run out of power. Georg would have to pinpoint his longitude/latitude, hope the battery held, and call back.

Georg dashed back inside the house and woke up Peter. Together they went back outside, and Georg got the required GPS reading while Peter wrote it down. Georg immediately called the colonel and gave him the configuration, then signed off again while the Americans confirmed the reading. Georg and Peter paced back and forth, uttering whispered prayers that they'd provided the right coordinates. Soon the colonel confirmed they had the exact location, and that the house was within a short distance of a large open space with no structures to obstruct a landing—the Special Forces could pick them up at that site. He gave Georg directions to get there and immediately signed off so Georg could save the power on the dying battery.

Early in the evening, Hamisha Zareef had left the SNI team under heavy guard, telling Georg not to expect him back that night. But as the time ticked down to midnight, Georg was in turmoil. The guards weren't letting anyone in—but they weren't letting anyone out either. There were high walls surrounding the house. There was sporadic gunfire coming from different parts of the city. He had tried to reason with the guards to let them go, and when that failed, he tried to get them to call Hamisha Zareef. The exchange ended in a stalemate. The rendezvous point was only a mile away from where he now stood, but it might as well have been a thousand miles.

Once again, Georg called the colonel to ask his advice. The American suggested they kill the guards, but that was out of the question. The group had been adamant that no one should be killed or suffer physical harm so the eight of them could be freed; even now, in this eleventh hour, Georg could not make an exception. The colonel told him the helicopters were en route at that moment to the rendezvous point; there was no turning back.

"Use whatever means necessary to . . ." Georg did not have the chance to sign off. Static and a weakened battery prevented him from hearing the last words from the colonel. His only recourse was prayer.

While the other members of the team remained in a common area attached to the side of the house with some of the family

members of the guards, Georg paced back and forth in the courtyard, imploring God for help. He was completely exhausted from
the internal pressure. And then . . . he came up with a bold idea. He
waited until the guards had gone back to sleep—and then he woke
them with the frantic news that he had informed the Americans by
satellite phone where they were located. The American soldiers
were on their way to rescue them! He waved the satellite phone in
the air, repeating the fact that the Americans knew their exact location, that the helicopters were on the way, that they were coming
here with Special Forces, and they would take the SNI team by force
if necessary. It worked. Georg got his desired reaction: the guards
were in total panic.

At that moment, orchestrated with God's perfect timing, fighter
jets flew over the city. This only added fuel to the fire Georg had
set. Everyone from the common room rushed into the courtyard,
and in an instant, the scene tumbled into chaos. Even the wives
and children of the guards who were staying in the house got very
upset and began to cry. Still, the guards refused to let the SNI
team go without Hamisha Zareef's authorization. Loyalty to and
fear of their chief rivaled the idea of facing a team of Special Forces
soldiers.

The Afghan guards argued with Georg while the Afghan women
cried and wailed their prayers. The SNI team filled the air with their
prayers for God to make a way of escape. Fighter jets circled overhead, with the thunderous sound of the afterburners roaring from
their engines. Georg had only thought to set off a controlled panic,
but it had become a descent into madness. The guards forced Georg
to make another call to the colonel and tell him not to send the
army; otherwise there would be a bloodbath.

"Too late," the colonel replied. "We know where you are. We are coming to get you. Tell them to let you go."

Georg disconnected the call and addressed the guards, taking on the persona of an angry father scolding his children.

"The Americans are on their way," he said. "I cannot stop them. They will take us by force, and you will all be killed."

This sent the crowd into near hysteria, but before the mayhem got completely out of control, everyone heard a vehicle stop in front of the house. A pounding on the front gate brought a temporary halt to the bedlam. No one could believe someone would be visiting this time of night. The guards opened the gate, and in flew Hamisha Zareef, with Saleem close behind. The sound of the fighter planes had roused them from their beds.

"You have to leave immediately," Hamisha Zareef shouted.

Georg first thought Hamisha Zareef meant to take him to the designated pickup site.

"The Taliban have come back into the city, and the people who brought you to Ghazni know where you are!" Zareef continued. "They plan to kill you. We must get you to a safer place."

Georg could hardly believe what he was hearing. There was no end to this terror. Yet something told Georg that Hamisha Zareef could be bluffing, that he knew how frightened they all were and could easily be demoralized into believing the worst. He asked the rest of the SNI members to return to the common room and pray fervently for the next several minutes while he tried to work things out.

Georg trusted no one. He was not sure of Saleem's reliability. And why should he trust Hamisha Zareef? His minimal investment in sanctuary and hospitality for the SNI team could prove a windfall profit for him should he choose to ransom them to the Taliban and al-Qaeda (or to their own foreign governments). Georg had had enough. Hamisha Zareef could not bully or intimidate him. He decided to match bluff for bluff.

"We are not going anywhere. Just let us go. If you do not, then shoot us right here and now," Georg exclaimed in front of everyone, to their horror.

That ultimatum would never have worked in Kabul. Too many would have obliged. But these people were still confused and unorganized.

An animated discussion ensued between Saleem, Hamisha Zareef, and the rest of his men; Georg could tell that they appeared to take him at his word, but were not likely to shoot the Westerners. When Hamisha Zareef stepped away from his men, it appeared as though he did not want to lose face before them.

"You must come with us. We cannot protect you here," he said again.

But Georg had lost all patience and any willingness to compromise. "I don't care if the Taliban are coming back. They can have us. We are not going with you," he said, his demeanor cold and calculated. "Shoot us now or let us go."

Georg did not have to wait long for an answer. While Georg went back and forth to the common room, everyone could hear the thumping, deep monotone of helicopter blades in the distance.

The moment Hamisha Zareef recognized the sound of the approaching helicopters, his demeanor changed completely. He was terribly frightened and began to move toward the front entrance, with Saleem at his heels. Zareef cast his eyes to the dark sky above and then stormed out of the gate. After a few moments,

Georg could hear the engine of Zareef's vehicle crank up, the driver gunning the engine, and then, inexplicably, the vehicle drove away.

Timing is everything, and once again, the timing of the sound of the helicopters was perfect. If Zareef had had more time, he surely would have forced the Westerners to go with him; and the longer they were on the ground in Afghanistan, the more likely they were to die. Yet the issue was still unresolved. Georg hesitated.

Saleem stuck his head around the door of the gate.

"He is gone," he said. "You must leave now."

That was all Georg needed to hear. He ran to the common room and told the rest of the group to leave now. They ran out of the gate and headed straight for the rendezvous point with Saleem; the guards were right on their heels. Georg suspected if anything went wrong at the pickup site, Saleem, under orders from Hamisha Zareef, might try to bring them back.

They ran through the streets, following the directions Georg had written down during his conversation with the colonel. The night was dark, and there was very little light coming from the other buildings in the area. There was an eerie quiet in the city, punctuated by the sound of the U.S. helicopters in the distance. When they rounded the last building at the end of the street, they made a mad dash for the open field. Nothing but death would keep them from arriving at their destination now.

Georg whipped out the satellite phone and made another call. "We are here!" he shouted. "We are here. We have made it."

The colonel was pleased to know the team had arrived at the designated location and asked if all eight had made it. When Georg affirmed everyone was present and accounted for, the colonel instructed Georg to have them line up in a row on the perimeter of the field and for anyone else to get back off the field completely.

"The helicopters will be there in five minutes," he said.

This was the final communication between Georg and the colonel. At that very moment, the battery died on the satellite phone. The five minutes felt like an eternity.

In their haste to get away, the team had left many of the things they'd hoped to carry with them. They had only one lantern and a few flashlights. They lined up along the edge of the field as the colonel had instructed and waited for the sound of the helicopter. They were also supposed to light a signal fire, but they had no way of doing that. To make the situation worse, many of the local militia groups had lit fires outside their homes to keep warm while standing guard against the return of the Taliban. What if all those fires confused the helicopter pilots? Would they just give up and go back empty-handed? Georg hoped that by waving the lantern and flashing their flashlights, their rescuers would see them.

Soon they heard the pounding sound of rotary blades, and in a few moments the enormous flying machines circled overhead. The impulse was to wave feverishly to get the attention of the pilots, but instead they all sat quietly, because they did not want to alert the citizens in any of the nearby houses. The only thing Georg had to signal the pilot was the small flashlight Mashuq had given him on the road to Ghazni. But the beam from the flashlight was so weak and the noise from the helicopter so deafening, it was impossible for the pilots to see or hear them, and after a few seconds of hovering above the field, the helicopters took off. This same scenario played out again and again; the helicopters would appear, circle the area, and then vanish in the darkness. For nearly an hour this situation repeated itself, much to the consternation of everyone on the ground.

From of the shadows, Hamisha Zareef suddenly appeared, with Saleem behind him. He approached the edge of the field and demanded that Georg and the others return with him. "They cannot see you," he cried. "They cannot find you. You must come back with us."

The temptation to return with Hamisha Zareef was strong. It appeared the Americans did not see them and did not want to risk hovering in the air searching for them—it made the helicopters an easy target. But they all knew staying in Ghazni was certain death now. The whole city would know of the failed rescue attempt; the rival factions, as well as the Taliban and al-Qaeda, would wage all-out war with each other to get their hands on the Westerners. The team was on the verge of desperation. The helicopters had to return.

When the helicopter made another sortie above the open area, Zareef and his crew hid out of sight and watched as the flying machines circled above and then once again disappeared from view. And once again while the SNI eight were quietly and patiently waiting and praying that the helicopters would return, Hamisha Zareef summoned Georg back to him. However, there was nothing Zareef could say to make Georg leave the field; freedom was too close.

The helicopters could not keep up this procedure indefinitely. It was time to take some drastic measures. When Georg rejoined the group, he found Heather digging through Margrit's purse until she found a pack of matches. Others were pulling off the extra clothes they were wearing and soaking them with the kerosene from the lantern. Heather piled the clothes out in the open, struck the match, and—at last, a signal fire! She grabbed the end of a burning head scarf and waved it above her head. Others found some wood in the field and threw it on the fire. Saleem, too, rushed on the field, hastily gathered some kindling and set it on fire, and began to wave it in the air. And finally, it seemed that the pilots saw them, because the helicopters circled right above their heads. The choppers descended so close to the ground that everyone in the field was blinded by the dust stirred up by the rotor blades. Heather was standing close to the fire; the powerful wind caused by the hovering choppers made the flames blaze up and catch her clothes on fire. As the group quickly extinguished Heather's burning clothes, they watched in horror as the helicopters disappeared once more.

The silent, black night was a crushing weight on everyone's soul. They were desperate for a miracle.

How could they have not seen us? Georg wondered. This highly sophisticated army with the best military equipment in the world? Why didn't the helicopters just land right there and scoop them all up? He felt like a man drowning in the ocean who was repeatedly thrown a lifeline, only to find that it was too short to reach him . . . and the sharks were circling, ready to strike.

After what seemed to be an excruciatingly long passage of time, someone shouted out of the darkness. "Do you speak English?"

Georg thought it could be one of the Afghanis trying to trick them, so he said nothing. But he could not keep Heather and Dayna quiet. Both of them screamed "*Yes!*" Georg told them to hush, but it was too late. From the blackness emerged men who looked as if they had arrived from outer space. Several of them rushed past the SNI team and secured the perimeter, their guns pointing at Saleem; all the others had run away.

"Don't hurt him!" Georg cried. "Don't hurt him. He helped us get here."

The Special Forces team was covered head to toe in gear, including night-vision goggles, and armed to the teeth. The leader was looking for eight Westerners; he counted out seven of the SNI team but kept excluding Georg because of the Afghan clothes he wore, and because he had not shaved his beard since their arrests 105 days ago.

"He is with us!" the others shouted, and at last the Special Forces leader had eight. He ordered everyone to line up. He paired each SNI member with a member of the Special Forces team, and the company scrambled away from the barren field and over the next rise.

The company moved too slowly for Georg, and he ran ahead of his Special Forces partner, promptly falling into a ditch. The soldier yanked Georg out of the ditch and back onto his feet, but Georg did not learn his lesson. He kept running ahead of the others, and when he saw the Chinook helicopter waiting for them, he could not help himself. He ran for what he thought was the entrance on the right side of the helicopter—only to discover, when he smashed his head against the protective shield, that it was not an entrance at all. The soldier took Georg's arm and led him to the rear of the aircraft. He stumbled through the entrance in the rear and fell onto floor of the helicopter. Completely disoriented, his head throbbing, Georg began to crawl on all fours toward what he thought was the front of the helicopter. A moment later, Heather crashed down on top of him, stumbling over him in the dark.

They both kept scrambling toward the front and crawled into a corner of the helicopter. The others quickly followed, spreading out on the floor of the Chinook. Georg did not even have time to catch his breath before the Special Forces team leader gave the order for the pilot to take off. The roar of the engine made the helicopter vibrate so much it felt as if it might fall apart . . . but when the chopper left the ground, rising higher and higher into the air, it begin to dawn on them that their nightmare, at last, was at an end, and the SNI eight began to shout, to pray, to laugh, to cry, and, by turns, to embrace one another and then those who had risked their lives to rescue them. It was pure elation.

Heather lay prone next to Georg, and she kept shouting into his ear as the aircraft began to pick up speed. "We are free! We are free!" From the bright glow emitted by all the electronic equipment, they could see the Stars and Stripes pinned to the ceiling, and it finally started to sink in. They had been rescued. The desperation and hopelessness were over. They were free.

A soldier reached out and patted Georg's shoulder, bringing him out of a daze.

"We were about to give up trying to find you," he shouted above the roar of the Chinook engines. "Once we spotted you, it was too dangerous to land where you were, too close to the neighborhood."

Georg nodded his head as if he understood, but he did not. His heart and mind were overloaded. What he was beginning to grasp was freedom. No more prisons. No more threats. No more Taliban. Freedom, and soon, very soon, reunion with those he loved.

"We have been praying for you all the time," the soldier shouted again. Georg shook his head in awe and gratitude. People around the world had prayed for them, and now, thanks to God, they would have the opportunity to thank the millions of people who held them before God through their long ordeal. Without those prayers, Georg was convinced they would never have survived.

EPILOGUE

Often when one is put in extreme situations, the opportunity to experience miracles becomes available. To the skeptic, a miracle might be easy to deny or rationalize (particularly if it is subtle), but when miracles come one after the other, it becomes difficult to explain as mere coincidence. That the SNI team survived being held by the Taliban—a hostile group that as a whole felt such animosity toward the organization that it had for years made concerted efforts to destroy their work—for 105 days was miracle enough. There were, of course, several officials within the Taliban that were sympathetic toward SNI. Over the years before their captivity, Georg and the other members of the team had taken great pains to establish and cultivate strong relationships among the Afghan people, including individuals within the power structure of the Taliban. That, too, certainly could be considered no small miracle, one born from love and long-term dedication to a people that required the risk of faith and a commitment to a call from God.

During their captivity, the SNI eight endured much privation and a steady threat of danger at the hands of the Taliban. While there were momentary breakdowns among the eight due to the stress, they were just momentary and understandable. What normal person would not have his or her soul and faith shaken by such dire circumstances? Yet the fact that they never completely gave up hope when hope could have easily been lost is a testimony to God's miraculous intervention. But it was in the last forty-eight hours of their detention that the sheer volume of miracles intensified.

From the beginning of their imprisonment, the SNI eight had a twofold, unified prayer: to be rescued, yes, but in the process that no one, friend or foe, should die so they might live, and that the sixteen Afghan SNI employees would be freed before they were. It was a tall order, given the volatility of the situation.

Mashuq, Georg's friend from the intelligence prison, was a hardened soldier of the Northern Alliance and sworn enemy of the Taliban and al-Qaeda. He was also committed to helping Georg and the others escape. Mashuq had befriended a few of the guards in prison who were not hard-line Talibs, and they, in turn, had provided him with a Kalashnikov in the final hours before he and the SNI eight were forced to leave for Kandahar. Mashuq would not have hesitated to use the weapon if it required him to fight for everyone's freedom, but it just so happened that when the Taliban came to collect Georg and the others, Mashuq was in another cell—without his weapon. He never fired a single round.

When it came time for the SNI eight to get into the vehicles that would take them to Kandahar, the Taliban wanted to separate the men from the women, but Georg refused, insisting the group not be separated. It's surprising that the Taliban acquiesced; their fingers were on the triggers of their Kalashnikovs at all times, and anything could set them off. Even though the SNI eight were crammed into one vehicle, one on top of the other, they appreciated the miracle of being together.

At different times along the way, there were occasions when their captors could have killed them. There was even an intense argument among the Taliban over that very thing, but since there was no consensus among the group, they kept the SNI eight alive and traveled on to Ghazni. Had they arrived in Ghazni just an hour later that morning, their Taliban captors would have seen the uprising by the citizens of Ghazni; they would have bypassed the city and headed straight to Kandahar—and certain death for the hostages. Once they were deposited in the Ghazni prison at 9:00 a.m., the SNI eight watched from their window as these supposedly fearless Taliban fighters fled, although no one was pursuing them— a divinely inspired panic. When there was a lull in the fighting between the Ghaznians and the Taliban, their captors could have come back and killed the SNI eight or left with them, but they did not. And when they were freed, the chance meeting with their Afghan Angel—in the midst of a city in jubilant turmoil far from where they'd last seen him—who gave Georg the satellite phone to contact the U.S. military, could only be seen as a miracle.

But the miracles had not run out. In the last hours before their rescue by Delta Force soldiers, the back-and-forth between the Afghan warlord who held them as "guests" in his compound (and did not want to give them up) was a true test of their faith. Had the fighter planes not flown over the city and awakened the warlord . . . had he not been able to get through all the checkpoints throughout the city to drive back to the compound . . . had the helicopters not flown over the compound at the exact moment the commander and Georg were in heated debate . . . had the commander not panicked at the last minute and driven away, leaving Georg and the others free to leave . . . they might not have made it to the rendezvous point. And do not forget the miracle of the battery of the satellite phone, which lasted long enough for Georg and the U.S. colonel to get the GPS reading and make final contact before the SNI eight left the compound. After all these circumstances one would think the miracle pool had run dry.

But there was a final miracle—the miracle of the match and the lantern. When they arrived at the clearing, the helicopter pilots could not see them, even after repeated sorties over the area. When they were safely back in Islamabad, the SNI eight learned that the helicopter pilots kept seeing lights flickering from dozens of rooftops in that area of the city. They were expecting a Taliban counterattack on the city, and these lights could have been signals for the enemy; the light from Georg's lantern only caused confusion. And after nearly an hour of trying to spot them, the helicopters had only enough fuel for one more sortie.

So Heather's frantic attempt to create a signal fire with clothing and kerosene is another miracle. That Margrit had matches and that someone had grabbed a lantern in the compound—these are miracles. The light from the blaze was enough for the pilots to make their final rescue attempt. And still there was one more miracle to be had. It was a four-hour flight back to the base, and as the helicopter was refueling in midflight, the pilot informed the SNI eight that the Taliban had just retaken Ghazni. They had been rescued in the nick of time.

Having endured one filthy prison after another; after being crammed into one vehicle and forced to sit on top of a rocket launcher and ride for hours along the dusty highway to Kandahar; after spending a night in a metal execution container; after spending another night in the compound of a warlord who did not want to release them; after a frantic escape and waiting in freezing temperatures for rescue; and after hours of riding in a helicopter . . . they arrived in Islamabad and were whisked away in luxurious Mercedes-Benzes

In their first few days of freedom the SNI eight gather for one
last photo before returning to their respective countries.
(L–R: Peter, Dayna, Margrit, Georg, Heather, Silke, Katrin, Diana).

to their respective embassies. It was a surreal ending to their incredible odyssey.

After phone calls to family and friends, reassuring them that they were indeed finally out of harm's way, the SNI eight appeared before the media for photos and to make brief statements of thankfulness. More in-depth interviews would come later. Georg would testify in one press conference that God had given them strength to endure, and through their faith in Jesus Christ, they had been able to survive the ordeal. And when he was asked about his feelings toward the Taliban, Georg was quick to say that he was human like everyone else and *did* feel angry for all the Taliban had put them through— but he and the others had chosen to forgive. "In the Lord's Prayer it says, 'Forgive us our sins as we forgive those who have sinned against us,'" he said. "We all decided to forgive the Taliban."

Their first night of freedom, the SNI eight were the guests of honor at a big gathering, with ambassadors from the United States, Germany, and Australia playing host. Diplomats, U.S. military, international officials, the leader of the Special Forces (who publicly thanked Georg for his leadership during the rescue efforts), members of the media, and many others celebrated the safe return of the hostages. When the guests learned that the SNI women had composed songs while in prison, the request was made that they be allowed to sing. The five women gathered and sang for all the dignitaries.

How great is Your goodness
That You have stored up
For those who fear You, oh God,

Which You have bestowed in the sight of men
On those who take refuge in You.

In the shelter of Your presence You hid us,
In Your dwelling You keep us safe.
Praise be to the Lord for he has shown
His wonderful love to us.

I was trapped in a city in my alarm
I said, "I'm cut off from Your sight!"
Yet You heard my cry for mercy, my God,
When I called to You for help.

Be strong and take heart
All who hope in the Lord.

In the shelter of Your presence You hid us,
In Your dwelling You keep us safe.
Praise be to the Lord for he has shown
His wonderful love to us.

Their brief miniconcert left everyone in the room speechless. After 105 days of captivity, the SNI eight could speak of forgiveness, and the five women could sing songs of hope and faith. It was a testimony that most of the dignitaries had rarely heard.

After a brief time in Islamabad, the SNI eight departed for their countries of origin. Each of them received a hero's welcome from family and friends, political and religious leaders, presidents—and from perfect strangers, those who had kept up with their plight and been vigilant in prayer throughout their captivity.

Less than six months after their release, several of those SNI workers who had been imprisoned or had successfully escaped before the Taliban could arrest them made plans to return to Afghanistan in the spring of 2002. Georg and many others had said repeatedly that what they had experienced was no deterrent to their desire to return to the country and pick up where they left off. It was a call of God they were compelled to follow, in spite of the reluctance from some family members to see them go. From psychologists to politicians to government officials, Georg and the others were discouraged from returning and warned of the dangers. While Georg, Marianne, and their sons, plus other members of the SNI team who had lived and worked in Peshawar during that time, were on retreat in Pakistan's Swat Valley, preparing for their reentry into Afghanistan, word came from the German foreign ministry that a new chief justice in Afghanistan had stated in an interview that if any of the staff from Shelter Now were to return, they would be arrested and put on trial again. After much prayer, the group decided they could not abandon this call from God. They would, however, wait until June 1, 2002, before returning, allowing more time for some of the hostile attitudes to calm. Len Stitt and his wife, Diane, were the first to return, with Georg, Marianne, their two sons, (Daniel and Benjamin), Silke, and a South African couple soon to follow. Fortunately, when the team moved back into Kabul, most of the tribal leaders and Afghan government officials welcomed them with open arms. The chief justice who had made the threats was a member of a more radical party with limited power, and consequently did not follow through. A few months later Margrit rejoined the group and stayed until 2007. Silke returned to Germany in 2004, and in 2007, Katrin and her husband and two children decided to join the team in Kabul. The two Americans and two Australians chose not to come back.

When the SNI team returned to their homes and offices in Kabul, they discovered the sad reality of the effects of a country at war. Most of their houses had been looted by the Taliban; the entire work of the SNI operation had been destroyed. When Georg and his family went to their house, they found it occupied. Even though they had paid the rent on the house through August 2002, they were not allowed to move back in, although the current occupants gave

A street market in Kabul, 2003.

them a few minutes for the boys to scurry up to the attic and collect the valuables they had hidden there. Right before she and the boys made their escape, Marianne had thought better of her decision to leave her treasure box buried in the garden, so she'd dug it up and had the boys hide it with their things in the attic. She was thrilled to see her sons holding the receptacle containing her photos and other valuables. Even though the Taubmanns had to find a new home, at least they had some of their most precious possessions.

It was a difficult time for everyone. All of them had to grapple with traumatic memories. Every day on his way to work, Georg had to drive past the prison where he and the others were interrogated and spent their first six weeks of captivity. Were it not for their faith, certainty of calling, and the strong community of believers who shared the same commitment and purpose, the challenges to start over might have been too much.

In the midst of coming to grips with having to start from scratch were two joyous reunions.

Mashuq had been able to slip back to Kabul and present Georg's letter to officers in the Northern Alliance and American armies, which had certainly helped legitimize their identity when it came to their rescue in Ghazni.

Later, when Mustafa (Mashuq's friend in prison and companion in their escape while on the road to Kandahar), heard that Georg and his family were back in Kabul, he sought him out. This reunion was made more joyful when Mustafa brought Mashuq and Georg back together. Once Kabul had been liberated, Mashuq devoted his energies for some time in helping to establish the fledgling democratic government until he decided to start his own business. The men who had shared some of the darkest moments in their lives now could share them as memories that only deepened their friendship over time.

Even more thrilling was the reunion with the Afghan SNI workers who had endured 104 days of Taliban imprisonment. Just before the Northern Alliance liberated Kabul (and at the same time the SNI eight were on the road to Kandahar), the Taliban guards at the Pul-e-Charkhi prison—where the sixteen Afghan workers were being held—fled for their lives. The day before, members of al-Qaeda had come to the prison and demanded the sixteen SNI workers be released into their custody, but the Taliban officials had refused to let them go—another miracle. Had the sixteen been given over to al-Qaeda, they surely would have been killed. And it just so happened that the sixteen shared a cell with a professional locksmith; after the Taliban guards left the prison, this man picked the locks on the cell. Along with six thousand other inmates, the sixteen SNI workers raced out of the prison and into the night. They had to hike through the night back to Kabul, careful to avoid land mines, friendly fire from the advancing Northern Alliance, and any Taliban or al-Qaeda stragglers. By dawn the next morning they were reunited with their families and were able to welcome the liberating armies into the city. The prayers of Georg and the others had been answered to the letter: all twenty-four members of the SNI team had escaped without anyone having to die; and the sixteen Afghan employees, who had endured far worse treatment than the SNI eight, had been set free before they were. It was a nearly perfect ending.

What has made it a perfect ending is the work that has followed the return of the SNI organization to Afghanistan. They have been able to rebuild everything that was destroyed and expand their work to areas of Pakistan. They have built houses and schools, water

SNI has returned to Afghanistan to rebuild. Here SNI employees in Kabul pour concrete for a foundation in 2003; Udo Stolte on the right.

supply systems, implemented agriculture and education programs, established medical and dental clinics, and set up outreach programs for the disabled. Since their return, people from eighteen different nations have joined their work in Afghanistan and Pakistan. And every year on November 15, as many as are able gather at the Taubmann home to celebrate their miraculous escape. Most of the sixteen Afghan employees who were in jail at the same time as the SNI eight come, as well as those previously mentioned when they were in the country. Some of the original SNI Afghan employees eventually found other work, but they rarely miss the November 15 gathering at the Taubmann home to celebrate their miraculous escape. Georg always reads Psalms 55:18, an important passage describing their mutual ordeal: "He ransoms me unharmed from the battle waged against me, even though many oppose me" (Psalm 55:18 NIV).

It was into this new world that Ben Pearson was invited to document their story. Not long after everyone was rescued, producers from Hollywood and other international film companies began to inquire about securing the rights to produce the Shelter Now story. However, the Shelter Now folks were skeptical about giving their story to just anyone. Author Stephen Mansfield happened to be acquainted with Georg and the work of Shelter Now in Afghanistan, and recommended that they contact film director Ben Pearson. Pearson

Ben Pearson arrives at Kabul airport in 2003 to film interviews with SNI personnel who had been held captive in late 2001.

flew to Germany with coproducer Steve Taylor to meet with Udo Stolte, and after a few days of conversations, a handshake sealed the commitment.

From a vantage point overlooking Kabul, Ben films while Georg tells his story.

In the summer of 2003, Pearson began filming, first in Afghanistan, spending the better part of a month there recording interviews with some of the SNI staff and employees and shooting different locations where the scenes of this story took place. He later flew to Australia, England, back to Germany, and then to Texas to film interviews with all the major players involved.

This work and travel is normally financed by a production company, but when Pearson made the commitment to produce and direct the documentary film of this story, no financing was in place. Friends stepped in with cash loans, others with in-kind services.

Credit cards were maxed out, bills mounted, but still Pearson never wavered. When one company said they would fund the project, Pearson took hope, but then, as is typical of securing funding for film projects, the financing fell through. Stepping out in faith like this is not for the faint of heart, and Pearson would not recommend this approach to other filmmakers, but by this point Pearson's "hand was on the plow, and he could not look back."

It was during the filming of *The Second Chance*, Pearson's first theatrical film, that Michael W. Smith, star of the movie, caught wind of the SNI story. The timing was fortuitous. Pearson had recently commissioned a translation of a German version of the story into English and sent this to his friend Michael. When principal photography ended on *The Second Chance*, Pearson sat down with Michael and showed him some of the raw footage of *KABUL24*. Michael was intrigued by what he saw, and not long after that screening, he called Pearson and committed to backing the project.

The process of making a film is never what it appears to be. Time can kill or enhance great ideas. In the case of *KABUL24*, time improved the story, just like an excellent wine. The process took Pearson much longer than expected, but this allowed him to ponder the bigger questions of this powerful story. He has attempted to answer them in thoughtful and profound ways while still telling a fast-paced thriller that keeps viewers sitting on the edge of their seats.

Another wonderful serendipity happened as the wait for funding dragged on. Michael W. Smith was able to secure his good friend Jim Caviezel to be the voice for the narration on the movie. Between film projects, Caviezel saw a rough cut of the film and immediately agreed to lend his talent to the project. Pearson believes the addition of Caviezel's voice brings a humanity to the story that completes the whole experience.

The story of Afghanistan is millennia old, rich in history and culture. In the last several decades, though, the country has been fragmented by violence and chaos. Since 9/11, Afghanistan has always been in the headlines—and it shows no signs of fading into the background. Again and again, the images we see are the devastating results of war.

What is often neglected is the work done among the Afghan people by organizations such as Shelter Now . . . organizations made up of people who quietly go about their commitment as peacemakers and servants of God to a country torn apart by conflict. This story celebrates many things, but above all, it celebrates the people who heard and obeyed the "still, small voice" that said, *Follow me*. It was a voice they could not resist. If they'd known what they would suffer and sacrifice, would they still have gone? Perhaps—because taking this sort of risk for Christ requires even greater courage. *KABUL24* is the story of a courageous few who, like the prophet Isaiah, said, "Here am I. Send me."

ACKNOWLEDGMENTS

The authors wish to thank many people for their dedication and commitment in helping them see this story become a reality in print and on film.

Were it not for Esther Fedorkevich, this book would never have seen the light of day. Inspired by a rough cut of the film, she approached the authors and said, "Here is a double dare. If you take the risk to write the book, I'll take the risk to get it sold." The gauntlet was tossed, and we all went to work. When the manuscript was done, Esther went shopping. In spite of polite but frequent rejections, she succeeded in landing a deal. We are eternally grateful that she has no shame in choosing to represent us and an above-and-beyond commitment in not taking no for an answer. Would that all authors were so served.

To the Shelter Now team who generously gave of themselves in ways that humble us all. We hope we've told their story well. To learn more about this wonderful organization, visit their Web site: www.shelter-now.org or www.shelter.de (click on the American flag for text in English).

To Stephen Mansfield, for introducing Ben Pearson to the Shelter Now team. To Steve Taylor, Matt Slocum, and Mark Stepp, who greased the wheels in those early days and continued their support throughout. To Michael W. Smith, who saw the rough footage and said, "Let's make history, bro." To Derek Pearson, whose tireless dedication as our film editor inspired us to settle for nothing less than excellence. To Joel Miller and the team at Thomas Nelson, for supporting us in every way from day one and helping us produce a book that makes us all proud. To Jamie Chavez, for her over-the-top editing skills; this book has her fingerprints all over it. She has made us all proud of the result. A special thanks to Elaine Pearson and Kay Arnold, who often commiserated during this long gestational period of getting *KABUL24* in print and on film, wondering when these creations would ever be birthed. They are the anchors we don't deserve—and we remain forever grateful.

Above all, we give thanks to God, who gave us our modicum of talent and the freedom to express it in countless ways. We hope this latest offering honors Him.

ABOUT THE AUTHORS

Henry O. Arnold has been a professional actor and writer for the last forty years. He co-wrote and produced the film *The Second Chance* starring Michael W. Smith and wrote the screenplay for the first authorized film documentary on evangelist Billy Graham, *God's Ambassador.* His recent novel *Hometown Favorite* received high critical acclaim, and he co-wrote and produced the documentary film *KABUL24* on which this book is based. He lives in Tennessee with his wife, Kay.

Photo by Derek Pearson

Ben Pearson is an acclaimed filmmaker and photographer from upstate New York with numerous awards, honors, and gallery shows to his credit. He has made his home in Nashville for the last twenty years, where he lives with his wife Elaine and their three children. Pearson co-wrote and directed the cinematography for the dramatic feature *The Second Chance* (2006–Sony Pictures Releasing). He recently made his directorial debut with the feature-length documentary *Kabul 24* (2009), a riveting account of the eight Western aid workers captured and held hostage by the Taliban in the weeks prior to 9/11. Ben is currently co-writing and preparing to direct the cinematography for the screen adaptation of the New York Times best selling memoir *Blue Like Jazz*.